Blackness as a Universal Claim

Blackness as a Universal Claim

HOLOCAUST HERITAGE, NONCITIZEN FUTURES, AND BLACK POWER IN BERLIN

Damani J. Partridge

[handwritten note:]

March 3, 20 3

Dear Austin,

Thank you for all of your guidance over the years. I hope that you enjoy the book.

Best wishes,

UNIVERSITY OF CALIFORNIA PRESS

University of California Press
Oakland, California

© 2023 by Damani J. Partridge

Please note that earlier versions of chapters 1, 2, 3, and 7 have been
published in the journals *Comparative Studies in Society and History*
(chapter 3) and *Transforming Anthropology* (chapter 2), and the edited
volumes *Refugees Welcome?: Difference and Diversity in a Changing
Germany* (chapter 7) and *Germans and African Americans: Two
Centuries of Exchange* (chapter 1). The chapters have been significantly
edited and updated for this volume.

Library of Congress Cataloging-in-Publication Data

Names: Partridge, Damani J., 1973- author.
Title: Blackness as a universal claim : Holocaust heritage, noncitizen
    futures, and black power in Berlin / Damani J. Partridge.
Description: Oakland, California : University of California Press, [2022] |
    Includes bibliographical references and index.
Identifiers: LCCN 2022006818 (print) | LCCN 2022006819 (ebook) |
    ISBN 9780520382190 (cloth) | ISBN 9780520382213 (paperback) |
    ISBN 9780520382220 (ebook)
Subjects: LCSH: Black power—Germany—Berlin. | Black people—
    Political activity—Germany—Berlin. | Noncitizens—Political activity—
    Germany—Berlin. | Holocaust, Jewish (1939–1945)—Influence. |
    Germany—Race relations—Political aspects. | BISAC: SOCIAL
    SCIENCE / Anthropology / Cultural & Social | SOCIAL SCIENCE /
    Anthropology / General
Classification: LCC DD78.B55 P37 2022 (print) | LCC DD78.B55 (ebook) |
    DDC 305.896043/155—dc23/eng/20220519
LC record available at https://lccn.loc.gov/2022006818
LC ebook record available at https://lccn.loc.gov/2022006819

32   31   30   29   28   27   26   25   24   23
10   9   8   7   6   5   4   3   2   1

To the four generations of women who have nurtured me intellectually, through their music, and through their love: Deborah Cannon Partridge Wolfe, Gwendella Allen, Josephine A. V. Allen, Sunita Bose Partridge, and Jasmine Josephine Bose Partridge

Contents

Preface

"Why is it so difficult to come into this society without being wounded?"[1] Mamadou, a young filmmaker, originally from Guinea, writes with chalk in the center of a busy sidewalk in a gentrifying neighborhood in Berlin.[2] Many passersby stop to read the writing next to the subway station where he used to live. One might argue that Mamadou has become "Black" as a result of his experiences in Germany. He has been told by lawyers and bureaucrats alike that the only way that he can stay is if he has a baby with a German woman or gets married to someone who holds a German passport. But he has resisted these avenues of tolerated existence and found another way to stay, at least for the medium term.

Shortly after his arrival in Berlin, Mamadou joined a theater group researching, writing, and performing a play on Black Power. Here, he learned to raise his fist like the Black American medalists Tommie Smith and John Carlos in the spirit of the 1968 Olympics. Mamadou has since become an actor in the full sense of the word: he is learning how to play a role and he is enacting social change. Regardless of whether or not he was Black in Guinea, Blackness has become a possibility, if not necessity, for him in Berlin. This is not only the phenotypical Blackness, but one that has allied him with a broad spectrum of POCs (People of Color) who often also make claims to Blackness and in the theater declare, "We are making history today. Do you remember 1968? Self Defense is no offense. No person is illegal. And the right to stay [should be] everywhere." Black-empowered claims would lead to his less precarious ability to stay in Germany. Blackness becomes a way to articulate his desire. Blackness also expresses his position in relation to Enlightenment claims to universal freedom, participation, and citizenship. Writing in chalk, Mamadou holds the immediate society accountable to him and people like him.

The point here, though, is not that Blackness should become the basis on which all racialized and minoritized people or subjects make political claims in liberal democracies, but that the claim-making tells us something about the systematic failures of these kinds of political communities, at least as far as those who claim Blackness are concerned. This book is aware of the problematics of what Jerod Sexton (2010) calls "people of color blindness," that the broad experience of marginalization or the original disavowal cannot get at the particularity of anti-Blackness as a slave-thingness. On the one hand, it recognizes that slave-thingness has not been historically stable, even if those of African descent are almost always central players in that dynamic. On the other hand, claims to Blackness, particularly when the historical and global persistence of anti-Blackness is taken into account, can be centrally understood as claims for the necessity of another kind of world that then also recognizes the originary exclusion of Blackness in spite of the persistent and continued insistence that Enlightenment freedom is universal. In this sense, claims to Blackness are the opposite of a return to ordinary, pre-populist democracy, but point to the need for something altogether different. This book is then based not only on the claim, but also on what that claim could and does mean in terms of everyday practice.

While the research that led to this book is situated primarily in Europe, and it seems to change the stakes compared to claims to Blackness in North America, the Caribbean, or South America, for example, the continued transnational connections also make Europe a relevant location from which to consider, claim, and mobilize Blackness. Even here, whether in subtle or explicit forms, state-organized or informal, expressions of White supremacy are no less odious. As Mamadou's experience demonstrates, woundedness (see also Brown 1995) is part of the condition of entry for those who become, if they were not already, Black. As Wilderson (2020) notes, thingness is as well. Articulating Blackness, this book will show, becomes part of the expression of finding life in spite of these bounds. The pursuit appears as part of what has become a universal claim.

In relation to Blackness, in Germany, in particular, the bureaucratic state holds itself accountable to the memory of its Holocaust, also known as the Shoah.[3] Today Germany stands behind the proclamation "Never again" through memorialization practices, including public education. Monuments, memorials, and classroom instruction work to prove the country's commitment to preventing future genocide. While neo-Nazi ideology and violence persist, there remains strong and continued efforts to counter anti-Semitism. In this regard, Germany has come to see itself as a global leader in opposing anti-Semitism and anti-Semitic violence, while increasingly focusing its educational practices on those perceived as "immigrants."[4] At the same time, activists fight to counter other forms of insidious contemporary racism (see, for example, Opitz, Oguntoye, and Schultz 1991; Terkessidis 2004; Aikins 2008; Arndt and Ofuatey-Alazard 2011; Langhoff 2011; El-Tayeb 2011; Florvil 2020).

Germany's World War II defeat forced West Germany, in particular, to atone for the form of racialized violence that led to the Nazi Holocaust; and yet, Germany maintains an image as overwhelmingly White and European. Attending to the contemporary dynamics of racism as they relate to the historical acts remains an issue. When other racialized people liken their experiences of exclusion and discrimination in Germany to the country's Nazi history, many Germans find themselves quick to counter that the non-Jewish, usually non-Black Other, is not experiencing genocide, and risks erasing the specificity of this prior form of atrocity. What I call the monumentality of Holocaust memory in Germany (see chapter 4) has meant that only certain forms of mobilization organized to fight against contemporary racism will gain traction. Comparison is taboo, but linking struggles, at least in some cases, seems possible.

For young people like Mamadou, even for those who don't appear as "Black," claiming Blackness offers a different way to articulate a noncitizen politics. This book thus examines how and why Blackness has emerged as a tool used by precarious people, Black people, and noncitizens to navigate and negotiate everyday marginalization, homogenization, and disavowal.

For many noncitizens, including Turkish or Arab Germans, Blackness is epitomized by American Civil Rights leaders like Martin Luther King, Muhammed Ali, Angela Davis, and Malcolm X. These historical actors and activists called attention to the hypocrisy of an America that fashioned itself a leader of global democracy amid segregation and rampant racial oppression. While Germany has gathered the moral authority, often expressed as a kind of moral superiority, even in the often unwitting sense of (racist) racial hierarchy, to become an anti-genocidal leader, the emphasis on the historical specificity of the genocide its former Nazi leaders perpetrated has made it difficult to think about and work in relation to multiple struggles simultaneously. As the accounts and articulations in this book reveal, Blackness has emerged in relation to multiple other struggles, transcending any one particular experience to become a universal claim. Blackness works as a different kind of assertion for the self-fashioning of noncitizens, that is, for those, regardless of official passport, who find little space to make claims to state and other resources, including schools, theaters, youth centers, and religious institutions.[5] Even while recognizing the universalized assertion of these claims, questions of accountability *vis a vis* anti-Blackness persist and will be addressed in the pages that follow.

Until now, my work has focused on how noncitizens get produced in contemporary life. In this book, I will explore how one (or a collective) can undo this production—not to become citizens, but to become a different kind of political actor. In general, I worry about the limits of citizenship, in that it necessarily produces and marks its opposite, that is those without resources or rights. Living, writing, and thinking as a noncitizen in Germany offers a unique vantage point from which to examine the relationship between Holocaust memory and Blackness. Focusing on noncitizens holds the reader, theorist, and the activist accountable to those not served by universalized Enlightenment claims. Blackness, as citizenship's originary outside (think slavery),[6] compels the minoritized and marginalized to think politics beyond citizenship and beyond the nation-state. Its everyday practice and articulations, as well as its particular histories, offer a place from which to mobilize and strategize anew.

Acknowledgments

I would like to especially thank Ahmed Shah and the members of both Theater X and Film X, who have shown what it is like to be part of a different kind of institution, and thus a different kind of world.

I am listing many of the real names of those with whom I worked on film productions with Theater X/Film X for Filming the Future of Detroit and Filming the Future from Berlin (see filmingfuturecities.org) and with whom we did exchanges between Detroit and Berlin, because we have worked on projects together that we then presented to broader publics in Berlin, Ann Arbor, Detroit, and online. While there are many more to thank, I would like to note these individuals, in particular: Ayla Gottschlich, Hagen Decker, Keryeschi Lorenso, Blaise Mbuh, Selvihan Bozkurt, Ousmane Diallo, Zeynep Dilek, Dalia El-Heit, Deniz Erdogdu, Melike Ertürk, Zarifa Evartone, Rohat Günes, Andre Iliev, Keryeschi Lorenso, Büsra Okumus, Kreshnik Ramadani, Sarah Seini, Ibrahim Balde, Medina Andre Toko, Jasmin Ibrahim, Helen Maynard, Ajara Hamidatu Alghali, Zeynep Oezcan, Hawlaane Noor Frances Sarr-Robbins, Whitney Smith, Filmmakers from Freedom House (Detroit), Ahmed Alashkar, Alix Bakilis, Roman Gelfand, Sheila Marretta, Mike Momo, Chibueze Mpamah, Seydi Sarr, Hawlaane Sarr-Robbins, Mazen Aljarboua, Roman Gelfand,

Mohammed Kello, Sheila Marretta, Zeynep Oezcan, Peggy, Abdulmajid Sedawi, Medina Andre Toko, Shayane Lacey, Maia Owen, and filmmakers from the institutions then known as the Jugendtheaterbüro Berlin and Refugee Club Impulse.

I would also like to thank the cast, mentors, and artistic directors of the film and play *Schwarzkopf BRD:* Ibrahim Balde, Dinah Büchner, Jamil Dishpan, Damla Eser, Jasmin Ibrahim, Esther Jurkewicz, Nurcan Khan, Katherine Kolmans, Mustafa El-Hussein, Mohammed Rmeih, Passart Salam, Ahmed Shah, and Ramon Smith. In addition, I am incredibly grateful to Riccardo Valsecchi who produced the film with Theater X, insisted that I take a formal part, and worked with the actors and artistic director to produce the image that has become the cover of this book.

For their collaboration at BALLHAUS NAUNYNSTRASSE and its Akademie der Autodidakten, both as mentors and as fellow filmmakers, I would like to thank Mely Kiyak, Neco Çelik, Ayla Gottschlich, Janine Jembere, Michael Götting, Hasan Adam, Elisa Asefa, Afida Asinot, T. Vicky Germain, Karina Griffith, Lewis Happy, Innocent, Sarah Mouwani, Amanda Mukasonga, Mirjam Pleines, Hannah Soma, David Sunda, Turgay Ayaydinli, Tuana Ayaydinli, Marlon Barlow-Lockward, Gerasimos Bekas, Giorgia Bonizio, Esin Colak, Bahar Demir, Serkan Deniz, T. Vicky Germain, Sophia Hoffinger, Taylan Kilic, Amanda Mukasonga, Yasmine Salimi, Frederick Schmidt, Zoe Schmidt, Philipp White, Okan Yilmaz, Davide de Feudis, Mehmet Can Kocak, Serpil Turhan, Mazlum Nergiz, Viviane Petrescu, Kerti Puni-Specht, and Cima-Nadja Samadi.

Even though Detroit is not directly a part of this book, I would like to thank my friends, supporters, and collaborators there as well, including Ajara Alghali, Seydi Sarr, Whitney Smith, Onricia, and Grace.

My longterm mentors include:

Judith Butler, with whom I am always in conversation, even when they are not aware of it. I am grateful both for their generosity and their inspiration.

Aihwa Ong, who continues to push me and always invites me (at least implicitly) to push back. I learn so much in the process.

Allan Pred, who is now gone, but whose work and community of former students continues to sustain me.

Paul Rabinow, who passed away the year I completed this book. Working with him as he taught Foucault gave me the framework to think both with and beyond certain forms of liberation.

While I never had the privilege of formally being her student, Leslie Adelson is such an incredibly generous scholar, who repeatedly reached out to me to invite my participation in communities for which I am eternally grateful. I am also grateful for the space that she worked to create in the academy for this kind of work. I am still trying to imagine how to recreate the kind of intellectual community she created in the form of a DAAD (German Academic Exchange Service) seminar one summer at Cornell. I have stayed in touch with many of the people who were there and continue to find out about others who are also connected to this seminar and to whose work I am indebted.

Fellow students whose work has deeply shaped my thinking:

I was in graduate school with Frank Wilderson and Jared Sexton, and I now wish that I had taken more advantage of that fact at the time. They, of course, weren't anthropologists, but we took classes together. Reading their work now, with my students, while also reading Saidiya Hartman (whose work I first heard in its early iterations at Berkeley) and Christina Sharpe, in addition to Jasbir Puar (who was already an elder at Berkeley when I arrived but who made me feel at home), along with (more recently) Ahmed Shah and Theater X members, all help me to think outside of (liberal) frameworks that, in their actual practice, work to oppress me and many others.

At the University of Michigan, I am appreciative of colleagues, current and former students, friends, collaborators, and mentors in the Department of Anthropology, including: Kelly Askew, Hakem Al-Rustom, Alysa Handelsman, Jacinta Beehner, Ruth Behar, Faith Bailey, Katie Berringer, Melissa Burch, Matthew Chin, Courtney Cottrell, Jason De León, Maureen Devlin, Jatin Dua, Abigail Dumes, Amal Hassan Fadlalla, Kriszti Fehervary, Tom Fricke, David Frye, Michael Galaty, Raven Garvey, Simeneh Gebvremariam, Hyatse Gyal, Matt Hiller, Benjamin Holenbach, Jennifer Hsieh, Cintia Huitzil, Matt Hull, Anneeth Kaur Hundle, Vitalis Im, Judy Irvine, Nina Jackson Levin, Webb Keane, Stuart Kirsch, Jennifer Larios, Alaina Lemon, Michael Lempert, Laura McLatchy, Yuchen Luo, Bruce Mannheim, Joyce Marcus, Mike McGovern, Barbara Meek, Yasmin Moll,

Erik Mueller, Maxwell Owusu, Anisha Padma, Alyssa Paredes, Holly Peters-Golden, Lauren Pratt, Elisha Renne, Elana Resnick, Leela Riesz, Liz Roberts, Irene Routté, Gayle Rubin, Noelia Santana, Sharmi Sen, Andrew Shryock, Sam Shuman, Jennifer Sierra, Carla Sinopoli, Taylor Spencer, Scott Stonington, Leigh Stuckey, Malika Stuerznickel, Julie Winningham, Lai Wo, and Laura Yakas, among many others.

The moment of Black Lives Matter that followed the murder of George Floyd was an especially important moment for my ability to speak more directly. Thanks to all of you who contributed to making that tragic murder into a moment that would institute a new direction for our collective struggle. We're already experiencing the backlash, so we'll need to push even harder now.

I really thank graduate students and undergrads at the University of Michigan who led by being outspoken in a way that made it possible for me to also be more forthright about what kinds of change would be necessary.

I am grateful for those students who also pushed me.

Both my undergraduate and graduate students in Filming the Future of Detroit, Filming the Future of "Diversity," Citizenship and Noncitizens, and Blackness and Universality helped to make the university a more bearable and (at least momentarily) revolutionary space.

In the Department of Afroamerican and African Studies at the University of Michigan, I would like to thank current and former colleagues and collaborators Omolade Adunbi, Kwasi Ampene, Naomi Andre, Kelly Askew, Marlyse Baptista, Bénédict Boisseron, Robin Means Coleman, Matthew Countryman, Angela Dillard, Frieda Ekotto, Amal Fadlalla, Kevin Gaines, Sandra Gunning, Nesha Haniff, Wayne High, Nancy Rose Hunt, Elizabeth James, Paul Johnson, Martha Jones, Lydia Kelow-Bennett, Aliyah Khan, Earl Lewis, Tiya Miles, Lester Monts, Derek Peterson, Ann Pitcher, Faye Portis, Sherie Randolph, Elisha Renne, Julius Scott, Xiomara Santamarina, SaraEllen Strongman, Heather Thompson, Jon Wells, and Magdalena Zaborowska.

Jazzaray James and Morgan Locke helped me create intellectual spaces both within and outside of the academy, first as undergraduate students, and now as those who are making spaces in their own right.

In German Studies and Black Studies at Michigan and elsewhere, I would like to thank Fatima El-Tayeb, Tina Campt, E. Patrick Johnson, Nitasha Sharma, Alexander Weheliye, Johannes von Moltke, Kerstin Barndt, and Kristin Kopp.

I am gratified by Marian Swanzy-Parker's willingness to read the beginning and end of this work at the last minute, ultimately providing me the confidence to turn it in, even if I did not respond to all of her queries and critiques.

I am thankful for my engagement with Heather Merrill and Lisa Hoffman, who included my work in *Spaces of Danger* (2015) and keep involving me and my work in ongoing conversations about racism and geography.

Katrin Sieg and Lizzie Stewart gave critical feedback on parts of the manuscript that addressed themes linked to their particular expertise on postmigrant theater and how German theater deals with race, racism, and processes of racialization. Ela Gezen, who also works on German theater, has been a perpetual collaborator.

I would also like to express my gratitude for Nora Haakh, who gave me advance access to her book on postmigrant theater and Muslim subjects.

Kristin Dickinson, at the University of Michigan (U of M), always invited me to German Studies talks and brought delicious mint tea leaves to our house in the middle of the pandemic while I was trying to finish this book.

Kira Thurman, also in German Studies at the U of M, brought me into conversations and communities in Germany and Ann Arbor in the midst of writing her own fabulous book.

Michael Rothberg, Esra Özyürek, and I have been traveling similar paths while being in conversation with each other in Berlin, online, and through our work. I am very thankful for the insights their work has offered this project.

I am also grateful to Bettina Stoetzer, Andrea Muehlebach, Nitzan Shoshan, Fred von Bose, Christina Schwenkel, Smaran Dayal, Anna Esther Younes, Saida Hodzic, Maria Stoilkova, Georges Khalil, Adam Benkato, Adelheid Krämer, Elke Bickert, Hans Kreutzjans, Bala Venkat Mani, Dace Dzenovska, Daromir Rudnycky, Hannah B, Heiko Henkel, Guillermo Atocha Arias, June Hwang, Katharina Schramm, Kristine Krause, Sander Gilman, Moritz Ege, Natasha Kelly, Nermin Celik, Pushkar

Sinha, Rosa Cordillera Castillo, Saba Mahmood, Sally Merry, Sarah Sebhatu, Saskia Köbschall, Siegfried Matti, Sultan Doughan, Tahir Della, Tmnit Zere, Trinh T. Minh-ha, Veronika Gerhard, Volkan Türeli, Çığır Özyurt, The BTWH (Berkeley-Tübingen-Wien (Vienna)-Harvard) transnational working group, and The Black Diaspora and Germany Network for the many conversations, invitations, collaborations, and critiques of this and other work.

This project has been funded by the University of Michigan, the Alexander von Humboldt Foundation, the German Research Foundation, the Mellon Foundation, and the University of Michigan Center for Emerging Democracies.

While working on the final stages of the book, Janet Ward at the University of Oklahoma made a platform possible to discuss coloniality, Blackness, and Holocaust memory with Esra Özyürek and Michael Rothberg as part of a German Studies Association transnational online conversation. I am tremendously appreciative.

I also want to thank David Turnley at U of M for allowing me to use his photograph of Nelson Mandela after his release from prison in my work.

I am grateful for Deirdre Spencer who has become an important collaborator in the fight against institutionalized racism at the University of Michigan.

Anjuli Gupta (now gone) and Biplap Basu shared their house with me early on during my career in Berlin. They helped me to escape potential attack by neo-Nazis while inviting me into critical spaces.

John Goetz has ben a constant friend. I am grateful for his humor, and all of those incredibly productive debates.

Miriam Ticktin and Patrick Dodd have been perpetual interlocutors. I wish they were still living in Ann Arbor.

Janice Williams Miller and Reuben Miller came to Ann Arbor, enriching our lives tremendously, until they returned to Chicago. Of course, Reuben's book gave me hope about the broader reception of academic writing.

Eka Neumann, Mandu Dos Santos Pinto, and Malia have been and will continue to be longterm friends, engaged from music to food to everything else that one requires to live and find moments of immense joy in Berlin. I can also count on them for both loving and rigorous feedback.

Rebecca Hardin, Arun Agrawal, and Naina have been critical to our nourishment and intellectual exchange in Ann Arbor, Michigan.

Kate Zambon has been a frequent interlocutor over the years.

Jonas Tinius, who I first met in Berlin, has also been a critical interlocutor.

Margareta von Oswald has been a gracious host and frequent interlocutor at the Centre for Anthropological Research on Museums and Heritage at the Humboldt University in Berlin.

Thanks to Austin Sarat, who keeps me refreshed as a perpetual student. Thanks also to Ute Brandes and Mary Brofenbrenner, German teachers at different stages of my life, who are ultimately responsible for taking me to the places where I ended up.

Amrita Basu and Jeff Rubin were also critical parts of my undergraduate career, and their courses on "Asian Women: Myths of Deference, Arts of Resistance" and "Sustainable Development" continue to shape my thinking to this day.

I am grateful for senior colleagues at other institutions, including John Jackson and Deborah Thomas at the University of Pennsylvania, for their mentorship and encouragement.

I would also like to acknowledge Reminder Kaur and Andrew Byron Kipnis at the journal *Hau* for their encouragement and deep critical engagement with my work related to this project.

Other friends, colleagues, and collaborators who provided contexts to help me think about this work in some significant way include Nan Kim, Jill Smith, Kimberly Arkin, Ela Gezen, Priscilla Layne, Jonathan Skolnik, Sharon Macdonald, Wolfgang Kaschuba, Silvy Chakkalakal, Jörg Niewöhner, Regina Römhild, and Arjun Appadurai.

I am grateful to audiences at the "Entangled Otherings" symposium at the University of Cambridge; the American Anthropological Association Meetings in Vancouver and Washington, DC; the German Studies Association meetings in Portland and in Indianapolis; the Johannesburg Institute for Advanced Study; the Royal Anthropological Film Institute in London; the London School of Economics; the Association for Asian Studies Conference (for sponsoring our panel on Black Lives Matter in South Korea); the American Anthropological Association "2020: Raising Our Voices" livestream event on "Embattled Europe"; the livestream event in Volkshochschule Muldental; Bowdoin College; the International Center Goa (India); the University of Michigan's Center for World Performance Studies; Boston University's Pardee School of Global Studies; the Heinrich Böll Stiftung for the Anthropology of Race and Ethnicity; the Network of the European Association of Social Anthropology; the American Comparative Literature Association Annual Meeting at Utrecht University in the Netherlands; Clark University's Centre de formation et de séminaires in Luxembourg; the Institute of European Ethnology and its Centre for Anthropological Research on Museums and Heritage at the Humboldt University in Berlin; the Modern Language Association Conference in Düsseldorf (2016); the Zentrum für Antisemitismusforschung at the Technische Üniversität Berlin; the Center for European Studies at the University of California, Berkeley; the Institute for Cultural Inquiry in Berlin; the University of Sussex; the Academy of the Jewish Museum in Berlin; the German Studies Department at the University of Pennsylvania; the Departments of German Languages and Literatures and Anthropology at the University of Toronto; the Departments of German Studies and Anthropology at the University of California, Los Angelas; Goucher College; the American Association of Teachers of German Seminar (2010); and Savvy Contemporary in Berlin.

In addition, I would like to express my gratitude for colleagues who took part in our "Interrogating 'Diversity'" symposium at the University of Michigan, including Jessica Cattelino, Seçkin Özdemir, Nil Mutluer, Esra Özyürek, Mayanthi Fernando, Ajanatha Subramanian, Anneeth Kaur Hundle, Matthew Chin, Ciraj Rassool, Gloria Diaz, Gabrielle Cabrerera, Carla Moore, Laura Yakas, and Rinaldo Walcott. I would also like to thank those who participated in our symposium on "Mobilizing 'Blackness.'" I wish that everyday life could be like that community. Thanks to Charisse Burden-Stelly, Fatima El-Tayeb, Nathalie Etoke, Ezgi Güner, Priscilla Layne, Alan Lentin, Jasmine Linnea Kelekay, Esra Özyürek, Fatou-Seydi Sarr, Mihir Sharma, Marian Swazy-Parker, Katerina Teaiwa, and Vanessa Thompson.

My experience writing this book with the support of the University of California Press has been amazing. I did not know that it could be this good. For this experience, and for making me know that I could be even more outspoken than I thought possible, as well as for her deep attention to my prose, I would especially like to thank Kate Marshall. Enrique

Ochoa-Kaup has also been fabulous. And, of course, the three reviewers. One remains anonymous, and I am eternally grateful for all three, including Kimberly Arkin and Esra Özyürek. Their work also inspires me. I am also very happy to have had Melissa L. Caldwell as an official press UC faculty reader, who encouraged me to write a manifesto. Just the thought made me know that the press had my back. Thanks also to my copyeditor, Catherine Osborne, and indexer, Derek Gottlieb.

In addition, I want to thank people outside of the University in Ann Arbor, including Nancy Lynn, Shonagh Taruza, and Kathy Macdonald in addition to long-term friends and supporters in Ithaca, NY, my home town, including Margaret Washington, Nancy Potter, and George Gull.

Finally, I am filled with gratitude for all of my friends, family, and friends who have become family. I already listed many of you above. Additional members include: Ehrhard and Barbara Friedemann, Bernadette Atuahene, Vera Grant, Jean-Paul Bourelly, Branwen Okpako, Nilambari and Anup Patil, Janet Lassan, Johaness Elwardt and their children, Sibel Istemi, Mustafa Dogan, Juline Dogan, Jensel Dogan, Silvana Santamaria, Bilal Athimni, Cecelia, Sevim Celebi-Gottschlich, Carl and Juliana Truesdale, and Aunt Gerald and Uncle Michael (Crowder).

Finally, I would like to thank my mom, my dad, my sisters, my brother, my brothers- and sisters-in-law, my blended and extended family, and Sunita and Jasmine. I love you. Of course, I am also grateful to you for reading my work, allowing me the space and time to write, for holding me accountable, and mostly for loving me in all of these ways and many more.

Introduction

"Anti-Blackness is universal, but is Blackness?"[1]

This question is the basis for this book. Is Blackness[2] universal? If so, what kind of politics can claiming Blackness enable? How might Blackness as a central basis for political life change the world?

This book is situated in postwar Germany, that is from World War II to the present, and set in a contemporary theater in Berlin. It is a theater founded primarily by non-Black People of Color where I observed, over the course of eleven years, Turkish and Turkish-German, Arab and Arab-German, and African and African-German people taking up Blackness in order to claim space in a predominantly White country that had both historically orchestrated genocidal violence but also become a global leader in the politics of atonement. Unfortunately, Germany's global leadership resulted in regulating what constitutes racism and who could demand redress. For many Turkish and Arab people (or those with Turkish or Arab heritage) residing in Germany, identifying their own experiences of racism becomes equated with Holocaust denialism. The underlying logic understands racism in Germany in relation to genocide, and therefore suggests that individuals not experiencing mass murder or anything directly linked to mass, systematic atrocity cannot claim racism. Claiming an affiliation with Blackness, though, has emerged as a way to create a different kind of globalized agency. It offers a critical way to engage the past, present, and future, linked to prior and ongoing examples of Black struggle. One could be Black or claim an affinity with Black struggle without denying the Nazi-orchestrated Holocaust.

Germany has thus become an important site for analyzing the efficacy of these claims while also highlighting the inadequacy of Enlightenment or post-Cold-War pronouncements of "freedom" to fully liberate Black people. Examining claims to universal Blackness is relevant, as one persistently sees, not just in Germany but also across the world. Importantly, universalized claims to Blackness must be held accountable to Black people, or to those who are the primary and persistent targets of anti-Blackness, or what geographer Ruth Gilmore (2007) describes as those systematically exposed to premature death.

This book thus links mutual struggle to political possibility. It worries about the universalized Enlightenment claims of "freedom" and argues that we need to make Blackness, not Enlightenment, the basis for assessing liberation. It's one thing to theorize liberation from the perspective of an Enlightenment philosopher and quite another to have to theorize it historically from the position of a slave—for whom it means something much less abstract (see Buck-Morss 2000).

Black people, and those who align themselves with a politics based on Blackness, are persistently being undone by the institutions—from schools to hospitals—that claim to both educate and protect them. Such institutions, however, can inflict violence or even death on those they profess to support. There are often certain truths that White peers and educators do not want to hear about the institutions they both produce and sustain. White supremacy is embedded in the everyday. In this sense, inclusion, even for Black people, means complicity with sustaining these institutions. Centering the present and future on Blackness, however, offers a different potential outcome.

THE THEATER

Who would imagine that theater would be so central to living? When I started this project, I began by investigating processes of democratization in contemporary Berlin, but came to understand that democratization usually means killing the spirit of those who are to be "included" in the democracy. If we begin with and center Blackness, then we feature a different orientation, a different roadmap, a different trajectory for political articulation. For Black people, living the contradictions of democracy is everyday life. Establishing other kinds of spaces becomes necessary to a kind of living that will not ultimately kill one's spirit at the same time. Otherwise, it seems a matter of time before that death ultimately comes.

I am thus writing this book to call for the establishment and funding of more spaces in which we, as Black people, can express our displeasure without fear, where we won't have to restrain our critique, where we can express the truths of our existence. The theater, as I will show, can provide a possibility for this kind of living. Here, the theater not only takes on the questions of democracy, but also the questions of capitalism and living space. Inasmuch as it also involves the body, it does this not only in terms of abstract theoretical trajectories, but also as everyday practice.

In this particular circumstance, as demonstrated in the following pages, because the theater's building was connected to a church, it was able to offer its noncitizen actors and local residents sanctuary (in this case church asylum, or *Kirchenasyl*). This meant that the police would not enter in the middle of the night to remove residents, which can happen in regular apartment buildings. Most recently, through one of the theater group collectives, also as a result of some struggle, being trans, or gender-queer, or non-cisgendered is openly discussed and lived in the theater. In all of these cases and in others, the theater offers a way to live.

Over a decade of doing research in and collaborating with Theater X, the same group of people, alongside many new participants, have remained. Officially, the theater gets state funding through pots established for youth work and youth theater. The stigma of "migrant" or post-migrant theater being viewed by arts funders as more documentary (Stewart 2021), based more on experience and less on artistic training or imagination, also applies here. But even if this theater does social work, it also wins prizes for its art. It sends members to famous acting and film schools. It collaborates with other theaters around the world. It also has established a film collective alongside its theater work.

Truth was at stake for this theater. This was and is not the polite, White, institutional, mainstream, form of truth, but the truth on which the collective's thriving was dependent. The participants wanted to get it right without regard for careerism. Getting it right meant establishing spaces where those who acted, made films, did the lighting, and organized the publicity would flourish.

BLACKNESS AS POSSIBILITY

This is what this book is examining in everyday practice. Beginning with the Haitian revolution and moving through the examination and even critique of "Diasporic Aesthetics" with Stuart Hall (1990; see chapter 1), this book thinks through Blackness historically, but also without trying to reproduce anything like national affiliation or loyalty. Black people need Blackness as a basis for establishing a different kind of world, not Blackness a as a limit. In this book, living with and thinking through Blackness with Theater X becomes a way to think about and establish a different world.

In observing and analyzing the politics of claiming Blackness, I have organized this book into three key sections. The first offers a historical and theoretical background to Black claims. It addresses the relationship between the particularity of Black suffering and how Blackness then becomes a universal kind of claim. This section thinks critically about the shift in Germany, Europe, and the world, from a rhetoric of Black men raping White women when the French placed French African troops to occupy the German *Rheinland* following the First World War (Campt 2004) to a shift in the reading of Black occupation. After the Second World War, many West Germans saw Black American occupiers as liberators they could trust. Because they felt that they were also being oppressed by White Americans, there was an additional opportunity for Black affiliation—an affiliation that corresponded with a global shift. The presence of Black occupiers also called attention to the contradictions in American occupation and thus American democracy. If Black people were not free in the United States, as Jim Crow was still law in the American South, what did American freedom and liberation mean in Germany? While "American liberation" addressed the specificity of German atrocity, at least as it concerned the politics of mass murder, it did not universally address racism.

Segregated clubs where White German women went to meet Black men and vice versa suggested a shift in the meaning of occupation, at least as it concerned these relationships. Black troops were also thought to be more generous to the German public—initially a starving public grateful for gifts of candy—than White American occupiers. Then the Civil Rights Movement and Black Power provided another opportunity for affiliation, again, even for White Germans, particularly those on the left (Ege 2007). Through historical events, political movements, and globalizing culture, including music, film, and television, Blackness gained a foothold in the popular imaginary and also found space for a different kind of allied affiliation.

The second section of this book brings these historical contradictions between democratization, rights, occupation, and participation into relation with Holocaust memory and processes of democratization in Germany. With the waning of formal American occupation, it shows how Germany began to master its own discourse of atonement and accountability. While this process began with the activists of the 1968 generation, in addition to holding the parents of that generation to account for their complicity with supporting the Nazis and anti-Semitism, it takes on the accountability of the children of the so-called "Guest-worker" generation (Chin 2007), including Turkish-Germans, and also the children of Palestinian refugees. Largely in schools and other kinds of formal and informal educational institutions, the '68 generation works to hold society as a whole accountable for the memory of genocide and the politics of perpetration.

When atonement for the Nazi-led Holocaust is linked to democratic participation, the consequences for Turkish, Turkish-German, Arab, and Arab-German (non)citizens becomes entangled with dominant assumptions that such populations are inherently anti-Semitic. This puts individuals and communities in a position of having to prove their trustworthiness in order to also have a say about the direction of the democracy. One might ask, however: how can they be held to account for a politics in which they, themselves, did not participate? Beyond the lack of historical participation, though, state actors, journalists, and others want people from Turkey and primarily Arabic-speaking countries, as well as Turkish-Germans and

Arab-Germans,[3] to account for and even admit to being anti-Semitic. As a country that led and orchestrated the Shoah, Germany feels responsible for administering a global kind of accountability. Within this system, claiming any kind of equivalence to the experience of genocide has been taboo. Claiming Blackness, though, has emerged as a different kind of possibility, which does not preclude one from also addressing anti-Semitism.

The last section of this book, then, thinks through Blackness as possibility, even for those who do not necessarily think of themselves as Black. Even in cases in which anti-Blackness is emergent, Black struggle suggests the possibility for mutual struggle (see also Alsubee 2020). In this context, images, sweatshirts, and t-shirts of Muhammad Ali are ubiquitous. Pictures, stickers, graffiti, and other public portrayals of the 1968 Olympics with Black athletes standing with raised and clenched fists, and images of Angela Davis, even in the 1990s and 2000s, also suggest a coming together of White, Turkish, Arab, Turkish- and Arab-German, and Black American affiliation.

This section further investigates the possibilities that emerge from these links. It takes seriously what these connections might mean amidst new trends in immigration, structured, in part, via the theater, a central site of this investigation, but also via the politics of the so-called "refugee crisis" beginning in the summer of 2015, when Germany formally accepted nearly one million refugees, most of whom had come from Syria. Between Blackness and noncitizenship, the last section challenges the reader to think critically about making Blackness more central as a means to open up space for engendering other, more accountable and more liberated, ways of living.

PART I   Occupying Blackness

1 After Diaspora, Beyond Citizenship

While I have been deeply influenced by Stuart Hall's (1990) cultural analysis of racism and his analysis of and hope for diaspora, I am also struck by the limits of the latter approach. Jacqueline Nassy Brown's (1998) notion of "diasporic resources" calls us to attend to the violent processes that these resources have helped alienated people to overcome. While addressing anti-Blackness, we need also to examine the extent to which diasporic resources, in this case Black resources, also apply to those who may or may not perceive themselves as Black. The communities built from Black resources that exceed Enlightenment and nation-state-like forms of belonging would likely seek to make a home wherever they are, and also develop transnational forms of organizing and affiliation. Because Blackness is different everywhere, we need Blackness as a critical stance, as the refusal of naive aspiration, as nothing like the nation-state. We need a different kind of power arrangement. Within these contexts and debates, the question is not just who defines themselves as a Person of Color, which I sometimes heard being discussed in Berlin theater and activist circles, but also how one attends to anti-Blackness. This is likely the motivation for Hall's calling for something like the nation-state to care for Black people, that is, not wanting to leave attending to anti-Blackness up to chance.

Rather, a truly novel articulation has to open up beyond the limits put on Blackness, or the limits Blackness as an identitarian kind of politics puts on itself.

Moving from Hall's and filmmaker Isaac Julien's (1994) analyses of "diasporic aesthetics" to post-diasporic practice in contemporary Berlin, in street scenes and in artistic performances, this chapter analyzes both the possibilities and the limits for coalition and social transformation through the practices and aesthetics of these art scenes. It looks at the multiple possibilities the Black American occupying presence helped enable *vis a vis* the mobility of African, Turkish, and Arab immigrants and post-migrants, Turkish-Germans, Arab-Germans, African-Germans, and Black people in Germany. Access to Black aesthetics and Black people means a different conceptualization of freedom, one that exceeds citizenship and opens beyond those who might be seen or see themselves as Black.

This chapter, thus, examines not only how "Black lives matter," but also the ways in which Turkish, Arab, African, and Black claimants come to take on and articulate Black positions as part of a universalizing process in which they demand change. It grows out of research on Holocaust memorialization and contemporary race. It argues against European claims to moral superiority, that is, the supposition that the mainstream German and European publics have mastered the past, atoned for their role in genocide, and asserted themselves with others through the pronouncement that "never again" will genocidal violence be repeated. European institutions and majoritarian subjects do this while demanding accountability for their relationships to the genocidal past from almost everyone living in contemporary Europe (excluding those who are the children and grandchildren of Holocaust victimization). But this obscures the possibilities for *suffering with* (my modification of the solidarity/pity paradigm) and, thus, organizing with those who see themselves as the descendants of the Shoah's horror (as opposed to its perpetrators), and other contemporary noncitizens.

Claims to Blackness become universal in the sense that they become one of the only ways for those without direct links to the Shoah to articulate experiences of contemporary racism without also being accused of Holocaust denial, with the Nazi-led Holocaust as the threshold for what one should understand as racism, or, in other words, what should never happen again. The logic follows that to call a contemporary experience racism is to make comparisons to the incomparable, as if experiences of discrimination are the same as genocide. In my research, I have been struck by how Turkish/Turkish-German and Arab/Arab-German youth in Berlin, Mizrahi Jews in Israel, Palestinians in and out of Israel/Palestine (see Hammad 2010), and African descendants in France use Blackness as their own vehicles for demanding social change. Because of the history of the American civil rights movement and the global circulation of African-American cultural forms, it is possible to articulate experiences of racism on these grounds (relating one's contemporary experience of racialization to Blackness in particular) without then being seen as a Holocaust denier. In contemporary Germany, articulations of Blackness rely on the postwar connection with the fight against American racism and the actual presence of African-American occupiers, who stood as a reminder of the contradictions inherent in the American-led effort toward post-Holocaust democratization.

Black Power acts as a resource (see Brown 1998, Partridge 2013) just as it reaches beyond any one diasporic experience.[1] The persistence of White European and American claims to cultural, economic, and moral superiority lurk in the background of an interaction that seeks an alternative and continues to demand change.

BLACKNESS, EUROPE, AND BEYOND

Given that Blackness has been a historical position that has traditionally been opposed to Europeanness (see Gilman 1985), this chapter examines the extent to which this oppositional positioning is changing. It lays out a path toward understanding the extent to which Blackness is changing Europe, and also the extent to which Blackness must change the world. From African-American occupation in postwar Germany to now, from aesthetic movements to the articulations of those still understood as migrants even if they were born in Germany, this chapter critically analyzes the efficacy of attempts to use Black aesthetics and the articulation of Black positions as part of a broader project of social change. It examines the extent to which these attempts are attempts to counteract noncitizenship, that is, the condition under which Black people live, including so-called migrants who might not otherwise be seen as Black, and including those who are not able to make accepted claims, beyond asylum, on the nation-state. This chapter argues from the position of being tolerated and often exoticized (see Brown 2006, Partridge 2012), but not understood to necessarily be the responsibility of the state or its normative citizens. It takes up the everyday articulations of Blackness to look at how the politics of citizenship as legal and social affiliation are changing. It is attuned to the relationships between everyday encounters, social movements, bureaucratic regulation, and the more abstract claims to freedom.

BLACK POWER IN BERLIN

I returned to Ann Arbor, Michigan, from Berlin in mid-autumn 2013, after having attended a theater festival with the theme: "Who here is educationally deficient?," a provocation based on the assumption that immigrants, postmigrants, and People of Color lack (democratic) education. The point had been to approach education as that which the normative institutions had failed to adequately deploy or receive. These institutions included schools, but also the state-funded theaters, all of which, among others, had failed to listen and to know the perspectives of People of Color (including Turkish/Turkish-German, Arab/Arab-German, East, Southeast, and South Asian/German, Palestinian, sub-Saharan African, Afro-German, Black, and Jewish youth). "Blackface" was prevalent on local and national stages; the German "N-word" was also defended broadly from the left to the right in the mainstream press (although later removed from some—but not all—children's books), and even in school classrooms, as if removing this word was robbing White Germans of their childhood memories, even while actively violating others. The famous German children's book *Die Kleine Hexe* contained this offensive word, which a Black immigrant discovered while reading the book to his daughter. He was incensed and complained. Then, the use of the same word was debated in relation to *Pippi Longstocking*. One German journalist appeared in prime time in Blackface on the most-watched state-funded news program in order to make his case. While the author of *Die Kleine Hexe* ultimately gave permission to remove the word from his book, many resented the original complainant. In one account, the complainant's daughter noted that the same word was used against her as an insult at school, and the teachers told the parents that there was nothing that they could do (Evans 2013).

In contrast, the theater festival, which was run by the youth and their advisors and coaches, highlighted the perspectives of postmigrant and racialized youth. It featured the present and future from the perspective of those who rarely find space on local or national stages, or in local or national productions, not to mention local, regional, or national legislative bodies or classrooms. In order to use this space, they had to create it themselves. The idea for the festival went further: they would be responsible for their own education.

This education went beyond the politics of representation toward exploring the possibilities for new embodiment. One poster created by an organizing committee featured a version of the famous picture of Darwinian evolution (see book cover). Instead of the evolutionary shift from ape to "man," the poster featured youth actors from a crouched to an erect position, ending with the raised and clenched fist of Black Power. Part of what is striking is the fact that not all of the figures featured in this image were phenotypically Black or male. And looking closely, a viewer would also see that the first, hunched-over figure has his hands behind his back as if he is trapped in the chains of transatlantic slavery.

Over the course of eight months, I had been a participant with the group that performed this progression in Berlin. I told them that I was intrigued by their theater and wanted to include their perspectives in a book I was writing on democratization (a process of incorporation that necessarily limits who can participate, and how one can do so). Part of my entrée into the group came through an invitation to help them explore the themes that they planned to include in one of their emerging theater productions on Black Power in Germany. I warned that I was not a specialist. But right away, in part because the artistic director insisted that there be no passive observers, I began acting with them, then preparing seminars with them on gender, Black Power, and intersectionality (see Combahee River Collective 1986; Crenshaw 1989, 1991). After eight months, I flew back to Ann Arbor, but went back a month later to attend and participate in their massive theater festival.

Ten days later, when I was back in Michigan again, a hip-hop music video from the theater group appeared on YouTube, showing a number that had been produced and performed by the group at the festival:

Moslem gleich Terrorist
Ich zeig Dir, was der Terror ist
NSA, NSU, Rollenscheiß, Blackface. . . .
Dicker Trauer ändert nichts
Mentalität Malcolm X
Kopf runter, faust Hoch,
Unser Wut ist auch so

Muslims called terrorists.
I'll show you what the terror is.
NSA, NSU [National Socialist Union], Stereotypical Shit Roles,
    Blackface. . . .
Self-pity doesn't change anything
The mentality of Malcolm X
Head down, fist high
Our anger is that way too

Having spent time in the theater, one would know that the group is made up mostly of those who might define themselves (or be defined) as Arab- or Turkish-German. The words allude to Malcolm X and Black Power, linking Turkish/Turkish-German, Palestinian/Palestinian-German, Arab/Arab-German, African and Afro-German lives to the politics of a conscious social change that would come through mutual reinforcement, an appeal to each other and others facing similar conflicts and experiencing a similar anger. Their bodies showed this in the video. While rapping the line about Malcolm X they made the X with crossed forearms; "head down, fist high," was the sign of Black Power. The group linked the necessity for this power to the series of National Socialist Underground (NSU) murders that took place over nearly a decade and then took even longer to solve, after the police and national media initially accused a "Turkish mafia" of killing each other. Almost all of the victims were Turkish/Turkish-German. Family members of those killed were made to think that their loved ones had been part of a mafia, while the police paid a far-right informant (who remained far right) and shredded

Figure 1. Angela Davis with Youth Theater Bureau/Theater X in Frankfurt.

evidence that could have led to solving the case much sooner, before more people died.

Also, after I returned to Ann Arbor for the second time, a picture appeared on Facebook with the theater group and coaches standing next to Angela Davis after an event in Frankfurt, holding their clenched fists high (fig. 1). Two of the young men wore black gloves, in the spirit of the '68 Olympics, a scene they had also performed in one of their key rehearsals and also less directly at the festival I had just attended. In one discussion before I left Berlin the first time, the group had talked about inviting a group of Black Panthers from Sweden and even Bobby Seale, who was visiting that group. Using the symbol of the raised and clenched fist was, then, more than appropriation. Appropriation would mean that they were getting more credit than the original (like Elvis Presley performing songs from uncredited Black artists and becoming famous as a result of his choice to perform these songs, not as a result of his ability to write them); their articulations had much more to do with the intended effect. They studied the history and acknowledged the originators. They were taking inspiration from a tradition that now also belonged to them.

In an African Studies conference on heritage at the University of Michigan in the early winter of 2014, visiting and local faculty and graduate students were treated to a tribute to Nelson Mandela by Pulitzer Prize winning photographer David Turnley. He showed his own images (fig. 2) of South African apartheid and its seeming defeat with the release of Nelson Mandela. Many of us held back tears as we mourned Mandela's then-recent passing in an era that now seemed to leave the future much more open than it seemed at the time of his prison release, an image to which one of Turnley's most prominent photographs refers, as if history itself were built around that fortuitous moment that put Turnley in the right place at the right time to capture it on film.

When he asked for questions, Turnley called first on the South Africans, as if they somehow owned the images in his photographs more than the rest of the academic audience. But to what extent do these photos belong to all of us (all people who identified with the struggle, including those who also suffered elsewhere)? To what extent do they exceed national pasts and futures? In the key photograph that had become the symbol of that moment of prison release and the beginning of the end of formal apartheid, Nelson and Winnie Mandela were standing with broad smiles and clenched fists. While these fists had also become the symbols of (at least on the surface) peaceful transformation, they were the same fists that the youth theater and Angela Davis were collectively upholding.

The teacher in a contemporary classroom at the end of Spike Lee's *Malcolm X* tells her students: "Malcolm X is you, all of you, and you are Malcolm X." In the film, all of the young African-American students stand up behind the desks, and, one after the other, declare: "I am Malcolm X. I am Malcolm X. I am Malcolm X." Then the film cuts to another classroom with different youth, this time with South African accents, declaring the same thing: "I am Malcolm X. I am Malcolm X. I am Malcolm X." The film then cuts to Nelson Mandela, himself: "As brother Malcolm said, we declare our right on this earth to be a man. To be a human being. To be given the rights of a human being. To be respected as a human being, in this society, on this earth, in this day, which we intended to bring into

Figure 2. Nelson Mandela coming out of prison with Winnie Mandela and a crowd to celebrate his emergence. Photo: ©David Turnley.

existence." The film then returns to documentary footage of Malcolm X uttering the words: "By any means necessary." (I will come back to this question about whether being a human being is enough, and the extent to which the "human being" in human rights excludes potential Black claimants. It seems to me that to call for change "by any means necessary" requires a different political orientation, one that is centered on Blackness as opposed to a general "humanity"—that, in effect, fails to center the fight against anti-Blackness.)

In the rehearsal space in Berlin, the young people had a poster with a picture of Malcolm X holding up his finger and pointing forward. It looked like a kind of picket sign, ready to use at the next demonstration, as if to remind those who might see the demonstration that, in spite of the broad accounting for the Nazi led and inspired Holocaust, their everyday lives were not "post-racial."

Blackness is a means by which one can articulate a different kind of future, a future built on a different foundation.

BLACKNESS AND UNIVERSALITY II

In addition to those philosopher and enlightenment theorist John Locke calls "children and idiots,"[2] Blackness becomes another historical figure that Europeans among others use to name an outside. Even though a historical production, Blackness as an outside designation that potentially empowers those who embrace the naming in some form must take into account the intersectional claims (desires, wishes, and dreams) of noncitizens.[3] One problem, here, however, is: to whom should one make these claims? In particular transnational circumstances, it makes sense to name Blackness, in particular, as a strategy that then becomes universal, which does not mean that it applies to everyone, but that it is the putative outside of the already articulated (and contracted) universalized claims to "freedom" and "democracy." Blackness has a material dimension onto which one can hold. In my analysis, it is necessarily a critically queer Blackness (see, for example, Ferguson 2004, El-Tayeb 2011), even if it is not always named as such. It is important, though, to refer to the particularity of its historical emergences. There is danger in the general and the abstract; lived and witnessed histories demand specific accountabilities. They hold particular institutions (rulers, privileged people, citizens, and themselves) responsible.

Here, Blackness stands in relation to the particularity of Whiteness as the unmarked category: "[W]hen the Enlightenment theory was put into practice, the perpetrators of political revolutions stumbled over the economic fact of slavery in ways that made their own acknowledgement of the contradiction impossible to avoid" (Buck-Morss 2000, 831). In quoting Buck-Morss, I am not advocating violent revolution, but pointing to the universalized articulation of *Blackness* in relation to the particular claims of unmarked "Whiteness." Inasmuch as it re-emerges in *Black Power* now, it is clear that this moment is not past, even if it has little space for articulation in the contemporary US-American context. The fact that it is being articulated in other places reveals a great deal about liberalism now and the necessity for making other kinds of political claims, even if it is not yet clear to whom these claims should be made. This is a dynamic I am working out in this chapter and in this book.

Further questions emerge: Shouldn't those claiming Blackness be the ones to make claims on each other (as opposed to "the state"), regardless of where they live? Wouldn't this exceed liberalism as a framework? We should think of Blackness, itself, as a political paradigm. If one were to make claims about justice, would it not be justice via Blackness as the possibility for noncitizens now? Buck-Morss (2000, 835–36) writes, "For almost a decade, before the violent elimination of whites signaled their deliberate retreat from the universalist principles, the black Jacobins of Saint-Dominigue surpassed the metropole in actively realizing the Enlightenment goal of human liberty, seeming to give proof that the French Revolution was not simply a European phenomenon but world-historical in its implications."

It is here where I depart from Buck-Morss, inasmuch as that universality relies on an (implicitly) Eurocentric vision, even if it does not articulate itself explicitly as such. The materiality of liberalism is colonialism and slavery. Equality, Fraternity, and Liberty stand for the production of the White French male bourgeoisie. Producing an outside is part of what it means to produce a welfare state to which Black actors only have limited access.[4] Again, the basis for their inclusion is exclusionary incorporation.

Blackness is more inclusive than citizenship, which stands in for Whiteness while claiming to be universal, as one sees in the case of pre-revolutionary Haiti or France or Germany now. Mobilized Blackness as a counter-articulation, on the other hand, is simultaneously local and global. It can be anonymous or forthrightly Black. It is necessary for some, a pleasurable aesthetic for others, or both for many.

ON THE COVER IMAGE

Mamadou, a young and hip refugee (see preface), stood with his head bowed and fist high at the end of the evolutionary picture made by the youth theater in Berlin, with people from the theater representing the evolution from slavery to Black Power. Toward the end of my extended stay in Berlin, he had been kicked out of his asylum house, told by German authorities that he must move to Dortmund. "But I don't know anyone in Dortmund. I want to stay here," he said in a meeting organized around how to make this wish possible. The youth theater was working on his behalf. They, with the help of lawyers and other participants, were making the case that he was an artist who had established his creative space and community in Berlin.

During the time of my main research in Berlin, this young man, with whom I immediately connected, had gone from becoming a soft-spoken and somewhat timid participant who did not speak any German and who spoke English only as a second or third language to someone who smiled often, gave everyone hugs, and shined on the stage of a packed theater at the federally funded cultural institution in the center of Berlin. He took on what had become a critical role in the performance of *Black Power*, featuring Malcolm X, Martin Luther King, Angela Davis, and what appeared to be his personal story of migration via sea, including his entrance into Germany and the initial (un)welcome that included, at least from the border guards in the play, repeated slams to the ground from the back of his head. "Welcome to Germany!" they proclaimed. In the end, he was also a member of the group who stood in Frankfurt with Angela Davis live with his, her, and their clenched fists raised high.

He was one of the people dancing, hip-hop style, with his fist over his head in the YouTube rap video filmed in Berlin.

Dicker Trauer ändert nichts
Mentalität Malcolm X
Kopf runter, faust Hoch,
Unser Wut ist auch so

Self-pity doesn't change anything
The mentality of Malcolm X
Head down, fist high
Our anger is also that way

I return to these words in the spirit of the song itself and the hip-hop refrain that keeps returning. The repetition is necessary to get the message across. It is also important that the video shows a collective that includes multiple connections to Blackness. The collective movement in the video is also an embodiment of the politics the group professes. Education, in this sense, exceeds the disaffection produced in classrooms of noncitizen students and White German teachers. We revisit the original protagonist's story here, not only to tell more, but also to show his connection to the collective experience and articulations of Blackness.

What are the conditions of possibility for joining the theater? What does "scaling up" mean in this context? What about those who cannot make it in this theater?

UNIVERSALITY AND LIMITS

As C. L. R. James (1938), Susan Buck-Morss (2000), and Julius Scott (2018) among others remind us, universality can be found in a limit. Commenting on the Haitian revolution, Buck-Morss notes: "Although abolition of slavery was the only possible logical outcome of the ideal of universal freedom, it did not come about through the revolutionary ideas or even the revolutionary actions of the French; it came about through the actions of the slaves themselves" (833). In other words, claims to Blackness became a necessary starting point for working toward a truly universal concept that is necessarily beyond citizenship, whose origins, must, in fact, precede it.[5] From the perspective of Blackness citizenship always appears to be caught up in its original failing. In everyday lives produced in milieus of racialization, one has to differentiate between the myths of meritocracy (Subramanian 2019; Sandel 2020) and what one with a collective sensibility needs to do to not only survive, but flourish.

For Black people and people being pushed toward the Black side of global incorporation[6], the assertion of a true universality that begins with the claims to Blackness might be more salient than these seemingly impossible claims to and assertions of flexibility or "flexible citizenship" (see Ong 1999).[7] In Berlin, this has to do with the color of one's hair in addition, often, but not always, to the color of one's skin. Of course, incorporation elsewhere might be very different from incorporation in Berlin or Germany, but the assertion of Blackness in the nation-state, even if by differentiated groups of people, is important. Asserting Blackness means producing political articulation beyond incorporation.

In the current moment, Blackness has become a means to express the particularity of suffering in various contexts, to respond to the predicament of the problematic of being or having become a noncitizen, or one who has been systematically removed from social and or legal claims of inclusion and supposed social and legal guarantees. A related predicament is what Wilderson (2020) refers to as anti-citizenship.[8] As I argue above, those who articulate a Black politics must be held accountable to Black people, which means accountability to those whose ancestors were slaves, and now those who face the persistent risk of police brutality, long-term imprisonment, poor physical and mental health, and disproportionate rates of premature death (Gilmore 2007, 28).

AFROPESSIMISM VERSUS BLACK POSSIBILITY

How does Blackness become possibility against the historical context of slavery? What was before slavery? Can there be something after? In his memoir, *Afropessimism* (2020) Frank Wilderson III makes a strong case for Blackness as an aporia to citizenship, even to humanity. In his line of thinking, it is not only that Black people are counter to humanity, but that theories of humanity require them in order to establish what the human is. Their loss would be the loss of the very definition of what is and what is not human. In Wilderson's account, Black people are not even "sentient beings." They are merely implements, tools, a means to an end. Wilderson (2018) argues: "Afropessimism is premised on a comprehensive and iconoclastic claim: that Blackness is coterminous with Slaveness: Blackness is social death: which is to say that there was never a prior metamoment of plenitude, never equilibrium: never a moment of social life" (see also Patterson 1982).

This book, though, focuses on Blackness and its possibility for mobilization. Even if slaveness is coterminous with the beginnings of Blackness[9], there are many points at which one can see the articulation of a counterpolitics generated by "the slaves themselves" (Buck-Morss 2000, 833). These are the points at which one must engage the history of the future of Blackness. "The most important thing about Afrofuturism is to know that there have always been alternatives in what has been given in the present," writes Alexander Weheliye. "I am not making light of the history of enslavement and medical experimentation, but black people have always developed alternate ways of existing outside of these oppressions" (cited in Womack 2013, 37). Within the history, present, and future I am tracing here,[10] mobilization is intent on distinguishing slaveness from Blackness, while nevertheless remembering and persistently standing against the re-invocation of Black bondage.

THE FAILURE OF ALTERNATIVE POSSIBILITIES

When talking or writing about racism, particularly in White spaces, one often hears the refrain, "But what about class"? This refrain usually means class eviscerated from race. In response, one might say, "What about slavery?" The danger of the "What about class?" discussion can be seen, for example, in assertions by one of the leading politicians of the German left. Sahra Wagenknecht, a charismatic national leader of the Left Party, used anti-immigration politics to attract voters during the 2015 "summer of migration," a period in which nearly one million refugees came to Germany and were initially accepted (particularly if they could show that they were fleeing war in Syria), a moment in which nationalists on the left and right openly opposed immigration. Here, "What about class?" became code for prioritizing White national citizens over everyone else. The reversion to the base/superstructure Marxist modalities does not work, then, particularly if class is referencing an unmarked Whiteness. Capitalism is *racial capitalism,* and in Angela Davis's formulation, racist capitalism.[11] As in the Haitian revolutionary response to "universal" citizenship, Blackness demands the need for possibility beyond the already existing forms of Marxist implementation.

Yet accountability remains an issue at play. The postmigrant theater, *Ballhaus Naunynstrasse,* was mostly a place of safety, but not always. As part of a project called "News from the Neighborhood" that always ended in a filled-to-capacity screening, we entered into a three-week-long film-making session mentored by a prominent Turkish-German theater director and a well-known Turkish-Kurdish-German journalist. We were making a series of films about ten neo-Nazi murders that took place over nearly ten years with the victims at first being accused of participating in a Turkish mafia. Around the same time, the journalist-mentor published an article that supported the use of the "German N-Word" in children's books during the incident recounted above. The mentor argued in favor of freedom of expression. But why did she support a form of "freedom" that undeniably injured those bearing the historical brunt of the hate speech, including some of those she was mentoring at the theater? Was this an opportunity to publicly define herself as not-Black? At the very least, relative to White Germans, growing up in the country, she had been Blackened (see Ong 2003).

Wilderson (2020) argues that, "Analogy mystifies Black peoples' relationship to other people of color. Afropessimism labors to throw this mystification into relief—without fear of the faults and fissures that are revealed in the process." He concludes, however, that "In such a void, death is a synonym for sanctuary." This is truly pessimistic. The current book is not only concerned with Blackness as a claim, but also the spaces in which this claim gets iterated and the significance of space to the politics of enunciation. If going to the theater is part of an everyday practice and that theater is organized by those who are also claiming, learning from, imagining, and living Blackness, then their politics can result in a different kind of articulation and possibility beyond death. I do note that Mignolo (2020) warns that once universality is claimed, it also immediately becomes oppressive. Mignolo offers "pluriversality," but I will stick with universality, here, as part of what is claimed in multiple global locations simultaneously.

SITES OF INVENTION AND POSSIBILITY

In an interview related to her work and the events of the summer of 2020, Hartman (2020) asks: "What does it mean to love that body? To love the flesh[12] in a world where it is not loved or regarded? To love Black female flesh. Breonna Taylor's murderers have still not been charged." Hartman goes on to point out that "The possessive investment in whiteness can't be rectified by learning 'how to be more antiracist.' It requires a radical divestment in the project of whiteness and a redistribution of wealth and resources. It requires abolition, the abolition of the carceral world, the abolition of capitalism. What is required is a remaking of the social order, and nothing short of that is going to make a difference."

This book is focused on the necessity for this remaking as well as work undertaken to orchestrate that process. Blackness, here, stands in simultaneously for possibility and necessity. This is not a comparative analysis, but one focused on particularity as it relates to and applies to universalized claims to resources and liberation. There are other points from which to begin, to focus, but Blackness (as experience and claim) is particularly urgent. Normative Germany, through a *Sonderweg,* an alternative route, imagines itself as having found a different path to Enlightenment, in which orchestrating genocide seems to have necessitated this different path, at least for Germany and as the historical home to the perpetrators of the mass killing of Jewish Europeans. I, like Hartman, Wilderson, and many others, am taking on the whole Enlightenment paradigm. If it begins with and hides its use of slavery, then the Enlightenment, even via an alternative route, will not liberate Black people. This analysis is based on connected and collective imaginations that have been and are being turned into lived realities. Here, the imagination and the material must come together to produce new kinds of practices, spaces, and worlds.

2 Exploding Hitler and Americanizing Germany

OCCUPYING BLACK BODIES AND POSTWAR DESIRE

This chapter traces the particular history of the post-genocidal emergence of Blackness in Germany/Europe, noting that the post-World War II occupation of Germany by Black American soldiers and new images of Blackness, representing a shift in how Blackness would occupy the continent. Through an analysis of the figure of the African American GI in film, in popular culture, and in the daily life of post–World War II Germany, I explore how the presence of this occupying Blackness reconfigured social imaginations. I examine the shift from an era in which Billie Holiday identified Black bodies as strange fruit swinging from US southern trees, to an era in which Blackness became a new way in which political possibility could be imagined.

One sees a critical movement from international outrage around Black occupation, as in the post–World War I response to Black French African troops occupying the German *Rheinland*, toward much more open desire after World War II. Tina Campt (2004, 52–53) writes about the widespread reaction in the interwar period:

As a Leipzig paper noted in a 26 May 1921 article titled, *"Die farbigen Truppen im Rheinland"* ["The Colored Troops in the Rhineland"]: what offends European sensibility in the use of Black troops is not their Blackness but rather the fact that savages are being used to oversee a cultured people. Whether these savages are totally Black or dark brown or yellow makes no difference. The prestige of the European culture is in danger. That is what is at stake. And precisely those peoples, those such as England and France that are dependent upon the dominance they exercise over colored peoples, should consider that with the degradation of Germany in the eyes of the colored, they degrade the white race and with this endanger their own prestige.

While there were also post-World War II critiques, the Weimar era had prepared Germans for the entrance of and even occupation by Black people. American Black soldiers, though, were received as not as "savage" or unfamiliar in the minds and representations available to everyday Germans. Germans openly desired and consumed "their culture" with the American occupation, unlike the earlier French one; the Americans also brought ideas (if not practices) of racial equality, candy, cigarettes, other consumer goods, and the Marshall Plan.

This historical context, alongside my own contemporary observations, has led me to examine the ramifications of having African-American occupiers in post–World War II Germany, and further, how the figure of the Black American soldier allowed German access to America, American capital, and Black possibility, not only for White German women, but also for Black and other people in Germany.

On the other side of Nazism and "America as the enemy" are the willingness and the desire to reach new possibility via Blackness. In the post–World War II moment, there seems to be a critical shift, inasmuch as the occupying Black soldier is now desired on a scale which no one would have previously imagined, at least inasmuch as this desire is expressed openly and in public. The desire itself is part of a process of rejecting the old nation in search of something or someone new and opposed to the dreams of *Der Führer*.

Leni Riefenstahl's films show this shift as emblematic of a national desire: from her emphasis on the *Führer*'s body in *Triumph des Willens* (*Triumph of the Will*) to her emphasis on Jesse Owens's in *Olympia* (about the 1936 Berlin Olympics), from the idealized Aryan body to her later fascination with the Nuba (see Müller 1995). Also in the World War II arena, Germans experience not only the defeat of their army, but the defeat of Max Schmeling by the African-American boxer Joe Louis. Again, one should note the presence of the Black GI and the subsequent social transformations experienced as a result of his occupation.

While other authors have pointed to the presence of African-American GIs in terms of troubling race and gender norms (see Fehrenbach 2000; Höhn 2002; Poiger 2000), too little has been made of the critical nature of this occupation (both mentally and physically) to processes of social transformation. I understand Americanization here in terms of the particular modes of consumption and desire. What Kaspar (1992) calls African-Americanization is not simply abstract or ideological, but also includes the success and dominance of Hollywood (see Fehrenbach 1995), the emergence of jazz and rock and roll (see Poiger 2000), the embrace of what West Germans eventually called "Black music," as well as the embrace of the anti-War and Black Power movements.

Uta Poiger (2000) puts Americanized consumption in a historical context and links its success to the willing participation of German youth. She notes: "While many US government programs in the 1940s and 1950s sought to prove to Germans that the United States was a land of high culture, East and West German officials, like authorities in the Weimar Republic and the Third Reich, grew increasingly worried about the impact that American movies, jazz, and boogie-woogie had on German youth" (32). Here, a youthful desire for pleasure exceeds the possibilities of formal regulation. Moreover, pleasure and desire as forms of occupation mean that at some point, African-Americanization could proceed without the threat of the military presence; and yet, the military presence in Germany has been crucial to physical accessibility.

Poiger, like others, gives a somewhat functionalist account of American GI/German relations—emphasizing official rhetoric as opposed to everyday encounters. But it is clear from the scenes of even pre-War German Jazz clubs and post-War desire that Jürgen Massaquoi, the son of a White German nurse and Black Liberian diplomat, describes in *Destined to Witness* (2001) and that persist in contemporary Germany (see also Partridge 2003, 2012) that pleasure and desire exceed function.[1] Poiger (2000, 36) writes:

During the 1940s, many of the relationships between German women and U.S. soldiers were based on a need for food, consumer goods, and protection. That is not to say that mutual affection could not play a role; certainly numerous relationships ended in marriage. But in the minds of many Germans, the food or nylon stockings that German women received from their American lovers, or the dances they danced with them, confirmed a link that had a long history in German anti-Americanism: the link between consumption and the oversexualization of women. And even more so than in the interwar years, Germans now related these phenomena to the weakness of German men.

However, the success of jazz, rock and roll, and American cinema in their official and unofficial articulations (including officially sanctioned jazz projects in postwar East and West Germany) that Poiger observes at a number of other junctures belie this observation, particularly when one takes into account the types of social taboos one had to break in order to enter into these relationships, particularly with African American soldiers. While American policy makers attempted to orchestrate the success and influence of American popular culture in Germany, it is clear that the success of the German embrace is deeper and more genuine than policy alone can account for, particularly given American policy makers' official distaste for relationships between African American GIs and German women, and their refusal in most cases to sanction their attempts to marry (Höhn 2002; Poiger 2000).

Exploring the types of dance scenes that Massaquoi describes in *Destined to Witness* in fiction film, through the movement from the desire for Hitler to the desire for Black America, Rainer Werner Fassbinder made *The Marriage of Maria Braun* (1986), a film that examines the life of a West German woman in the World War II and postwar periods.[2] In the very first shot of *Maria Braun*, the image of Adolf Hitler that fills the screen explodes. It later becomes apparent that this explosion is necessary to make room for the entrance/imagination/body of the African American soldier. While Maria, the main character, marries Hermann Braun (a German soldier) in this first scene, the marriage—the union between the White German woman and White German masculinity—is troubled. In the ceremony, the objection to this union comes in the form of an American bomb that forces the couple to dive for cover, and signals their eventual separation due to the war. Then, the administration of the state-sanctioned marriage itself explodes as a close-up reveals the *Standesamt* (civil registry office) sign being propelled to the ground and papers flying everywhere. Maria, determined to complete the official state-sponsored ceremony (a determination that mirrors the West German determination for national consolidation), asks as she finds a loose sheet of paper on the ground: "Where should I sign?" Cries of a screaming baby foreshadow the birth of a new and troubled nation, inalterably (as we will learn) penetrated by various forms of Americanization. Within this context, Maria learns not only to desire, but also to perform, moving from desire to "self-sufficiency" and towards future explosions. She learns new forms of consumption, new forms of desire, and the English language. She becomes cosmopolitan through lessons administered by the African American soldier Bill.

Through the visual and aural language of this film, one begins to understand Black occupation in multiple senses. This includes the sense in which the Black presence becomes an occupying force, but also the sense in which Blackness occupies the social imagination, and furthermore, the sense in which occupying Blackness becomes a possible if not necessary mode through which people in Germany might mobilize a different future.

In one scene, Bill teaches Maria English. She repeats his words, in a bout of seeming confusion, before he eventually corrects her when she says "I am Black and you are white." "No," he counters, "I am Black and *you* are white." "I am white and you are Black," she concludes. Here, it takes going through the Black body to become white again. It takes occupying Black bodies—that is, proceeding through a phase of national "inferiority"—in order to find the new German nation.

In her book *GIs and Fräuleins: The German-American Encounter in 1950s West Germany* (2002), Maria Höhn gives a historical context for how the relationship between Bill and Maria Braun might have been seen in the 1950s.

> Even more troubling [to conservative German commentators and officials] than the prostitutes were the many German women from respectable backgrounds who nonetheless associated with American GIs. Their Americanized demeanor and behavior evoked much consternation, and their willingness to live in common-law marriages with white and Black American GIs

marked them as sexual as well as racial transgressors. Conservatives reserved their greatest outrage, however, for their own charges. Instead of expressing outrage over the goings-on in their communities, the local population was busily figuring out how to participate in the American-induced boom (10).

Höhn focuses on the presence of African American and White American GIs in the immediate postwar period and the outraged response of conservative commentators. She is also interested in the ways in which these relationships challenged American Jim Crow norms. However, her analysis often stays close to official debates, with less emphasis on the transformative power of unofficial desire.

Nevertheless, pointing toward the accessibility of Black GIs, in comparison to White soldiers, Höhn suggests:

> Germans were stunned at how well the Black soldiers treated them, but Black soldiers were equally amazed that most Germans approached them with much more tolerance than did white American soldiers. In the aftermath of Germany's bitter defeat, many Germans preferred the Black GIs to the white soldiers, because Black GIs were more generous with their food rations. Black GIs also did not approach the defeated Germans with the sort of arrogance that many of the white soldiers displayed. Because of the humiliation of their defeat, Germans also experienced a certain kinship with the Black GIs, convinced that Black GIs, just like themselves, were treated as second-class citizens by white Americans.
>
> The encounters of Black GIs with Germans were so positive that the African American press in the United States repeatedly described the experience of the GIs in Germany to indict American racism at home. *Ebony,* for example, reported in 1946 with much surprise on how cordially most Germans treated Blacks: 'Strangely enough, here where aryanism ruled supreme, negroes are finding more friendship, more respect and more equality than they would back home—either in Dixie or on Broadway.' While providing wide selections of photos of interracial fraternization, *Ebony* concluded, 'Many of the negro GIs . . . find that democracy has more meaning on Wilhelmstrasse than on Beale Street in Memphis' (90–91).

Part of what Germans liked more must have also related to their desire for "palatable" Black bodies as opposed to pure "African" ones, particularly when one considers the then recent success of Jesse Owens and Joe Louis in their very public defeats of Adolf Hitler and Max Schmeling (see also El-Tayeb 2001 and Campt 2004).

What Höhn (2002) describes as a preference for Black GIs is substantiated by the image and accessibility of Mr. Bill in *The Marriage of Maria Braun*, compared to the official American all-White military establishment pictured in the form of the military tribunal that sentences Maria's husband to prison after he takes the blame for her killing Mr. Bill when the husband finally returns from a Soviet war prison and finds his wife in a sexually explicit encounter. The introduction of a new kind of establishment also promoted scenes of accessibility, not just to African American music, but also to Black bodies. In spite of the presence of underground jazz clubs in the Nazi era, "another new kind of enterprise that suddenly appeared in the villages of both Kaiserslautern and Birkenfeld counties was the nightclub" (Höhn 2002, 111; see also Poiger 2000). The presence of night clubs next to American Army bases, even in German villages, represents a movement of clubs from the underground to the mainstream, from the city to the rural enclave. Here, one finds a genealogy the clubs where African men and German women went to dance with each other after the end of the Cold War. The stakes, however, have been transformed. In the 1950s, processes of Americanization were articulated through the need to fulfill American, and be fulfilled by Americanized, desire as part of the process of gaining access to economic capital and American bodies. The other side of this process relied on the ways in which Germans learned not only how to produce the products, but also how to consume. Furthermore, they began to understand consumption not as a privilege, but as a right unequivocally associated with what they then, learning from Americans, called "freedom." A transformation of German gender norms and the significant desire of German youth were critical to this process (see Poiger 2000).

Along these lines, Höhn observes: "Young women also flocked to the garrison communities because they had read colorful descriptions in the national press of the never-ending dollar supply of the American GI. The descriptions of Baumholder as the 'el Dorado of West Germany' or as the 'Alaska on the west-wall' in the national press always stressed that this was 'the land where milk and honey flow, that is, where the $ and the DM roll'" (2002, 128). Note the confluence of disdain and desire mobilized by the national press attention to relationships between GIs and German women, with a particular emphasis (according to Höhn) on relationships between Black GIs and White German women. Höhn goes on to note, "At a time of high unemployment, especially for women, many desperate souls responded to these enticing tales" (128). It seems both interesting and problematic, however, that Höhn refers to these women as "desperate," in the sense that she assumes the rhetoric of the conservative critics. Furthermore, as noted above, the emphasis on dollars and desperation could potentially lose sight of the critical importance of pleasure and desire in these encounters.

Höhn suggests later in her work: "Church-affiliated welfare workers worried incessantly that parents were not up to the task of protecting their young from the seductions of the dollar" (163). "In order to protect young German women from the GIs and their dollars, church-affiliated welfare workers also spun a tight web of surveillance around all those families considered at risk." In fact, it was "the nation" as a whole that was "at risk," and the nation as a whole, if one takes German unification into account, that succumbed. Again, one needs to move beyond the dollar as the only, or even primary, motivation for the ensuing "adventure." The imagination of a Black threat became, in the post–World War II context, the articulation of a national desire. This is the story underlying Höhn's narrative of moral resistance from conservative Germans.

Policing the sexuality and desire of young White German women was not merely an afterthought or side effect of German conservatives guarding against a larger process of "Americanization"; to the contrary, protecting and determining sexual practices is central to national self-definition. In this sense, the success of processes of Americanization do not depend solely upon the desire for Coca-Cola or the desire to consume in toto, but more importantly upon how access is obtained—that is, through the bodies of Black American GIs who were more accessible, more resisted, and thus more intriguing and more desired (due to the broader social belief in their increased sexual danger). In a number of places, Höhn notes the disproportionate attention the national media paid to relationships between African American GIs and White German women. In some sense, this attention both backfires and comes too late. The tabooization and attempts at social policing are restricted by the fact of occupation. The ensuing relationships are made possible by the types of "freedoms" that African American GIs would not be able to enjoy in the United States, but that became tenable in Germany as a result of their having fought in the war, the transportation of African American images to popular German media, and, according to Höhn, the American military's response to communist critiques of American racism. In Germany, America was more accountable to its claims of freedom than laws, social rules, and authorities allowed in the United States, which, in the 1950s, still enforced anti-miscegenation and Jim Crow laws in a significant number of states.

Finally and critically, "Due to the occupation statute, German police officers could not conduct vice raids without the assistance of American military police (MPs). Unless accompanied by the MP, German law-enforcement officers could not check the identification of a German woman if she was in the company of an American GI" (183). Höhn adds, "The limits put on their authority was particularly abhorrent to German police officers if the woman was in the company of a Black soldier." While this law was later changed to allow German authorities to at least police German women, it is significant in terms of the history of German authorities' inability to police the desire for the occupation of Black bodies. Furthermore, one should note that the Black-only bars next to post–World War II Army barracks did not mirror their American equivalents in the sense that they weren't, in fact, Black-only, but allowed White German women.

In many ways, this process was prefigured in the Weimar-era success of jazz, a type of music, as Poiger (2000) notes, simultaneously associated with modernity and Blackness, and that exceeded the formal dimensions of what is understood today as a narrower art form. It included spirituals, instrumental music, and even nascent rock and roll. The presence of African American GIs in postwar Germany as occupiers and victors suggests a new legitimacy for a desire previously suppressed, particularly in the Nazi era, where jazz had to be Germanized in order to be legal (Poiger 2000). The presence of "real" African Americans in the German landscape suggests the possibility of "authentic" access, the fulfillment of a historically repressed/suppressed desire.

Regarding the relationship between American GIs and presumably White German women, the film historian Annette Brauerhoch (2003, 1) writes about "'*Fräuleins*' [the German women who desire American GIs] as a representation of 'nation.'" If this is true, then, as I have argued, the nation was desiring Black men. In the film *Fremd Gehen* (Heldmann

1999), Brauerhoch plays the contemporary White German woman who sleeps with a series of African American GIs on a US Army base near Frankfurt in almost daily encounters with the Black soldiers. She also wrote the script for this pseudo-autobiographical documentary film. In the related academic piece, she notes: "Most of the accounts of this phenomenon of the '*Fräuleinswunder*' have concentrated on a view from the outside, relegating the women under consideration to the status of objects of history" (2003, 1). Here, one should note the linguistic relationship between "*Fräuleinswunder*" and *wirtschaftswunder*.[3] In other words, inasmuch as the occupation by African American soldiers is desired, Germany/she can have unlimited access to wealth and "liberation."

Along these lines, one should note the ways in which Black GIs become objects in Brauerhoch's analysis, her film, and the broader national social imaginary. In the talk she gave in 2003, she opened by saying that "This paper will try to take their perspective as subjects who can be considered as foreigners in many aspects of the 'Americanization' of Germany." Brauerhoch refers to these as "foreign affairs," implicitly making a link between actions taken in bedrooms and the transformation of foreign policy. Noting links between conflicting forms of Americanization, she writes: "The Hollywood production code with its rule against representations of 'miscegenation' was in its main outlines copied by the guidelines for the German voluntary Board of Censors (*Freiwillige Selbstkontrolle* was established in 1948)" (3). And yet, ironically, it was not antimiscegenation laws, but the act of desiring Black bodies that became one of the only avenues through which many German women (and men) experienced Americanization, and thus the possibility of personal and social transformation.

Brauerhoch continues: "In departing from norms of proper female behavior by actively pursuing sexuality, and leading promiscuous lives without marriage, the Fräuleins established a form of female subjectivity which was threatening to an emerging concept of a developing new national identity, in which gender roles served to restabilize the system" (4). To some extent, this claim is overstated, inasmuch as the entire nation embraced processes of Americanization. German women who desired American GIs began a public negotiation not only of their gender roles, but also of the nation and its Americanization. Brauerhoch refers to the *Fräuleins* as "protofeminist rebels against normative gender restrictions and Nazi-induced racial propaganda" (1). In many ways, this is the type of resistance that could be predicted, inasmuch as that which is most forbidden is often that which is also most acutely desired. Curiosity is aroused by the power of repeated denial. However, Black American male occupation changed the significance and meaning of this desire.

CONCLUSION

In this chapter, I have pointed to some of the multiple ways in which the figure of the Black American soldier and the fact of his occupation, both his militarized presence in Germany and his appropriation through performance and desire, became critical to postwar German transformation and processes of African-Americanization. The desire to occupy and be occupied, to love one's occupation, were predicated on his presence, as they were also predicated on the presence/absence of of the cis-gendered heterosexualized figures of German women, German men, African American women, and those Tina Campt (2004) refers to as "other Germans."

And yet, after the fall of the Wall, as African American GI numbers diminished, there has been again an increased tension between national self-determination and Americanization. The desire, however, is no longer facilitated by the actual presence of African American bodies in large numbers, but by the persistence of an imagination linked to the ever-increasing consumptive possibilities.

3 Occupying American Blackness and Reconfiguring European Spaces

NONCITIZEN ARTICULATIONS IN BERLIN AND BEYOND

Thinking further about Black occupation and social transformation, this chapter works through the circulations and transformations American Blackness continues to undergo after the immediate post–World War II period. It considers further the extent to which this occupying Blackness has become increasingly relevant to those who may or may not be considered Black. It examines the extent to which Blackness becomes a vehicle for making claims, and to which mobility and liberation become more central to the kinds of claims people articulating Blackness make in both local and global arenas. Even if a sometimes objectifying desire tries to limit and reduce, the fact of occupation suggests multiple possibilities for the ways in which those Black articulations begin to carry social weight.

One should note that this is not simply a chapter about images or representations. It analyzes these dimensions of occupation as they relate to performance, embodiment, and ultimately also to social mobility and the possibilities for social change, addressing not simply the possibilities within liberalism or liberal democracy, but also as a necessary alternative to them. The occupying presence of American Blackness in what I describe below takes on social, psychic, and physical dimensions. Reading the early reception of MTV and Hollywood in Germany are not enough to sustain this analysis, and occupation is not only significant as a result of its military history.

OCCUPATION AND EMBODIMENT — BECOMING AMERICAN BLACK

In *Destined to Witness: Growing Up Black in Nazi Germany,* one sees Hans Jürgen Massaquoi, the son of a White German mother and a Liberian diplomat, remembering not only his identification with, but also his impersonation of an African American GI in the immediate post-World-War-II period (Massaquoi 1998, 320). Fresh from masquerading as an American GI and then being evicted from a US Army base, he entered another scene of (African) American occupation. He and a White German friend decided not to wait for their train with the Allied personnel but in the German waiting hall, where travelers seem much less affluent than their military occupiers. Mistaking them for Americans, Black MPs approached Massaquoi and his friend and tell them to move to be with the Allied personnel and away from the Germans.

Massaquoi's Blackness, which had exposed him to racial exclusion under the Nazis, then had a transformed meaning. In the era of postwar occupation, his Blackness meant that he would be read as Black American. This interpellation came through the enforcement power of occupying Black American military police.[1] The MPs and others' reading of his body as Black American had the effect of changing his life. In fact, Massaquoi ultimately turned this postwar performance, one that originated in an attraction to and performance of American jazz, into a vehicle for his movement to the United States, where he ultimately became a middle-class American and managing editor of *Ebony* magazine.

African American occupation since World War II in Germany, in particular, was simultaneously military and imaginary. Its efficacy was established in the movements of the otherwise marginalized alongside postwar Americanized reeducation programs, including military funds to promote American film and American jazz. The programs also included the performances of Negro spirituals at US State Department-funded America Houses in Germany:

American officials seeking to convince Germans of the quality of American music favored spirituals.... The capstone ... was an African American choir's 1949 tour of every major city in the American zone.... In Munich, '[o]ver 800 people jammed the theater and the hall immediate[ly] outside the theater and gave overwhelming applause to the Choir.'... [According to the US information center, in Heidelberg,] [t]he audiences for the performances grew from at least 800 at the first concert to 2,000 at the second (Schroer 2007, 159–60).

The point here is not to valorize Americanization or militarization, but to think critically through the ways in which African American, as opposed to simply American, occupation shifted the dynamics of occupation, Americanization, and social mobility.[2] Americanization is not always unmarked, as is often imagined. It is not simply the expansion of private property, free markets, or imperial Whiteness, but also involves African American (among other hyphenated) occupiers. Furthermore, it means not only the occupation merely of territories but also of imaginations. In this sense, this chapter examines the unexpected possibilities this occupation reveal, and the unanticipated audiences who gain access to social mobility, and thus get transformed in the process. Complicating the position of African American occupiers themselves, as Heide Fehrnbach points out in *Race After Hitler* (2005), many Black soldiers found the notion of postwar German "occupation as liberation" contradictory, inasmuch as they felt freer in Germany than they ever had in the segregated Army or under Jim Crow in the United States. Moving from the immediate postwar period to the present, this chapter examines the relationships between contemporary aesthetics, postwar African American military occupation, and German citizenship. It looks at the extent to which the doubly displaced performance of and desire for Black American bodies figures in relation to the European performance of citizenship. It examines further how the desire for and expressions of Americanized Blackness relate to the success of this performance, and how African American presences get transformed in their German translations. Finally, it interrogates the political possibilities of these reconfigurations as well as the new prospects for coalition.

Moving from the immediate postwar period to Stuart Hall's analysis and articulations of "diasporic aesthetics" to their actual practice in contemporary Berlin, through street scenes, artistic performances, and their representations, I will analyze both the possibilities and the limits for occupying Blackness as it relates to coalition building and social transformation through the practices and aesthetics of these art scenes. In what follows, I examine the multiple shifts in position as the Black American soldier's body helps to reconfigure the national gaze and mobility of other Germans and Germany's Others. I end by analyzing how these expressions are also always gendered.

AFRICAN OCCUPYING AFRICAN AMERICAN

In a conversation several years ago in the United States with a theater director from the Congo about my research on hypersexuality and Black bodies in Germany (Partridge 2012), I learned that even in sub-Saharan Africa, young men planning to migrate to Europe were practicing their performance of Black American masculinity, learning to dance, speak, and move like "African Americans." In my own observations (beginning in the mid-1990s) in contemporary German clubs and asylum hostels, I saw African men wearing American baseball caps and FUBU jackets, dancing to what Germans called "Black music" (R&B, hip-hop, and soul). In the mid-1990s, I began to realize that this performance was one of the only ways in which African men could be intelligible as relatable (not starving, humanitarian-aid-dependent) beings in post-World War II Germany. Even if White German women seemed to be saying it was really Africanness they desired,[3] Americanized Blackness offered the reassurance of something familiar. English became the mode of speech. Hip-hop clothing became critical attire, and grinding to R&B became central.

In many ways, a history of African American occupation suggests the possibility of national recognition for contemporary African men through an African American-centered performance. Of course, as Judith Butler (1993) notes, recognition always comes at a cost (see also Partridge 2008).[4] In the 1998 student film *Falsche Soldaten* (*Fake Soldiers*) the Benin-born director Idrissou Mora-Kapi depicts the ways in which African immigrants in Germany begin to impersonate American GIs by speaking English, carrying fake IDs, and driving American cars to gain access to, and social and legal recognition by, White German women. The possibility of Africans finding a legally recognized place in Germany, often by marriage to German women, then required occupying the symbolic space of African American bodies. In these cases, the possibility to emerge as a different kind of self gets lost in translation.

OTHER MODES OF OCCUPATION: TURKISH-GERMANS EMBODYING BLACK AMERICANS

A *New York Times* article entitled "A Bold New View of Turkish-German Youth" (Bernstein 2003) reported on a new film by Neco Çelik:

> The film '*Alltag*' [*Everyday Life*] has been criticized by some in the German press as too American in its sensibility and direction. But Kreuzberg's[5] youth culture is strongly influenced by Hollywood and by the presence of Americans in Germany. It was also shaped by the black urban subculture transposed onto the children of Turkish immigrants in Germany, a force adapted by Mr. Çelik into his movie.
>
> 'Everything has to do with American movies,' he said. . . . 'In the 1980s, everybody saw *Scarface*, and everybody here called himself Tony Montana,' Mr. Çelik said. He was talking about the ruthless drug trafficker played by Al Pacino.
>
> Hip-hop was introduced to the neighborhood by the children of American servicemen stationed on Berlin's outskirts. 'They showed up as rappers at hip-hop parties,' Mr. Çelik said of the Americans, 'and hip-hop and gangs belong together.'
>
> Mr. Çelik's own gang was called the Thirty-sixers, named after the last two digits of [his] Kreuzberg postal code.[6] There were battles with the Black Panthers, a rival Turkish gang from Wedding, another heavily immigrant district of Berlin. . . . Then, in another adaptation of urban American culture, Mr. Çelik became what he called a graffiti sprayer.

In a prior conversation with Çelik in 2002 at a film conference at the British Council that featured Turkish-German and British Asian filmmakers, I asked him how he had managed to become a filmmaker and get funding without acquiring any formal film training or attending one of the prestigious German film schools. He remarked: "Have you seen *Training Day?*" "Yes," I said. "You know how he [Denzel Washington's character] said you have to be like a wolf? I was a wolf." Çelik's invocation of extra-human embodiment did not refer to the actor directly, but to his hyperbolic performance of Black masculinity, and the necessity of this performance to make it in Germany.

In both these interviews, Çelik participates in his own authentication as a recognizable figure, demonstrating his potential by demonstrating his Blackness. In this sense, one must read *Training Day* (Fuqua 2002) as a training film not only for Ethan Hawke's character, the White American rookie who Denzel Washington's character trains to police the urban LA streets, but also for Neco Çelik. As he explained to me, Çelik's training and authentication comes through an identification with oppositional youth culture in the United States as transported through the bodies of occupying Black youth in Germany: the children of American GIs in preunification (pre-1989) West Berlin. It is worth noting that he refers to the actual physical presence of these youth and not only to popular processes of Americanization as they are experienced in German movie theaters or on German TV.

Çelik came of age in the *Naunyn Ritze* youth center. As he noted, "I am, myself, a graffiti artist from the eighties." This is the same place where he later became a youth worker. He recalls that the youth center was a project started by the Allies to teach democracy. And then, Çelik points out, the "guest worker children" came, "and they had other problems." The occupying presence, however, also had an impact on these unanticipated actors. As Çelik's artistic initiation as graffiti sprayer suggests, the occupying Blackness provided real possibilities for transnational affiliation of an aesthetic politics that counteracts forces and feelings of displacement. He moved from youth participant, to youth worker, to film, theater, and then opera director. On the other hand, inasmuch as the Turkish-German never quite achieves the status of becoming Black American, Çelik had to insist even more on the authenticity of his performance (as Black) to gain broader social recognition—to be on center stage.

In his article, the *New York Times* journalist Richard Bernstein compared Çelik to the Black American filmmaker Spike Lee. Soon after, a German national newspaper article entitled "Der Spike Lee von Kreuzberg" ("The Spike Lee of Kreuzberg") (*Frankfurter Allegemeine Zeitung*. 2003), took a tone that at some points seems mocking, perhaps reflecting a broader public skepticism about the place of Turkish-Germans, even the refusal to recognize that such a hyphenated possibility could or does exist. Clear, however, even in the title of the article, is the central place of African Americanness as a model. Çelik's authenticity as Black is at stake in understanding his presentation as recognizable.[7] American Blackness becomes the grounds through which a more recognizable articulation *vis a vis* the broader German public can be achieved. These grounds are critical both for Çelik and for the journalist, which might explain the latter's insistence on referring to Çelik's Turkishness and refusing to authenticate his Americanized Blackness, his becoming Spike Lee. The critical tone, which reflects the broader relationship to Turkish-Germanness, is found in the full title of the article itself: "The Spike Lee of Kreuzberg: Earlier, Neco Çelik was in a gang, today, he makes films, tomorrow, he wants to be world famous."

> 'It's a long damned way from Kreuzberg to Hollywood,' one wants to say to him. 'It could be that one lifetime is not enough for this long trek.'
>
> But if Neco Çelik had told one ten years ago that he wanted to make films, real feature films with real actors, closed-off streets, and a crane that carries the camera into the sky above Kreuzberg, then the reply would have assuredly been the following: 'Grow up Neco, get your Abitur [pre-university high school degree], or learn something practical! Filmmaking is a dream, on the order of becoming a jet pilot, or the captain of a tanker. You don't have a clue, Neco. You don't have any connections. You don't have a chance.'
>
> This is the way, or nearly the way, that Neco Çelik's father speaks today. As the son was filming, the father was invited onto the set. 'Look here, Kreuzberg is blocked off for three weeks. Look at the big lights and the actors and the whole film crew. Of all of these people, I'm the boss.' His father was not impressed, Neco Çelik explains: His brothers had acquired more practical skills. One is a mechanic, the other a police officer. This impresses his father, who came in the seventies from Anatolia.

Here, the journalist, Claudius Seidl, contrasts the film industry (read Americanized life, values, and dreams) with the values, dreams, and hopes of rural Anatolia. He contrasts Neco Çelik and his father, creating fake quotes to suggest that "traditional" practicality impedes Çelik's ambition.

In the end, it seems that establishing gang affiliations and connections to the children of African American soldiers was part of establishing authenticity and place. Spike Lee was a mark of intelligibility for a mainstream German media. This was also so for Çelik. For the *Frankfurter Allegemeine,* though, it was not yet clear whether or not Çelik had succeeded, whereas for *The New York Times,* he had already demonstrated the never-ending presence and (at least at the time) supposed "superiority" of Americanized desire and Black American becoming. Çelik's film *Alltag* subsequently aired on ARD, the most-watched German television station. In a later conversation with me, he pointed out that it was only after the interview and review of his film appeared in *The New York Times* that German journalists began to change their opinion about him and the film. "Since when did *The New York Times* become the *Maßstab* (standard) for the German press?," he queried.

Yet, through the process of becoming publicly recognizable, through the release of his first feature film, on the path to establishing his authenticity by connecting his work and his life to the American "ghetto," to American Blackness, Neco Çelik has, according to his own observations, begun to be recognized as a German filmmaker. Inasmuch as Turkish-Germans can become Germany's "Blacks," inasmuch as they can be consumed, they relink Germany to an Americanization process which simultaneously includes consumption, modernity, and globalization. In many ways, the persistence of this reality remains part of the national subconscious. "[T]he cultural hegemony of the United States was perhaps never as dominant as it is now, but—and this is my point—it is not perceived as such. For West German artists and intellectuals in their twenties and thirties, the import of American culture is not part of a cultural imperialism or an unwanted Americanization but, rather, an accepted part of life" (Gemünden 1998, 210).[8] What is significant about Çelik's and the related cases I have described thus far is that incorporation happens through the occupying power of Black Americanness, in particular.

If one watches German TV, goes to the German movie theater, or listens to much of German popular radio, one experiences the undeniable persistence of what Timothy Brown (2006) has called "(African) Americanization" in German everyday life. More broadly, "In recent years American films have accounted for 75 percent to 85 percent of the German market, whereas German films make up about 10 percent of the domestic exhibition market" (Gemünden 1998, 203). Furthermore,

"Since the introduction of cable television in the mid-1980s more and more American programs have been imported to fill the greatly expanded time slots" (204). Within this context, the presence of Black bodies is critical not only to processes of Americanization but also to the possibilities of social mobility. After all, many of the imported images are also "Black." The question still remains: To what extent will the mobilization of this Blackness be able to change the conditions of noncitizenship altogether? To what extent will it address the specificity of anti-Blackness? If incorporation is always exclusionary incorporation (Partridge 2012), is the occupying presence of Blackness enough?

OCCUPYING BLACK POWER

Informally called the "Turkish Malcolm X" by German critics (see Güvercin 2008), Faridun Zaimoglu introduces his book *Kanak Sprak: 24 Mißtone vom Rande der Gesellschaft* (*Kanak Talk: 24 Dissonant Tones from the Edge of the Society*) with the figure of American Black Power, to intervene in the German literary imaginary. In fact, this move made Feridun Zaimoglu a German celebrity. Çelik calls him his favorite author in Germany.

Zaimoglu writes: "Analogous to the Black consciousness movement in the USA, the individual Kanak subidentities will increasingly become aware of overlapping relationships and contents. The demystification has been introduced; the way to a new realism has been set. In the middle of a mainstream culture, the first raw proposal for an ethnic structure in Germany has come into being" (2000 [1995], 17, my translation). Here, an African American social movement, a movement that followed the Second World War, provides a model for Kanak articulation in Germany. "Kanak,"[9] referencing German and European colonial history and simultaneously referring to another kind of Melanesian Blackness, has also become a racist term in the German context, usually used against Turkish- and Arab-Germans and Turks and Arab people in Germany, standing for a particularly German form of positioning that immediately points to the contradictions of national citizenship, in this case, for Turkish and other racialized Germans, through the analogous contradictions of African

American experience. Again, it is through the occupation of and by Black bodies that a form of enunciation can take place.

Linking Zaimoglu's published work to his public interviews, literary theorist B. Venkat Mani (2007, 127) notes, "The journalistic portrait of Zaimoglu as a young author established him on the one hand as an assimilated Other who can communicate and can be comprehended in the language of the majority, indeed, in the vocabularies of assimilation, and on the other hand as the Other who protects and sustains his Otherness through a persistent defiance of assimilation." As in the case of Çelik, Zaimoglu achieves popular recognition and is viewed as "authentic," not as a result of the perception of some authentic Turkishness but via the language of the African Americanized street: "[H]e defines [his] public work as a process of empowerment of minorities and the reclaiming of cultural hegemony" (132).

I read this "reclaiming of cultural hegemony" directly in relation to a process of occupation, which then also exceeds the initial relationships established in the postwar moment. It reformulates how one can be in Germany and beyond. It means that one need not only think of effecting social change as it relates to the context of the federal government or formal politics. It offers different political possibilities. Graffiti, also as articulated, for example, in Çelik's films and other artistic works, operates as a form of occupation, as does the reconfiguration of the German language offered in Zaimoglu's books, Çelik's films, in schools, youth centers, and on the street. Of course, the difference between the other aesthetic renderings and the street formulations is that the mainstream (normative) public no longer sees the theater, film, and published versions as negative. In these articulations, it is critical to understand occupation in the double sense I have been suggesting thus far, that is, both as a physical and as an imaginary (psychic) form. Graffiti occupies physical space and is simultaneously an aesthetic that occupies the imaginations and desires of Berlin and other cities. There are government policies to remove it and yet there are also special paid tours to go see it. It reconfigures the significance and meaning of the spaces it inhabits.

On the West side of the Berlin Wall during the Cold War, graffiti was seen as an articulation of "freedom," while the East German side was, of course, unmarked. As the Wall was falling and street hawkers began removing and selling pieces, the most valuable pieces were those that had been spray painted. In fact, in Berlin in 1989, after renting a chisel to get my own pieces of the Wall, I noticed that to make them appear more valuable, men who were selling the interior pieces would spray paint them before removal, as if the suggestion of graffiti would insure their authenticity. Also in 1989, an artists' project known as the East Side Gallery was commissioned to organize international artists to paint a large portion of the formerly unmarked East side. Twenty years later, the (street) artists were invited back again to renew their work. Now, uncommissioned graffiti on gentrifying housing blocks may be responsible for keeping rents down, as one sprayer put it, according to a tour guide of Berlin graffiti and street art.

THE NECESSITY TO OCCUPY REVEALED IN THE IMPOSSIBILITY OF BECOMING "WHITE"

In addition to the physical marks left by graffiti to aesthetically and symbolically claim space, in this chapter I have been using the term "occupation" to mean a form of embodiment—noncitizen youth embodying Americanized Blackness through postures and positions, writing, dancing, and dress. I have also been using the term to describe a particular history of military occupation in which claims of liberation carried with them a necessary reconfiguration of globalized racial politics in a way that American postwar planners had not anticipated. Furthermore, I have been using occupation to think through the reconfiguration—including the opening up of—social and physical space as the normal rules give way (at least in part) to the rules of occupation, including those of and enforced by the Black occupiers. Finally, I have been thinking about the cultural politics of occupation. In this case, occupation is not only significant because of its military presence but also because it is involved in the creative reformulation of consumption and desire. But to a large extent, occupation is necessary, because noncitizenship persists.

In this respect, it must be noted that Germany has only recently defined itself as a "country of immigration." Even if immigration has been a critical part of its history (see Herbert 1990), those who did not blend in, with the exception of a few officially recognized minorities, have historically faced severe sanctions. While the citizenship law was liberalized in 2000 to make it easier for those with parents with permanent residence to become legal citizens, the social regimes that regulate incorporation have been dragging their feet, so to speak, on the possibility, even the pretense, of full inclusion. (Full incorporation, itself, is likely an anathema, leading back to the need for Blackness as a different kind of articulation.) Within this arena, Turkish-German filmmaker Fatih Akin has been an *Ausnahme* (an exception). He is arguably the most famous contemporary German film-maker, both nationally and internationally. He won the Golden Bear, the highest and most prestigious prize, at the Berlin International Film Festival in 2004 and the award for the best screenplay at Cannes in 2007. In 2008, he was the president of the Cannes jury. Nevertheless, in a public discussion with Feridun Zaimoglu at the Free University Berlin (Zaimoglu and Ayata 2008), Neco Çelik recalled his own difficulty with the reality of Fatih Akin's success. Speaking about the making of his first short films and trailers on the path to making his first feature, Çelik recounted:

> At the same time, I was working on a feature film in which I wanted to tell a story from the neighborhood. Then, Fatih Akin came and made his films— *In July, Solino, Head-On.* And the people said: 'Yes, but Fatih Akın has already made that kind of film. We don't want any more Turk films.' I said, 'I'm not making a Turk film. This is Kreuzberg [Berlin]; that is Altona [Hamburg]. What's the problem? I'm Neco and that's Fatih.' They still came back and said, 'No, it's too much. . . . '
>
> After five years, I came to the understanding that this story, even though I had never noticed it, was in fact a Turkish story. I then rewrote it as a German story (135–37, my translation).

In this instance, telling a "German story" meant not veering too far away from normative tropes. If one does, one needs permission.

In another articulation of this story in a conversation with me, Çelik revealed that the producer told him that the majority of the German audience could not identify with the story if a "Turk" were the main character. While keeping it a story about his neighborhood, Çelik relented and rewrote the main character as a White German. Until he did this, the producers, who had the power to decide whether or not Çelik's film would be financed, rejected it precisely because of their perception of its Turkishness and thus perceived lack of appeal to the German mainstream. On the other hand, what film theorist Barbara Mennel (2002a, 2002b) identifies, problematically, as a "ghetto" milieu (but what Çelik himself calls a neighborhood film, in the spirit of Spike Lee) is appealing to the mainstream funders, perhaps precisely because of Lee's success. In a discussion about the interview in the *Frankfurter Allgemeine Zeitung*, Çelik told me that he thought it was an honor to be compared to Spike Lee. In other words, the sociocultural space that Lee occupies in the German imagination makes some breathing room (if not total liberation) possible for Çelik.

Addressing the problematics of racialized film production in Germany, a number of Germanist film scholars have written about the links between the funding available and the particular genres in which Turkish-German film directors are able to operate. In these analyses, the critics point out that funding for film in Germany primarily comes from television—the principal moneymaker for German-produced film/video productions (see Halle 2008; Mennel 2002a, 2002b; Göktürk 2003). This funding, in turn, has been primarily public—supplied by federal and state sources. In other words, as with the politics of occupation and the promotion of Black aesthetic forms, artistic production becomes a state matter linked directly to the contemporary politics of democracy and citizenship, a realm that Blackness suggests (as subsequent chapters will also show) that we still need to get beyond if Black liberation is really at issue.

Fatih Akin began his career by complying with some of the then-acceptable African Americanized formulas, including what Mennel (2002b, 134) calls an aesthetic of "ghettocentrism and auteurism." While Mennel and Randall Halle (2008) see auteurism (in which the film director establishes a distinctive aesthetic) as a European dynamic, I would argue that the mix of ethno-racial neighborhood dynamics and auteurism is also part and parcel of the success of filmmakers such as Spike Lee. Deniz Göktürk (2003) and Barbara Mennel (2002b) argue that the aesthetic forms that Akin used were already a departure from the ethnicized Turkish productions, what Göktürk, adopting a model from the British case (Malik 1996), identifies as a (potential) shift from a "'cinema of duty' to 'the pleasures of hybridity.'" (I will return to the problematic terms "hybridity" and "ghetto" below.)

Describing the shift from "duty" to the contemporary "ghetto" form, Mennel (2002b, 136–37) writes: "The 'cinema of duty' remains for [Sarita]

Malik 'social issue in content, documentary-realist in style, firmly responsible in intention.' It 'positions its subjects in relation to social crisis, and attempts to articulate "problems" and "solutions to problems" within a framework of centre and margin, white and non-white communities." As both Mennel and Göktürk (2003) note, the films associated with this genre emphasize the social and spatial boundedness of Turkish immigrants. They thematize problematic gender dynamics, including women cut off from the society by dominant men. Although made by Turkish, Turkish-German, and White German directors, these films, both Göktürk and Mennel suggest, leave both the male and female (but primarily the female) Turkish immigrant as voiceless victims with little power to change their situation. The significance of the cinematic form here has to do with the fact that while fictional, these films take the place of documentary, fulfilling mainstream expectations about the "backwardness" of the immigrant Turk.

Furthermore, and this cannot be emphasized enough, the fact that these, as opposed to other, films get made at all is linked to the vision of the state-backed funders. Göktürk (2003, 182) notes that "*schemes of film funding (Filmforderung)* on a federal or regional level, as well as coproductions with television, mainly with the public broadcasting channel Z.D.F. *(Das Kleine Femsehspiel)* sometimes proved to be counterproductive and limiting in the sense of reinforcing a patronizing and marginalizing attitude towards Ausländerkultur, the culture of foreigners." The already existing supposed "sociological perspective" is authenticated in fiction film, which gets read as documentary—with the "authentic" behind-the-scenes images now supplied to the White German viewer.

One such film thematizes a Turkish woman who joins her Turkish husband in Germany, perhaps in line with the family reunification policies of the German government since the early 1970s. The film takes place entirely in one room until the end, when the female protagonist kills her husband. Confirming the power of this image, Göktürk writes that "*40qm Deutschland [40 Square Meters of Germany]* (1986) . . . received the *Bundesfilmpreis* [the Federal Film Prize] in 1987, an award given by the Federal Ministry of Internal Affairs—dutiful national acknowledgment, which paradoxically seemed to cement the subnational status of '*Ausländerkultur*'" (2003, 183–84). If there were just one film, perhaps this portrayal could be seen as the exception, but, as others have demonstrated, this became part of a trend with films made by different filmmakers, all of whom received official backing.

In the 1990s, however, the commercial success of a number of African American filmmakers in the United States opened up new possibilities for Turkish-German cinema. Spike Lee, the Hughes brothers, and John Singleton (among others) in the United States reconfigured the possibilities for filmmakers and writers such as Çelik, Akin, and Zaimoglu in the sense that the films linked to these artists then became viable as forms that had already proven to be popular. Ed Guerrero (1993) refers to a "black movie boom" which consists of American films of the early 1990s. Mennel (2002b) problematizes the domineering male-centered dimensions of these possibilities (from the perspective of how minoritized filmmakers enter the mainstream). Of course, Turkish-German filmmakers realize these possibilities, just as the broader public and the German mainstream media continue to express their displeasure via frequent discussions and portrayals of the Muslim/Turkish/Arab woman covered by the headscarf. In Akin's, Çelik's, and Thomas Arslan's[10] films, though, Islam is not a primary emphasis. Despite the German stereotypes about Islam and Muslim subjectivity, women are sexualized in these films, some even as prostitutes. In *Gegen die Wand*, Akin's breakthrough film, a major controversy emerges, connected to the fact that the lead female actress had appeared previously in pornographic films. Emphasizing Çelik's boundary-pushing, a lurid scene in *Alltag* resulted in someone calling security at the University of Michigan as the film was transferred to another video format. The complainant apparently said that they had been exposed to explicit sexual images—even though no nudity actually appears in the film.

Writing about this period in German cinema, Mennel suggests, "performing the pleasures of hybridity might just have become the new duty" (2002a, 53). In the examples above, this involves sensationalizing the representations of the "migrant" in film and popular culture. It follows that the most well known Turkish-German films of this period then get stuck in a new problematic dynamic of what Ed Guerrero (1993) has called "neo-Blaxploitative" filmmaking.

Moving beyond this point, I ask: To what extent is the German national culture itself imprisoned in and by its own images of the Turkish-German Other? How might this imprisonment reduce possibilities for a more vibrant exchange and even more vibrant aesthetics? On the other hand, how does the occupation by and of African American Blackness shift this dynamic, providing some grounds for a conversation, even if it involves translation and transposition? Ultimately, Turkish-Germanness via Blackness offers a different potentiality for the wider distribution of Akin's, Çelik's, and Arslan's artistic production. Occupation via American Blackness becomes the condition under which the two audiences—White German and racialized Germans—get brought together. This coming together, however, is not equivalent to assimilation. Even as the Turkish-German filmmakers gain new audiences, they cannot become normative citizens with access to the full range of creative possibility. While it opens up space, the occupation of and by American Blackness[11] also constrains movement. These filmmakers have not (and most likely cannot) become White.

IMPORTING A MODEL OF ETHNIC SUCCESSION? A BLENDING OF THE FILMIC AND THE REAL

Hamburg, where Fatih Akin grew up, was not, in fact, part of the American zone of postwar military occupation. In Akin's films, as compared to some of the others we have seen, America (and specifically American Blackness) is less immediately apparent, although the tropes of ethnicized and racialized Americanized possibility remain central. Akin's feature *Kurz und Schmerzlos* (*Short Sharp Shock*) blends Hollywood's stylized Italian-American mob tropes with an African American aesthetic backdrop. It was shot on location in Hamburg and includes urban surfaces decorated with graffiti and a dance club scene that revels in hip-hop and places its racialized youth squarely into modernized urban life.

Thinking more concretely about how Italian-American Hollywood tropes fit in relation to American Blackness and ultimately recognition in Germany (the possibility of success that also comes at a cost), one should have in mind American models of "ethnic succession": "a set of expectations that in a just and moral world, ethnic minorities will attain entry to the mainstream of American society through gains achieved in successive generations" (Ong 2003, 3). In these examples, there is an important parallel between ethnic and racialized immigrants and histories of labor migration in Germany and the United States. In the American context, however, one identifies ethnic succession not only with the process of becoming a formal citizen, as Ong notes (2003, 11), but also with the process of becoming White (Roediger 2002 [1991]).[12] Furthermore, Roediger (2002 [1991]), and Rogin (1996) have linked Jewish and Irish ethnic succession to the successful performance of blackface in the United States. By performing blackface, one distances himself or herself from Blackness, unless one is seen as the "authentic" Black person.

A central concern for this chapter is the extent to which Turkish-Germans can also fit this model of ethnic succession, particularly in a context in which there is much less space for hyphenated belonging than in the United States. The other question is: To what extent has American Blackness opened the possibility of at least partial incorporation? What possibilities does this incorporation exclude? Again, can incorporation be anything more than exclusionary incorporation for the noncitizen? Akin's artistic repertoire blends the filmic and the real. The filmic is represented via the form of his first feature film, inspired by Martin Scorsese's first feature *Mean Streets* (1973), a film, like Akin's, featuring a story of friendship and the (Italian) mob, but shot in New York as opposed to Hamburg. *Kurz und Schmerzlos* also portrays the ethnicized and criminalized fringe; it includes pimps, prostitutes, and a portrayal of friendship among characters who are immediately identified via onscreen titles as Greek, Serb, and Turkish. The mobster foreground finds its place in Germany via a hip-hop background (in music and images of graffiti in the diegesis) representing the materialization of everyday ethnicized life in Germany. Akin does not make an explicit issue of this background in the film, but it is very visible in the frame, and he has commented publicly on his affinity for hip-hop, among other musical influences.

The question, however, remains: To what extent can the racialized other become a White German and find a permanent place in the German mainstream? To what extent is this desirable? While the Turkish-German main character in the film suggests that he will give up and escape to Turkey, the filmmaker himself remains in Germany and does this to great acclaim. In fact, in his filmic oeuvre, the tension between origin and *Heimat* (homeland) remains a constant theme, with characters usually traveling to Turkey to recover or redeem some part of themselves that has been—perhaps permanently—lost.

Given that Akin has never become a White German filmmaker, even if he has become a German one, it seems that this is possible precisely because of the space that American Blackness (in his case implicitly) opens up for the possibility of being in the social imaginary. Hip-hop is the springboard for racialized incorporation as opposed to ethnic succession, in which, as Michael Omi and Howard Winant (1994) argue, the term "ethnicity" as opposed to "race" suggests the possibility of becoming White. In the context of Berlin, and particularly Kreuzberg, actually part of the formally American-occupied zone, the relationship to American Blackness is less abstract. As Çelik recounts: "The next thing that I was involved in was the hip-hop scene. . . . I did graffiti" (Zaimoglu 2008, 129–31, my translation). Even in the narration of his story, there is an important relationship between the filmic model of ethnic succession and his production as a German Black artist, revealing the open but constrained (and problematic) possibility of recognition. In his interview, conducted as part of his residence at the Free University, an educational institution that is itself a result of American occupation and postwar rebuilding,[13] Zaimoglu introduced Çelik as follows:

> He was hyped by the American media as the 'Spike Lee of Germany.' Neco and I met a couple of years ago. One should picture it in their mind as follows—even if it is not so nice for him that I put it this way: It was something like a scene in the film *The Godfather*. I have seen it a couple of times. Real thugs and fighter types—at least by their looks—came to him, kissed him on the hand, and said: 'Big brother Neco . . .' (The audience and Zaimoglu laugh.) So we should call him: 'The Godfather of Kreuzberg' (Zaimoglu 2008, 118, my translation).

Çelik, though, immediately played down Zaimoglu's stylization of their initial encounter: "Okay, about the hand kissing: That was my younger nephew [general laughter] who kissed my hand because he wanted to show respect, because I'm his uncle. I told him: 'Stop that!' He [Çelik signals toward Zaimoglu] is, of course, dramatizing that moment" (118, my translation). The dramatization which Çelik tries to soften is, of course, the staging of himself as a mob-type figure. While he might have been involved in a neighborhood gang as a youth, Çelik is now a stylish, easy-going, sharp but friendly artist and youth worker. The play between the models of ethnic succession and American Blackness, however, is important to the strategy of making it in Germany. In *The New York Times* article that launched Çelik on the global scene, we can see the ways in which he himself plays with this ethnic/Black American dynamic.

Blackness, however, represents both the possibility and the limit of ethnic succession in Germany (and the United States). The Black American referent and its popular global consumption means that the German public at large will be able to distinguish between Çelik and his father, whose background is rural Anatolia. This differentiation, however, reifies his father's marginality—even if Çelik vehemently fights against this, as he does.

It is important to note here that in spite of this occupation with and by Blackness, in everyday life, there can simultaneously be a distancing from African diasporic people.

> NECO ÇELIK: The hip-hop scene is—especially here in Berlin—shaped by youth of Turkish descent. This issue of 'honor' is implanted by their parents who come from Turkey and raise their kids traditionally. The youth use these words, but they don't do anything to back them up.

> AUDIENCE MEMBER: Does it have something to do with the feeling of being an underdog? Like the Blacks in the USA, who stylize such terms? Is that practice adopted here?

> NECO ÇELIK: Yes, surely MTV plays a huge role. MTV rears our kids. The youth in the *Naunyn Ritze* [the youth center where Çelik has worked] won't have much to do with with Blacks. But strangely enough, they rap. They want to be like the Black rappers on MTV. It's a paradox (Zaimoglu 2008, 139, my translation).

Çelik was born in 1972, and the youth about whom he speaks were presumably born in the 1980s and 1990s. One wonders about the extent to which the absence of actual African American occupying troops in the post–1989/post–Cold War era contributes to the distancing of contemporary Turkish-German youth from the politics and the physical presence of African diasporic Blackness. While American Blackness may continue to act as a social resource in Germany and beyond (see J. Brown 1998 and my modification in chapter 1), the distance from its physical presence as an occupying force produces new challenges for coalition.

OTHER TENSIONS OF COALITION: GENDERS OF OCCUPATION AND AFRO-GERMANS

While African American GIs and a hip-hop aesthetic emphasizes a masculinization of African American occupation, the Black bodies by and through which occupation has taken and continues to take place are not necessarily male. As the authors of *Farbe Bekennen* (*Showing Our Colors*) note, part of their response to the exclusion by White West German feminists in the 1980s was to assert their place as Afro-Germans and to point to the necessary links among race, racism, gender, sex, and sexism. This intervention is inspired, empowered, and informed by the US Civil Rights movement and the presence and articulation of Black women: "With Audre Lorde we created the term 'Afro-German,' borrowing from Afro-American, as the term of our cultural heritage" (Opitz, Oguntoye, and Schultz 1991, xxii). Lorde herself recalls the context: "In the spring of 1984, I spent three months at the Free University in Berlin teaching a course in Black American women poets and a poetry workshop in English, for German students. One of my goals on this trip was to meet Black German women, for I had been told there were quite a few in Berlin" (1992, vii).[14]

Since the end of the Second World War, it has been through the term *Besatzungskinder* (occupation children), that many Afro-Germans have come to be popularly known. The term invokes the occupation of Black American bodies, even if this is not the sociological reality. The *Showing Our Colors* authors write that "after World War II there was hardly any further mention of the Afro-Germans born before or after 1919" (Opitz, Oguntoye, and Schultz 1991, 79). They refer, here, to the so-called *Rheinlandbastarde* ("Rheinland Bastards"), the children of French African troops and White German women born after World War I, and the disappearance of their existence from social memory, following their sterilization and stigmatization. However, the shift in the social imagination from

"Rheinland Bastards" to "Occupation Babies" suggests a significant shift in the possibilities for Black articulation in Germany, even if the term "occupation" in this context is sometimes understood and used negatively.

As historian Heide Fehrenbach (2001, 164) notes: "As federal and state officials became all too aware, their response to the children [of White German mothers and Black GI fathers] was an important early testing case for postwar German democracy." She continues:

> What emerged from reports by native local authorities were not narratives of German female victimization similar to the 'black horror' stories that circulated after the First World War or tales of mass rape by Soviet troops in the East during the spring of 1945, but narratives of national disorder that linked racialized American masculinity with unrestrained native female sexuality, criminality and materialism (168).

These qualities, at least those of materialism and female sexuality, would eventually be embraced by critical components of the German public in the post–World War II (African) Americanized era.

Beyond this initial move toward the possibility of acceptance, as the authors of *Farbe Bekennen* make clear, the presence and politics of Audre Lorde in post–World War II Berlin became critical to processes of Afro-German politicization in their attempts to effect a broader social transformation beyond the scope of military occupation. Lorde recalls:

> Afro-German. The women say they've never heard that term used before.
>   I asked one of my Black students how she had thought about herself growing up. 'The nicest thing they ever called us was "warbaby,"' she said. But the existence of most Black Germans has nothing to do with the Second World War, and, in fact, predates it by many decades. I have Black German women in my class who trace their Afro-German heritage back to the 1890s (1991, vii).

In spite of this history, it was only after the Second World War that a social space for Afro-Germans, even if as "war babies" or *Besatzungskinder*, became part of the broader social imaginary beyond the post–World War I obsessions with racial purity and eugenics. This later occupation provided the grounds for social reconfiguration in multiple unanticipated directions.

CONCLUSION

I have pointed to many of the ways in which African American occupation is linked to processes of social transformation—the reconfiguration of social and physical space, shifting positions of Blackness from ones of marginality to those anthropologist Jacqueline Nassy Brown (1998) calls "diasporic resources" (see also Campt 2004). But here, these resources are rearticulated to include not only those originally perceived as being of "African descent," but also those in other spaces of displacement or noncitizenship; many of them also reference Blackness in relation to their own experience and possibility for political articulation.

Furthermore, while this chapter is heavily influenced by the specific histories of military occupation, in the end, that is not the most significant meaning of the term "occupation" or its potential. It is only a starting point for thinking about articulations and limits, histories and futures. Through this research, it has become clear that transformative occupation must possess both material and imaginary dimensions. It must both inspire displaced subjects and occupy dominant space. Occupation itself can become a position from which to speak, but speech alone will not be adequate.

In conclusion, I would like to return to Stuart Hall (1990, 236–37): "We have been trying to theorize identity as constituted, not outside but within representation; and hence of cinema, not as a second-order mirror held up to reflect what already exists, but as that form of representation which is able to constitute us as new kinds of subjects, and thereby enable us to discover places from which to speak." To what extent can occupying presences constitute us as new kinds of subjects? Including but also moving beyond film, how might the aesthetic dimensions of occupation, and an occupying Blackness, open up real possibilities for social change, even beyond representation? Were we, often the descendants of former slaves and figured as colonial tools (see Wilderson 2020), ever the subjects of democracy in the first place?

While emphasizing specific histories and relationships, this chapter has suggested some possibilities for and articulations of unanticipated alliances. To think more specifically and more strategically about occupation, in particular, might advance the efficacy of these social forms, already in process. While this chapter has pointed to Black potential, as Neco Çelik's among other commentaries suggest, these alliances, for the most part, are not yet formed strategically as such. Their infrastructures are thin and there is too little thinking about the political economy of their sustenance or a more forthright politics of accountability—that is, not only using Blackness as a possibility but also holding oneself accountable to Black people. Occupation as a political strategy, of course, means more than the simple adoption of aesthetic forms that happen to flow as the result of market forces. Critical occupation with and through Blackness must be based on consciously coordinated efforts, planning, and articulations with specific goals in mind.

PART II Holocaust Memory and
Exclusionary Democracy

4 Holocaust *Mahnmal* (Memorial)

MONUMENTAL MEMORY AMID CONTEMPORARY RACE

In this and the next chapter, I will briefly break away from the idea of an occupying Blackness in order to understand how Blackness, again, becomes necessary for political possibility beyond the more narrow Enlightenment forms of democratic participation. In these possibilities, democracy must be called to account for its repeated failures and original exclusions. This chapter examines the relationship between contemporary racialized beings in Germany and the process of Holocaust memorialization. It asks why racialized youths cannot see themselves in the process of Holocaust memorialization, a process that is linked, in Germany, to political participation more broadly conceived, and why that process fails to see them in it. The argument is not about equivalences between everyday racism and genocide, but instead examines how the monumentalization of Holocaust memory has inadvertently worked to exclude both relevant and potential participants from the process of memorialization. That process, as a monumental enterprise, has also worked to sever connections between histories, memories, and contemporary racisms.[1] The monumental display of what presents itself, at times, as moral superiority does not adequately attend to the everyday, mundane, repeatable qualities of racialized exclusion, either today or in the past.

My motivation to write this chapter originated with an investigation I conducted on citizenship and noncitizens in Berlin schools at the turn of the twenty-first century. I was struck by the general disconnect between left-leaning, 1968-generation teachers and their Turkish/Turkish-German and Arab/Arab-German Berlin-based pupils.[2] One tenth-grade math teacher at the *Haupt/Realschule*, a lower-tier secondary school that I was observing, told me that he had expected to be working with working-class (implicitly, White) kids. He had hoped to help to transform their socioeconomic circumstances, but in his first year he was instead confronted with an entirely "Turkish class." A history teacher for the same grade and school was dismayed by her students' indifference to her lessons about the Second World War and the Nazis. The secondary school and its students and teachers were situated in Kreuzberg, the so-called immigrant neighborhood, notable for its beautiful canals, nineteenth-century apartment buildings, hip restaurants, Bohemian bookstores, trendy student hangouts, and anarchist graffiti. The milieu was part of an emerging problematic concerning the place of German history in contemporary German life. Ironically, it seemed to me, these teachers were more likely to sympathize with a prototypical White German working-class student who had begun to outwardly identify with skinheads than with the majority of their students, who were Turkish-German or Arab-German.

Over the course of the 1999–2000 school year, the tenth-grade science teacher was scheduled to lead a class trip to the nearby former concentration camp, Sachsenhausen, and I decided to accompany them. As with the school as a whole, most of his students were children of immigrants, predominantly Turkish and Arab, while a minority were White Germans. When I arrived the morning of the trip I was disappointed to find only two or three students there, all of them White Germans. The other students had said that they would come, but they did not show up and so we went on without them. The science teacher thought his students were apathetic, and I went along with his assumption that the absent students had simply taken the opportunity for a vacation from school. On further reflection, though, I wondered to what extent their absence was due to the event itself and the way in which the Holocaust is taught in German schools. To what extent was their absence linked to the failure of the perpetrator discourse to include them,[3] with its emphasis on (implicitly mainstream,

White) German guilt? I wondered if the identificatory terms of the memorialization of Nazi genocide were creating new impossibilities of association or horror. I was struck by how the discourse about the Holocaust, perpetration, and guilt, among not only teachers but also Germans more broadly, was fully retrospective, and avoided any connections between the genocide and contemporary circumstances. I observed also that the implicit demand for affiliation with the guilt of historical perpetration was producing new specters of exclusion.

MEMORIAL TO THE MURDERED JEWS OF EUROPE

In 2009, I accompanied a group of Palestinian/Palestinian-German and Turkish/Turkish-German youths on a trip to the recently constructed Berlin Memorial to the Murdered Jews of Europe (see fig. 3). The young people were part of a program funded by the federal government and organized by a national antiracism foundation to address "gaps" in "democratic education," particularly among right-wing male and immigrant youth. The group I accompanied was scheduled to go to Auschwitz in the fall, and in preparation for that trip the foundation liaison had organized a series of events over the intervening months in Berlin. Previous gatherings had included an exchange of personal histories (including histories of Palestinian refuge in Germany); a documentary film about a German family's confrontation with its own Nazi SS legacy; and a visit to an unconventional memorial in a middle-class Berlin neighborhood that recounted the daily intensification of anti-Semitism during the Nazi era.

On that Sunday afternoon, ten out of sixteen youths showed up. We began with brunch at the foundation, about an hour away from where the youths lived, then proceeded on a guided tour of the German Reichstag (the national parliament building) and the visit to the Memorial. The youth center's director and the social worker who usually accompanied the youths told me that no one had dropped out of the program, even after several months. This surprised me, since the social worker had previously told me that the program had been motivated partly by what she and others perceived as the youths' latent anti-Semitism. The director, who was also a social worker, participated in planning the program, but the main

Figure 3. The memorial covers an entire city block and looks out onto Berlin's enormous Tiergarten park. Photo: Author.

organizer was the foundation liaison. She said that in everyday conversation the youths had suggestively asked, *"Bist du Jude?"* ("Are you a Jew?"), or forthrightly proclaimed *"Du Opfer!"* ("You victim!") as an insult. She said that this rhetoric, or at least the direct references to Jews, had stopped after the first few weeks.

On the day of the visit to the Memorial, the liaison was annoyed with the youth for play-fighting in the Reichstag, which they also did at the youth center. The official guide had warned them to use appropriate language and behavior. On our way through the building, one of the young men struck a hip-hop pose behind an FDP (liberal party) podium as his friend and I took pictures. When we got to a part of the Reichstag where victorious Soviet soldiers had used charcoal to etch their names into the building,[4] the same young man gave the commemoration a modern twist by pretending to shake a can and spray-paint his name below the historical Soviet graffiti.

As we left the guide to take the elevator to the glass dome atop the Reichstag, which famously bears the racialized words "*Dem deutschen Volke*" ("[For] the German Folk") at its entrance, she said to the youth, "I'll see you again, when you're parliamentarians." Whether she meant this as an ironic jab or a form of motivation I could not tell, but I recalled her admonition about "appropriate behavior." Was hip-hop bravado unwelcome in this house of democracy, or would the democracy itself have to be transformed by the hip-hop messengers in order to become a more truly democratic institution? In other words, does not the demand for proper (democratic) comportment also exclude? How could the possibility of opening up the democracy be configured in relation to our next stop—the Memorial to the Murdered Jews of Europe?

Between the Reichstag and the Memorial, the foundation liaison gave a talk to the youth about their behavior and said they needed to do better. Though he was not harsh, he had told me on the side that he would not go through with the trip to Auschwitz if such behavior continued. After their first meeting with the group, the social workers and the foundation liaison had both wondered if the youths' parents would let them continue with the program if they knew that it was about a history relating to Jews. Although the youth were excited about the prospect of going to Auschwitz, the liaison said that he was going to introduce the Jewish dimensions of the project slowly. In the first meeting, he told the youth only that the project was about history. On the day of the Reichstag visit, as the time approached for going to the Memorial, he seemed particularly agitated and nervous about the possibility of an inappropriate incident there.

After a short break, we all walked past the Brandenburg Gate and the new American Embassy en route to the Memorial. The official Memorial guide contained pictures of the previous site, where the *Reichskanzlei*, housing the Chancellor's office, had stood before its destruction in the war. The liaison also showed the group another, failed proposal for the Memorial and asked them to evaluate it. He eventually asked them to walk into the Memorial and come back after five minutes. In the period before entering, one young man had fallen asleep on one of the Memorial's stelae. When another talked on his cell phone, the guide retorted, "If you have questions, you don't have to immediately pick up the phone to call information." During the guide's presentation, though three youths talked among themselves, most listened and answered questions; they were much more attentive and respectful than were the youth from the eastern German city of Magdeburg whom I had observed on a previous day.

When the Berlin youths came back to the guide after exploring on their own, the guide led a discussion about the possible meaning of this memorial, one that, as the guide pointed out, had no names or words. We then proceeded underground to the "*Ort der Information*" (Place of Information), where a display of names, images, and text narrated a more formal history of internment, deportation, and extermination. On the way down, before the security check, the foundation liaison poked his finger into the back of one youth and told the social worker that he would not take him to Auschwitz. The social worker had asked the liaison how he thought things were going, but I did not see what the young man had done. He did not respond immediately to the finger in his back, but seemed hurt after the incident. It was not clear to me whether this was a warning, or if instead the liaison meant what he had said. The guide told the youths to explore the exhibit on their own, after which I saw the social worker gathering the group together for a private discussion. Meanwhile, the foundation liaison spoke with the guide.

After we had returned upstairs and outside, the social worker, emerging from the conversation with the youths, told the foundation liaison that they had something to tell him. On the corner of the Memorial, in response to the youths' mea culpa, the liaison proceeded to say that he would go through with the next meeting, but that if the group's behavior did not improve, he would end everything after that. He wanted each person to sign a contract agreeing to behave appropriately. One youth said that the activities had been too much for them for one day. The liaison responded that in Auschwitz there would be even more, and they countered that Auschwitz would be different because they had not been there before.

Things seemed to end on a more positive note. We walked back to Brandenburg Gate, and all of the youth proceeded to the S-Bahn, the regional train, to take it back to their neighborhood. I was anxious about the possibility of failure: that the program might end before the youths made it to Auschwitz. In comparison with the previous meeting I had observed, I thought that they had been less engaged, and, when they tried to participate more, they had been made to feel out of place, particularly in the Reichstag. Their experience at the Memorial was more of a lecture than a conversation. When asked to interpret the stelae, many said they saw them as mere abstract concrete blocks, a place to play hide and seek. The guide gave his own interpretation of why people were tempted to play at the Memorial, that they were overwhelmed by the horror, and that play put things back into a manageable order, but this reading sparked no epiphanies among the youth. My own sense was that there was still too much distance between the events the blocks were meant to symbolize and the youth who were supposed to be affected by them. The interaction had agitated the liaison, although he did say, on the side, that it was up to the experience itself, including the guides, to engage the youth. While one young woman did offer an interpretation of her own, most simply gave the guide polite answers to his questions: "It's gray." "We had fun playing tag." They all continued to demonstrate a desire to go to Auschwitz, even if the Memorial had failed to reach out and touch or connect with them directly.[5]

MEMORIAL PLANNING AND FAILED CONNECTIONS

In speaking at the opening of the Berlin Memorial to the Murdered Jews of Europe on 10 May 2005, Dr. Paul Spiegel, then president of the Central Council of Jews in Germany, observed that the site "honors the victims of National Socialist tyranny, but it does not directly implicate the perpetrators. On a visit to the Memorial, the perpetrators and supporters from that time and their contemporary ideological compatriots do not have to feel as if the Memorial is speaking directly to them" (Spiegel 2005).

Against Spiegel's claim, one might argue that the decision to put the Memorial in the center of the city—next to the site of what is now the American Embassy, Potsdamer Platz (a major commercial, shopping, and entertainment center), and the Brandenburg Gate (the entrance to the traditional city center), and along the road leading to the Reichstag (the main house of the German legislature)—suggests a permanent confrontation with questions of perpetration. On the other hand, perpetration seems to be less and less a problem for those who claim non-Jewish German heritage but were not active themselves in committing genocide. It is true that the perpetration issue is mildly sustained by national anxieties about renewed complicity between past agents of atrocity and young neo-Nazis who vandalize Jewish tombstones and attack so-called foreigners. But largely absent from discussions of memorialization or the monument is any reference to everyday racism, in either its institutional or intimate varieties, as part of the historical genocidal logic. Connections are rarely made between genocide and racism today, and other histories of atrocity. Part of Spiegel's point seems to have been that a confrontation with perpetration is one not only with the specific events of the Nazi Holocaust but also with what it means to be a perpetrator now, and how one might continue to be complicit in acts of racist violence.

More pointedly, contemporary monumentalization of and distancing from Holocaust memory is necessary for contemporary modes of normalized racial exclusion. Europeans gain contemporary legitimacy by signifying a historical break from a genocidal logic, despite their building new (asylum) camps (see Agamben 1998). In other words, the technology of the camp has not been banned altogether, only its particular historical use. I am not arguing that the Nazi camps and contemporary asylum camps or deportation prisons are equivalent, or that asylum camps commit the same kinds of violence as did Nazi-era concentration and extermination camps, or, as Agamben suggests (1998, 2005), that refugees in asylum camps are completely excluded from universal rights or political life. Rather, I want to draw attention to the ways in which a nationalist logic persists, not just in Germany, but also in Europe, the United States, and beyond, which differentiates types of citizens and qualifies the universality of rights.

In this chapter, I do not imagine Europe (politically embodied by the European Union) as the site for a reemergence of a Holocaust. But I do think that setting the Shoah as the standard for what should never happen again contributes to a monumentalization of an antiracist, anti-anti-Semitic logic that solidifies the legitimacy of Europe and European nation-states while still excluding Others in practice. It even can exclude while partially incorporating them (see Partridge 2008, 2012). Here I include as "Others" those who already reside within the nation-state and Europe. My main objective in this chapter is to point to a gap that is being produced between Holocaust memorialization and the recognition of contemporary racisms.[6] The discussion of memorialization that I address in what follows is wrapped in guilt. Yet it simultaneously relegates any confrontation with racism cum genocide to a past (see Olick 1998) that is now monumentalized, standardized, and made useful for contemporary purposes without addressing contemporary racisms in their complex European (or American) varieties (see Balibar and Wallerstein 1991; Pred 2000; Özyürek 2009; Bunzl 2007, 2005).

Paul Spiegel added another dimension to the process of Holocaust memorialization and its contemporary implications when he argued at the opening of the Berlin Memorial:

> The occasionally emotionally taxing conflict [over where, how, and why to build a memorial] has produced many noteworthy contributions to the German-Jewish dialogue about the still burdensome past. Unfortunately, this discussion has been in danger of producing a hierarchy of the victims and the losses suffered. In the face of torture and death, there is no hierarchy. Pain and sorrow over the losses suffered in every affected family are tremendous. Therefore, I emphatically support the proposition by other victim groups to have public sites of remembrance.

How the discussion about the past takes place now is significant for the present and future of antiracist (not to mention Jewish, Black, Indigenous, or POC-affirming) politics. Spiegel refers here to a larger controversy in which Lea Rosh and other advocates for a memorial (which ultimately opened in May 2005) argued that it should specifically honor the Jewish victims of the Holocaust, rather than all of those targeted by the genocidal Nazi logic. This discussion, of course, has relevance not just for how the past is remembered but also for contemporary life.

MONUMENTAL MEMORY AMIDST CONTEMPORARY RACISM

I now want to shift my attention from historical relationships to a contemporary one: that among Berlin's Holocaust Memorial, German Holocaust memory, and those racialized in contemporary life, particularly so-called Turks, Turkish-Germans, Arabs, Arab-Germans, and Palestinian refugees. I will also briefly address African-American and Latinx youth in the United States. I want to explore several key questions: (1) How can the racialized, and the analyst, relate to what Viola Georgi (2003) calls a "borrowed memory," that is, the borrowed memory of the implicitly White, non-Jewish German, but also European genocidal perpetration and victimization of genocide? (2) To what extent are the nation-state and the supra-nation (Europe) being asserted and reasserted in this necessity for remembering via a major memorial? (3) What work does the memorialization of a violent racist history do to serve the contemporary nation and supra-nation (Europe)? (4) How does the Berlin Memorial contribute to the rupture between racialist history and contemporary racism? (5) Does the Memorial work as a form of absolution and forgetting (see Olick 1998; Edkins 2003) while solidifying national and European consciousness?

In addition to addressing these questions, I want to note that one can read the Holocaust Memorial as something akin to what Benedict Anderson (1991) called "print capitalism." That is, the Memorial works like a novel, allowing people to read and argue over the same book in the same language at the same time, to come together as those who can—as opposed to those who cannot—discuss and read and be the national audience.[7] In this way, the Memorial and the discussions about it contribute to producing the nation.

In the spring of 2008, I decided to return to Berlin for the third anniversary of the Memorial's completion. On the Memorial's website I had seen that a concert was to be performed within it, and more importantly (it seemed at the time), the most prominent advocate for the Memorial project, Lea Rosh, would speak. For many, she was at the center of what had become a very controversial project over the course of the seventeen-year planning and advocacy process. The Memorial was contentious due to its large size and its location in the center of the city, because it differentiated between Jewish and other victims, and because the company that had supplied the anti-graffiti agent for the Memorial owned a subsidiary that had supplied the lethal gas for the Nazi extermination camps. Furthermore, for seventeen years Rosh had held on to a tooth from a Nazi extermination camp in order to bury it in the Memorial, a proposal that was ultimately abandoned because, many argued, it violated the Jewish law that calls for immediate burial of Jewish body parts and outlaws any instrumental use. Rosh had also begun the fundraising campaign for the Memorial by placing a provocative billboard on its eventual site, which read: "*Den Holocaust hat es nie gegeben*" ("The Holocaust never happened").[8]

ENTERING THE MEMORIAL

As the project's New York-based architect Peter Eisenman has suggested in many statements, the Memorial to the Murdered Jews of Europe, while monumental, is not a classic monument. It is a field of gray pillars that appear to guides and visitors alike as if they were tombstones.[9] Unlike a cemetery, however, walking toward and into the pillars one is enveloped by them, until the surrounding Berlin cityscape disappears from view. The experience is profound, but to experience this profundity, or any connection to the Shoah in its richness, one must bring along one's own memories.

When I returned to the Memorial for its anniversary, a Catholic youth group was reading aloud Elie Wiesel's and others' accounts of the Shoah. The young volunteers were dispersed throughout the field of stelae with yellow scarves tied round their necks like American Scouts or East German Young Pioneers. The scarves were close to the color of the Stars of David that Jews were forced to wear during the Nazi era. In the early afternoon, passersby were confronted with these readings or with accounts of the numbers thought to have died in the Nazi camps across Europe. One young woman stood at a podium at the edge of the Memorial reading into a microphone. Others read deep within the Memorial, invisible from the street. One woman wore a Palestinian scarf over her yellow one (recalling a German fashion of the late 1980s to mid-1990s that had come back), but she refused to answer my questions about her decision to wear the scarf at this event, saying that the two scarves were unconnected and directing me to speak with the organizer about the readings.

Speeches by Lea Rosh, Wolfgang Thierse (former president of the German Bundestag), and a representative of the Israeli Embassy were followed in the early evening by an orchestral concert, a piece especially composed for the event (see fig. 4). The concert, like the readings, took advantage of the space and the acoustics of the monument by using the sounds of horns, voices, strings, and tympani to create a new aura in a space that is ordinarily much more silent, without its own voice or speech to direct or "correct" interpretation.

In its everyday life, when it is not at the center of a special occasion, the Memorial makes few direct statements on its own. Although it covers an entire city block, the announcement that it is the Memorial to the

Figure 4. For the orchestral concert the audience and the orchestra stood dispersed among the pillars. One could hear the musicians, but not see them or the conductor. The orchestra watched the conductor on video screens. Photo: Author.

Murdered Jews of Europe is subdued and only appears on the small street that parallels the main one that leads to other tourist attractions, including the Reichstag, Potsdamer Platz, and Brandenburg Gate (fig. 5). You might not see the sign at all unless you know where to look. Furthermore, traditional symbols of the Shoah play no role in the aboveground structure. As Eisenman (2005) put it, "We did not want to prescribe what [the visitors] should think; on the contrary, we wanted to make contemplation

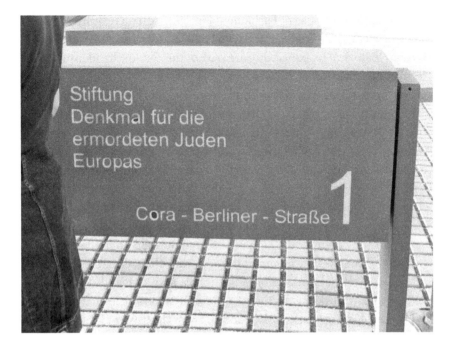

Figure 5. This sign reads: Foundation of the Memorial to the Murdered Jews of Europe, and gives the address. Photo: Author.

possible."[10] Following this logic, Eisenman was initially against having the *Ort der Information,* which gives an historical account of the European dimensions of the Shoah underground, beneath the field of "2,711 stelae made of high-quality concrete, each measuring 0.95 m in width and 2.38 m in length, hollow, with inclinations of between 0.5° and 2°" (Stiftung Denkmal 2008).

PLANNING THE MEMORIAL FOR THE MURDERED JEWS OF EUROPE

On the planning foundation's website, the most frequently asked question has been: "Why is the Memorial dedicated solely to the memory of the murdered Jews?" The foundation responds: "The decision to dedicate the Memorial to the murdered Jews of Europe was taken by the German

Bundestag [lower house of Parliament] in 1999 after a lengthy debate. It makes it clear that the recognition of the singularity of this crime and German historical responsibility are part of the core of the identity of the German nation-state."[11]

This framing of "singularity" and "responsibility" as part of a national "core identity" brings us closer to some of the tensions underlying the disconnect between 1968-generation teachers and so-called immigrant students. The terms of the relationship to the Memorial and to the history it represents are predefined for those who want to claim belonging or citizenship. This was done in part to combat the danger of Holocaust denial, which is a crime in Germany, but it also closes off other kinds of connections to Holocaust memory, simultaneously producing both the victims of Nazi genocide and their descendants as non-German noncitizens.

That the Memorial's planners thought that the German nation-state should be so crucial to the project's rationale says a great deal about how the monument works in "nation space." It also makes clear that the nation and the state, and not antiracist politics, are at the center of the process of memorialization. A 2005 discussion between the monument's architect Eisenman and *Spiegel Online* highlighted these ideas:

SPIEGEL ONLINE: Who is the monument for? Is it for the Jews?

    EISENMAN: It's for the German people. I don't think it was ever intended to be for the Jews. It's a wonderful expression of the German people to place something in the middle of their city that reminds them—could remind them—of the past.

SPIEGEL ONLINE: An expression of guilt, you mean?

    EISENMAN: No. For me it wasn't about guilt. When looking at Germans, I have never felt a sense that they are guilty. Clearly the anti-Semitism in Germany in the 1930s went overboard and it was clearly a terrible moment in history. *But how long does one feel guilty? Can we get over that?*

        I always thought that this monument was about trying to get over this question of guilt. Whenever I come here, I arrive feeling like an American. But by the time I leave, I feel like a Jew. And why is that? Because Germans go out of their way— because I am a Jew—to make me feel good. And that makes me feel worse. I can't deal with it. Stop making me feel good. If you are anti-Semitic, fine. If you don't like me personally,

fine. But deal with me as an individual, not as a Jew. I would
hope that this memorial, in its absence of guilt-making, is
part of the process of getting over that guilt. You cannot live
with guilt. If Germany did, then the whole country would
have to go to an analyst. I don't know how else to say it.

SPIEGEL ONLINE: The monument is specifically devoted to remembering the
Jews who died in the Holocaust. Do you think it's right that
the other groups victimized in the Holocaust are excluded
from this monument?

EISENMAN: Yes, I do. I changed my mind on that a few months ago. The
more I read about World War II history, the more I realized
that the worse the war went in Russia, the more Jews were
killed by the Nazis. When the Nazis realized they couldn't
defeat the Bolshevists, they made sure they got the Jews. Now
I think it's fine that the project is just for the Jews (*Spiegel
Online* 2005, my emphasis, original English).

In what follows, I explore further the relationship between guilt and
responsibility and the implications of getting over guilt, particularly for
those who can feel neither guilty nor responsible.

GUILT REQUIRES ABSOLUTION

"Thousands of Germans," he [then Chancellor Gerhard
Schröder] said, "were prepared to take part in the mass
murder of the innocent."

Today's European Germany has learned from these
crimes, that they could never grow tired of repeating the
phrase: "Never Again" (BBC, 2002).

Within the context of thinking about the break between genocide and
contemporary racisms, guilt becomes a central issue. This is expressed
most explicitly in terms of the guilt of "Germans" in relation to what "they"
did to "the Jews." This formulation is itself a serious problem because of its
connection to an ultimate call, even if it is only implicit, for national absolution. When, the German politician wonders, will it be all right to act in
the world without guilt, to make foreign policy (and even domestic policy)
without atonement as the central rubric of what is acceptable on the world

stage, where some still have low expectations for Germany and suspect hidden German desires for military aggression.[12]

Atonement is a problem because it does not directly consider the fact that racist thinking and policies persist, even if they are not equivalent to genocide. If atonement means getting over guilt, and that guilt is tied to getting over a history of racism, then atonement also potentially means not recognizing contemporary racism because the nation can be and has been forgiven.[13] Sharon Macdonald (2009) found in a study of the contemporary impact of the Nazi Party grounds in Nuremberg that "Even well-intentioned attempts to openly face the past can end up telling redemptive stories" (190). Furthermore, as many have correctly pointed out, the generation that was directly involved with the Nazi genocide is dying out. Increasingly, it makes little analytical or political sense to carry over guilt from one generation to the next, particularly when the 1968 generation did so much to protest against their parents' complicity with genocide. That guilt is being gotten over can be seen, in part, in Germany's increasing willingness to participate in global military missions, even though its military is legally bound to a defensive posture. Additionally, the formulation of what "Germans" did to "Jews" is problematic in the sense that at least some, if not the majority, of those Jewish people who were murdered or had to flee Europe were also German, and only made primarily Jewish by the Nazis and their European sympathizers.

Finally, if atonement is so central to the framework of Nazi genocide and its contemporary recognition, then the fall of the Berlin Wall and German unification play critical roles in potentially bringing about the ultimate forgiveness for which the guilt, and possibility of atonement, have been calling. The trust that Germany has recovered was symbolized in the Allied agreement to the 1990 German unification, and eventually in a return to global military, now "humanitarian," intervention in countries like Bosnia, where Germany was on the "right side" of genocide, and later Afghanistan.

Domestically, as I have pointed out elsewhere (2008), atonement may also allow Germany to end a refugee policy that was initiated, in part, to make up for the sins of genocide as part of a broader European process (see also Pred 2000, on Sweden). Since the Asylum Compromise of 1993,[14] it has been much more difficult for non-European people to come to Germany or to the other Schengen countries, claim asylum, and gain legal status. In other words, the implicit call for atonement as a central rubric of a post-racist European future is embedded in a refusal to recognize contemporary racisms as central to the logic of the nation-state and Europe. Racism is linked to a particular historical moment that mainstream Europe now imagines it has largely overcome and left behind.

RACIALIZED GERMANNESS?

The monumental effort to get beyond racism reveals the persistent reassertion of a racial logic. Eisenman, for example, experiences a split between contemporary, "regular" German and global Jewish subjectivity (*Spiegel Online* 2005). Even in the present, Jewishness remains an exceptional subject position. This separation is standard in the German context, but the difficulties that it presents are not confronted, even by the Monument's primary organizer, Lea Rosh, who has also publicized her own genealogical relationship to Jewishness. She refers to her Jewish grandfather in some discussions, including one with another attendee at the third anniversary celebration which I overheard. In that brief conversation, Rosh said that she stands by this genealogical fact, which links her personal history to the event being commemorated (and to her advocacy for the Memorial in the first place), and yet leaves her as an exceptional figure in her biological connection to Jewishness and mainstream recognition in German life.[15] The monumentality of Holocaust memory stems partly from the enormity of loss, reinscribing the problematic separation between Germanness and Jewishness.

In this context, Germany, in both mainstream media and the everyday conversations of Germans, produces new racialized positionings, while denying its participation in the re-inscription of processes of racialization (see also Chin et al. 2010; Fehrenbach 2005). Why else would Eisenman feel so Jewish when he comes to Germany? On the other hand, Eisenman's discussion and other mainstream accounts like it miss the opportunity to make connections to other contemporary subjects undergoing processes and experiences of racialization and racism. While Turkish-German leaders have attempted to make such links, they are often rebuked, and they certainly are not addressed in the mainstream discussion (see Peck 1994; Yurdakul and Bodemann 2006; Margalit 2009). The monumentalization of the past turns it into something that can only be discussed dangerously.

MONUMENTALITY AND INACTIVITY

Monumentality also produces a problematical forgetting. The monumental as forgetting (see also Huyssen 1996) is palpable in the notion that the Memorial to the Murdered Jews of Europe is the first and will be the last monument to tie Holocaust memory to the specificity of German planning and European perpetration. An implicit conclusion follows: "We have paid our dues. We have put the monument in the center of the capital." There is an implied teleological progression in the monument's completion. When the monument is ultimately built and dedicated, the seventeen-year controversy about its erection ends. On what basis could an active discussion of this magnitude continue? Given that the logics of perpetration are not the same as those of guilt, how can a discussion of the changing nature of perpetration go on, either as a historical or contemporary problematic, which remembers but is not limited to genocide as its defining feature?[16] How does the nation-state ultimately protect itself from contemporary accusation by building the monument as an historical artifact that primarily serves the contemporary function of memory?

Put differently, the Holocaust Memorial does, to some extent, seem to provide an anchor for a German and European future via its monumentality and centrality. But an active relationship to contemporary politics working to simultaneously address the foundations and persistence of racism is absent nonetheless. There are no events at the Memorial that regularly thematize this connection, and no active youth center at the Place of Information underneath the Memorial. Racism, thus, serves as a past moment from which one progresses. With the erection of the monument, both the Holocaust and its memory are pushed into the past. "We remember for the culpability of our ancestors, not our own." In this sense, the monument seems to achieve Eisenman's goal of "getting over guilt," but at what costs? Is there not some more critically engaged way to address the relationship between memorialization of Holocaust memory and contemporary racism, without insisting that successive generations need to suffer guilty consciences? Would continuing to raise the question of perpetration, as Paul Spiegel suggests, make Holocaust memory more active and differently relevant to the present condition?

Anyone who even casually followed the debate over whether or not to build a monument, and then where to build it, knows that seventeen years passed between the initial period proposal and the actual construction. Then-Chancellor Helmut Kohl liked Eisenman's winning design, but some people felt that "the discussion [itself] is the Mahnmal [the memorial]" (Till 2005). Implicitly, discussion is ongoing, while the erection of the monument represents an endpoint, a finality that seems as if it will last forever, and not, in fact, require new, unanticipated discussions that reach into not only the past but also the future. Edkins (2003, 130) has added a European dimension to what has traditionally been imagined as a distinctly German problem.[17]

> In the case of the French memorials of this [an earlier] period, there is no reference to the shared responsibility for the mass deportations or the French collaboration with Germany (Wiedmer 1999). They make concrete a particular reading of events that has little to do with living memory but rather replaces it, as Pierre Nora argues (1996). As products of an official, state-led commemoration, 'rather than encouraging active remembering on the part of the community, these memorials remember for the community' (Wiedmer 1999, 33). Unlike the sites that evoke a popular response, like the Cenotaph or the Vietnam Wall, these monuments stand as evidence of a problem solved. We visit, ponder a while, and then turn our backs: 'under the illusion that our memorial edifices will always be there to remind us, we take leave of them and return only at our convenience' (Young 1993, 5).

One can push these observations further and observe that memory alone, even communal living memory, will not suffice inasmuch as living memory requires a type of witnessing that will be increasingly difficult to obtain as survivors die out. And, of course, those killed under the Nazi regime can never recount their own experiences of horror; the murdered cannot actively participate in the ongoing discussion, as Edkins notes. What is

needed is a way to stage the contradictions and problematics of a genocidal logic so that they can be accessed not only as a historical problem but
also as one that affects the present. It must be connected to the specificity
of the Shoah but also understand perpetration and implication[18] as ongoing problems.

There have been efforts in this direction. In Berlin's Jewish Museum
computer screens have displayed questions about contemporary prejudice, such as a dislike of Jews among one's friends or family, and provide
an instant tally of how other visitors have answered each question. The
Museum has used Turkish-German guides to speak to general audiences,
and also to predominantly Turkish-German school classes, about the histories of Jewish presences in Europe.[19] These approaches evince willingness to link history more directly to the present, and this sets them apart
from the normal process of memorialization (see Topkara 2009;
Frankfurter Allgemeine Zeitung 2008b; *Deutsche Welle* and *Qantara*
2008; *TAZ* 2008).[20]

Interestingly, Eisenman himself claims that he resists monuments:
"Actually, I'm not that into monuments. Honestly, I don't think much
about them. I think more about sports" (*Spiegel Online* 2005). He nonetheless agreed to design this one and sees it as one of his major achieve-
ments. It seems important to think through Eisenman's claims both that
this is a monument for the German people "devoted to the Jews who died
in the Holocaust," and that it is, at least for him, about getting over guilt.
While the monument was being built, how did the process of getting over
guilt work? If guilt ends, does the meaning of the monument change?
How does the German production of Eisenman as "a Jew" really relate to
this guilt, and further, to contemporary racism and anti-Semitism (often
expressed via a kind of philoexoticism)? One can take these questions a
step further and, returning to Anderson's (1991) reading of the novel, ask
how the reading of the monument works in translation. Can new audiences be created? Can other Others enter the discussion? How do translations relate to the monument's reading, and the creation of a common
community with an implicit common fate? Why was the *Besucherordnung*—
the official guide to how one should behave at the monument (see
fig. 6)—originally only in German, while the Information Center, its
pamphlets, and the monument tours are all in multiple languages,

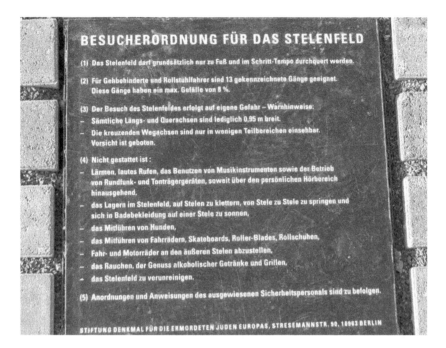

Figure 6. Original guide to how to behave at the memorial. (The guide is now also in English.) Photo: Author.

including English, Hebrew, Russian, and Turkish? (On my first visit I did notice the absence of Turkish and other languages.) Did the monument itself initially need no translation? Does the politics of translation imply its own gap?

FROM MONUMENTAL ARCHITECTURE TO MONUMENTAL FILM — FROM GERMANY TO THE UNITED STATES

The relationships between distance, "being touched" (in the sense of being both physically and emotionally moved; see Adelson 2005), Holocaust memorialization, and contemporary racism are not just German but transnational problems. The relationships between history, memory, memorialization, and citizenship can be fully understood only by examining them within different national settings and also in their complex international manifestations. Let me illustrate the former with a case drawn from the United States, of a high school visit to a local movie theater's screening of Steven Spielberg's *Schindler's List:*

> A group of students from Castlemont High [in Oakland, California], mostly African American and Latinx, went to see "Schindler's List" as part of a class trip. About an hour into the matinee at the Grand Lake Theater, a boy shouted as a young Jewish woman was slaughtered on screen.
> 'Oh,' he said, 'that was cold.'
> Laughter followed. A couple of dozen other moviegoers—some whose family members had died in the Holocaust—besieged the theater manager to complain (Spolar 1994).

After the laughter, the film was stopped, the lights came on, and the owner asked the students to leave. According to the newspaper article, "As the 73 students walked out, some of the patrons, obviously angry, gave a standing ovation" (see also Parker 2018). The *Oakland Tribune* took up the incident as one of racial significance, of "Blacks" laughing at slain "Jews." While some movie-goers commented on "the pain caused by them laughing," some of the students defended themselves by saying, "We always talk at the movies." The high school dean said that the laughter had to do with the students having been desensitized to violence, both on screens and in their neighborhoods. Steven Spielberg agreed. The owner of the cinema said that it was simply an issue of what was "proper behavior" at the movie theater, not anti-Semitism. The teacher who arranged the visit revealed that he had taught his students nothing about the Holocaust before the theater trip, and that many of them had wanted to see *House Party* (an early hip-hop film) instead. It seemed that a number of students had gone in anticipation of the ice-skating trip that was to follow the cinema event.

The most revealing statements come from the students themselves:

> 'We were just expressing ourselves—to relieve the tension, to do what we do in movies,' Tracy said. 'We're used to going to a movie theater and just talking. The media tried to turn this into an anti-Semitic thing, but it wasn't that.'
> 'Some people said we were too young for the movie, but I knew about the Holocaust in sixth grade,' said Danielle.

'We could understand. . . . What I didn't like was it was a three-hour movie—*in black and white*—with no credits or anything in the beginning. When a teenager goes to a movie, you want to see something interesting' (my emphasis).

Here, it becomes clear, there was little possibility for "touch." From the perspective of the students, *Schindler's List* reifies the fourth wall (the impossibility of their entering the life of the film) through the sustained use of black-and-white images. Like an archival image, the film forced itself into irrelevance for the teenage spectators, as something past and not "now," and this alienation was highlighted by the film's juxtaposition of black-and-white and color. The spectators who jumped up to applaud the students' forced removal clapped, not primarily because of the world the film had created, but because of their knowledge of what the film symbolized. The mimicry of documentary evidence employed by the film's use of black-and-white nonfiction-like footage demands the respect of the "knowledgeable" spectator, and yet the high school students refuse to be taken—they see it simply as a film: "It wasn't like people were laughing because people were dying. The woman who got shot *fell funny* and people just laughed. I mean we react differently in school than we do outside of school" (my emphasis). The student continued: "When it started you could just see a candle. . . . I mean, what is that? That's not interesting. . . . I think the teachers should have told us more. And I don't think they should have taken us there on Martin Luther King Day. No way. None of us is Jewish." Here, one should note the distance (lack of touch), in the student's words, between the commemoration of Martin Luther King, Jr., and the cinematic memorialization of genocide.

As with Eisenman's refusal, not only does the film fail to create the possibility of what Kaja Silverman (1996) calls an "identificatory lure"; it also fails to create a space where the unknowledgeable spectator might feel a part of the world of the film. The feeling of utter sadness that informed spectators feel when they leave the theater is largely based on their memories of other images, documents, and stories. The film triggers these memories, as opposed to making immediate touch possible or challenging spectatorial subjectivity. The uninformed spectators do not experience the film. They are not touched. Their own memories are not brought into the conversation. Can concrete memorials be more effective in connecting to what Viola Georgi and Rainer Ohlinger (2009) have called "*crossover geschichte*" (crossover histories), or what Michael Rothberg (2009, 11) refers to as "multidirectional memory" as opposed to "memory [in] competition"?[21]

BACK IN BERLIN

> According to Richard Serra [an artist commissioned to
> participate in the original competition to design the
> Memorial in Berlin], putting sculpture on a pedestal in a
> public square meant that the object of art was separated
> from the lived world of the onlooker. Sculpture on a pedestal
> transmits 'the effect of power without distinction'; it requires
> a subdued, even invented, audience to accept an idealized
> topic defined by the art community as worthy of
> commemoration (Till 2005, 183).

In Berlin, even though one can walk into the Holocaust Memorial and disappear, does it really ever escape the problem of being like "sculpture on a pedestal"? Does it undo the monumentalization of racialized history? Does it allow for unexpected touch?[22]

One should also ask if Turkish/Turkish-German and Arab/Arab-German kids not going to the Memorial, or African-American or Latinx children laughing during *Schindler's List,* are employing forms of resistance, or are necessarily anti-Semitic. When German teachers insist on a certain form of memory, are they reproducing nationalist memory and securing national sovereignty? Is any heroism to be found in Berlin's Holocaust Memorial?

Political theorist Jenny Edkins (2003, 4) argues that "What we call trauma takes place when the very powers that we are convinced will protect us and give us security become our tormentors: when the community of which we considered ourselves members turns out against us or when our family is no longer a source of refuge but a site of dangers." In the Turkish/Turkish-German and Palestinian/Palestinian-German cases, the family (sometimes only in a reconfigured sense) is a potential site of refuge; but that family can also, either as the nuclear unit or as the broader "community" sustained by the nation-state, be the systematic purveyor of violence via multiple forms of abuse including the violence of unemployment, or the persistent threat of deportation either of oneself or one's family members (on "deportability" see De Genova and Peutz 2010). The sometimes ambivalent intensity of the reliance on the biological family, especially when the nation-state persistently makes one feel alien, and also on the nation-state, which is supposed to protect those within its boundaries, becomes more acute under conditions in which, "Battered women would not recognize the picture of the family as a source of protection and stability," and further, "States abuse citizens on the battlefield, in captivity, in concentration camps. The modern state cannot be assumed to be a place of safety, any more than the patriarchal family can" (Edkins 2003, 7).

In this respect, given their experiences of alienation in the school setting, one could argue that the Turkish-German and Arab-German students distrust the White German teacher's account of German memory. They do not trust or identify with the teachers' empathy or potential horror. The Turkish-German and Arab-German students who do not show up, and the Black and Latinx kids who laugh, are not touched, because no hand is reaching out to them directly to recognize the connections between these past events, their own histories, and their contemporary social injuries. They are greeted instead by society at large with a pessimistic response to "their cuture," which is assumed to be anti-Semitic.[23]

In line with the Memorial project's dominant actors, Eisenman did not think about designing the Memorial for an audience beyond "normal" Germans, or in terms of a more complicated relationship to the specificity of Jewish victimization. His vision limited the scope of the way in which the arguably monumental architecture could move and touch people. On the one hand, it leaves the interpretive field too open; on the other, it closes it off too much. Even though Eisenman argues that he wants to be understood as an individual and not only as a Jew, when he travels to Germany, his interpretation of the process of memorialization sees Jews as Jews, and not as Europeans or German people who are also Jewish. While Jews were murdered for being Jewish, perhaps the Memorial should do more to suggest lives in complex negotiation with this identification and even with the contemporary lure of perpetration. Otherwise, one is left with an abstract representation of victimization that does not and cannot reach beyond those who already remember, or at least partially know.

NEW DIRECTIONS, NEW TOUCHES: FROM NATIONAL TO POST-NATIONAL IDENTIFICATIONS

The national space constructed by the Memorial, Hollywood film, and national literature creates networks in which people imagine themselves belonging to the same community without ever actually meeting each other (Anderson 1991). The irony is that local Turkish and Arab, or African American and Latinx, youth are made to feel foreign, as if they have nothing to contribute to the conversation, even though they have long-term claims to the communities in which they reside. Immigration and identification are thought of not in terms of local affiliations but as national and diasporic phenomena. And what about touch? In addition to the possibility of being moved, if touch were taken more seriously in the local, tactile sense, then processes of memorialization would be transformed (Adelson 2005). They would be taken off of their pedestal. This does not mean that they would be without conflict, but perhaps conflict would also become part of the process of being moved.

As the local dimensions of memorializing touch are beginning to be taken more seriously in Berlin, new things are beginning to happen. In a project called *Stadtteilmütter* (city-quarter mothers), carried out via programs with local and national support, so-called immigrant mothers engaged their local environments and German history in new ways. They learned about the relationships between familiar local buildings and Nazi perpetration—that the local department store once fired all of its Jewish employees, that an old factory was once a site of forced labor, that Jewish residents had been deported from a building in which or next to which they now live.

In its turn to history, this program had, like others, failed to consider relationships between past and contemporary experiences of racism and exclusion, but the mothers themselves made the perpetuation of this failure impossible. In their daily lives as well as in their assessments of the program, they actively demonstrated the multiple dimensions of touch. As one mother put it in an interview following a public presentation of the project, in the same district where the *Stadtteilmütter* project took place: The experience of this history "was horrible. We cried a lot." At the event itself, another mother said: "We have become more sensitive. We ask 'Who lived here before?' 'Who was deported from here?'" One of the women said, "Those who were born in Turkey, they didn't learn a lot about this history." One of the leaders of the seminar continued: "We don't feel as if we belong to this society, because we are not allowed to become a part of it."[24]

After a film was shown about another group of mothers from the same district who went to Auschwitz as part of their program, a heated discussion ensued. In the film, the mothers recounted how, when they went to a synagogue near Auschwitz as part of their trip, some local people near the synagogue insulted them with words such as "Headscarf woman" and "*Kanacke Raus.*" The latter insult, "Get out, *Kanacke,*" used a racist term for Turks, one we have already seen. "We were afraid to walk alone on the streets through the city," said the woman onscreen.

Following the screening, a woman who identified herself as Palestinian got up to speak: "We're always living in our past. The same thing and even worse is happening now. . . . It's happening with German weapons. . . . I want to say a word for peace." After her speech, the audience of just over two hundred people clapped loudly. A White German woman spoke next: "We have to differentiate" between what happened then and what is happening now. The audience applauded after her speech as well. Then a German-Jewish Holocaust survivor spoke: "There is a huge difference between comparison and making equivalent (*vergleichen und gleichzusetzen*). . . . It disturbs me when I hear people say Gaza and Auschwitz are equivalent. I have been trying for years to make contact with Palestinians. I don't have any Palestinian acquaintances/friends. I want it to stop with the demonstration signs, 'Kill the Jews.'" To a suggestion that a group dialogue was needed between Jews and Palestinians in Berlin, the Palestinian woman said to the Holocaust survivor, "I agree with you." After a long back-and-forth with audience members and among the mothers about questions of comparison and whether or not the Shoah can be compared with other historical events, one of the organizers of the history project intervened: "One can't get away from comparisons. The point is not just to educate from one perspective."[25]

Weeks later, I managed to interview the Shoah survivor. I asked her, "On what grounds, or on what basis, do you think that dialogue could take place?" She responded: "I don't know on what basis, really. Um. I think it is necessary that people express their prejudices. Like me, I think I have the prejudice that people who come from Arab countries and Turkey know little about the Holocaust, if anything at all, and that they are anti-Semitic . . . and that they have anti-Semitic concepts. This is my prejudice. If somebody would please tell me theirs, about me, so that we can then establish a dialogue to learn to what extent these prejudices are true or not."[26]

To what extent can the Memorial to the Murdered Jews of Europe also be used as a local rather than an exclusively national space, in order to begin this type of dialogue, which would then also address relations between the conditions of the Shoah and contemporary life? Such meetings and dialogues could reconfigure what we mean by memorialization, as well as the effectiveness of touch. The emerging discussion will raise new questions that cannot be easily contained by established discourses. New touches also mean new challenges, but also potentially personal and social transformations. In the end, we need to connect the monumental to the local and make historical memory continually active. We cannot relive the Holocaust, but we can be moved by its memory, particularly when it is directly connected to how we are living here and now. To experience this connection, we should not have to think of ourselves as national citizens, or only as ancestors of perpetrators or survivors. Powerful connections can be established through new experiences of this history in relation to our contemporary condition.

OŚWIĘ CIM, OCTOBER 2009

Let us now rejoin the youth group that we met earlier, to travel beyond the sites of recent memorialization to the actual sites of mass murder. After an overnight train trip and two switches the next morning, we arrived at the Polish city the Nazis named Auschwitz. At one stop Polish commuters had stared at us, a group of fifteen youth (ranging from sixteen to twenty-three years of age), two organizers, a social worker, two interns, and me, all shell-ing and eating sunflower seeds, searching for coffee, and talking loudly. Walking from the final train station, we eventually arrived at the German-Polish meeting center, built before the end of socialism. It was more like the campus of a small American liberal arts college than the youth hostel I had expected. Our rooms were in several different buildings, with a large center at the entrance where we would eat, and eventually meet with a Holocaust survivor to hear about her experiences in the camps.

That same day we walked to Auschwitz I—not the center of mass mur-der, but the center of its local organization. Our Polish guide spoke perfect German and said that we could take pictures, even though this was offi-cially forbidden. We followed him with earphones as he spoke into a port-able microphone, rattling off numbers and facts, leaving, as I wrote that evening in an anonymous assessment of the day, no time for emotion. It was pitch black before we left Auschwitz I. I think what I wanted most at the end of that day was just to be held and comforted, having been exposed not just to numbers but also to rooms full of children's shoes, suitcases bearing family names handwritten in large letters, children's clothes, domestic pots and pans, and a massive collection of human hair. One young woman from our group refused to enter that room, and another immediately burst into tears. While in graduate school I had read about the hair in a *New Yorker* article (Ryback 1993), but its author had failed to adequately enunciate its impact, and perhaps to do so is impossible. I was struck by the smell, a human smell of age, decay, and loss. On that day at Auschwitz I, I could not sustain my anthropological role. Critical dis-tance was impossible. I could not observe, but only feel.

A number of the young men in our group proceeded directly to a liquor store they had spotted on our walk there. One of the young Palestinian-German men got drunk for the first time. He started not with beer, but with vodka. The next day one of the trip leaders told me that this was a normal response to Auschwitz. She had observed on many trips that alco-hol was often turned to as a coping mechanism. This trip, however, was complicated by the fact that most of the youths' parents forbid alcohol. The next night, as they sat around smoking, drinking, and talking in the main building of the center, the social worker asked that same young man about his ability to recite the Koran, to which he simply responded, "I'm drunk." His facial expression implied less that he was unable to recite than that it would have been disgraceful to do so given his condition.

On the first evening, a woman who regularly led trips to Auschwitz and who worked for a major memorializing institution in Berlin led the discussion by asking everyone to write or draw a picture on small pieces of construction paper in response to the following questions: "What moved you the most?" "What irritated you the most?" "What most annoyed you?" "What made you the happiest?" Everyone, with the exception of this trip leader, participated in the exercise, which allowed us to remain anonymous. The answers were as follows:

The excursion to the concentration camp was very informative. Moved by: child poverty. Children's shoes; ashamed for the people who, the crimes. . . .

That lots of people looked at us strangely. The Children who were murdered.
Three of us received glances because of our [Palestinian] scarves.
The city tour was too short.
I was moved by the perspective of the people in the concentration camp, all of what they had to endure.

I hope that we don't have to walk so much tomorrow.
Thorough tour, informative, the children's clothes.
CHILD. [The foundation liaison told me later that this is what he wrote.]
Positive: that everything was explained to us thoroughly; negative: all of the walking. I learned enough for today.
Death by starving.
Hair.
Hair; the exhibit wasn't in the German language. [The social worker later mentioned being surprised by this fact.]

Harrowing, professional tour.
The cells where prisoners could only stand.
Experiments with children!!!
Black wall [the Execution Wall]; children's clothes
Hair.
Emotion without time. [This was my entry. Although I did not reveal this publicly, I did tell one of the young men, a sixteen-year-old, and the group leaders.]
The Standing prison—4–5 persons.

This last person also drew someone with a whip (a guard), a person on all fours with a dog mouth, and someone standing in front of a wall, probably the shooting wall, saying something. On top of the picture was written "Empathy." On the bottom the person wrote: "That we didn't have a smoking break. When the man [the guide] wanted to go, we had to go."

That evening, we discussed what was meant by my (anonymous) phrase: "emotion without time"; about the murder of children, and then at length about why other youth were at Auschwitz I with Israeli flags draped around their shoulders. The female organizer said that she disagreed with this "instrumentalization of the Holocaust." The young men were disturbed by the way that the apparently Israeli bodyguards stared at them and their Palestinian scarves. The discussion then moved briefly to the politics of Israel and Palestine, until the female organizer ended it.

The next morning we drove in vans to Auschwitz II, the center of mass murder, which has been, to the extent possible, preserved in its original postwar state. We saw the barracks, a train car that transported people to their extermination, and then the remains of the crematoria. The Polish guide pointed to white flecks on the ground and told us that these were the remains of human bones. "Allah, where have you brought me?" asked one of the young Turkish-German women. I, myself, was left speechless after learning the purpose of a large wheelbarrow in the only exhibit at this camp, alone in a room behind glass. I had assumed that it was to transport clothes, since this was also the building in which the prisoners were made to exchange their clothes for the camp uniforms. When I asked the guide what the barrow was used for, he told me: to transport human ashes.

That evening, we watched *Schindler's List*, at the suggestion of one of the young Palestinian-German men. Seeing it after Auschwitz, in Auschwitz, was a totally different experience, as the foundation liaison also observed. Both of us had always been critical of the film, but seeing it now gave daily life a presence beyond the ends of the preserved death camp. It made the sense of loss even more visible. The film re-inhabited the camp, the chambers, the barracks, the lone train wagon, with living souls. The same young woman who had cried in the room of hair, cried again throughout most of the film. "How could people do this to each other? What would I have done for my family members if I were in the same situation?" she asked later. The experience—not just that of the film, but also of being in the camps, listening to the survivor's account the next day, and being in the town—sparked other memories of trauma, of families going hungry in Palestine, of seeking refuge from political repression in Iran, and even of a father who had abandoned his daughter and left a rage in her that she did not know how to deal with, other than letting it out on those close to her.

Throughout this experience, it struck me that what was absent in the contemporary German discussion of racism, expressed in terms of immutable "cultural difference" and the "failure of integration," was humility and love. There may have been and may continue to be a lingering anti-Semitism among some of these young people. One of the Palestinian men, the one who refused to recite the Koran while drunk, whose family had lost their home in Israel, said, "The Jews then are different from the Jews now. . . ." He added, "The Germans then are also different from the Germans now," suggesting that they were no longer Nazis. But such anti-Semitism might best be overcome by constructing a safe space of care, which not only teaches these young people but also learns from them, in conversation with their contemporary experiences.

The foundation liaison worried about the future of these youth who he had now brought to Auschwitz. At one point, I heard him ask the social worker what would happen to them after they got too old for the youth center. He said that this trip alone would not be enough. He was referring here not simply to their education, but to their future prospects in the nation. At one point the other organizer asked the youth if they would go back to Palestine if offered the chance. A number quickly raised their hands, indicating that they would immediately go back. "What else could they say?" the foundation liaison asked me rhetorically later, when, back in Ann Arbor, I talked to him on the phone. Even if most of them had been born in Germany, and had German citizenship, Germany was offering them no strong vision of a possible future. I told him about my research in the schools in which the teachers, too, saw no future for their so-called immigrant pupils. The liaison, whose family had been away for the first few days after he returned to Berlin, told me that he had been feeling depressed, not just about Auschwitz, but also about the future of these young people. On that day when he asked the social worker, "What will happen to the youth," she had answered that they would need to start getting ready to move on, to make way for others at the youth center.

Just before leaving Auschwitz, the liaison had asked me to tell the group more about my work. I talked about how impressed I was with how loving and close-knit the group was. Later, however, it occurred to me that this community was ephemeral, a temporary form of companionship made tighter by a new experience of trauma that would tie them more to each other, but not to the nation-state that wanted them also to remember. The foundation liaison briefly worried about his participation in nation-building, but then quickly added that for these youth that was not the point. The point of the state-funded program was simply to make them less irritating residents within the nation-state. It was not to make them more equal members who would be given a larger platform from which to speak to their experience in relation, if not in comparison, to this history.

5 Democratization as Exclusion

NONCITIZEN FUTURES, HOLOCAUST HERITAGE,
AND THE DEFUNDING OF REFUGEE PARTICIPATION

Citizenship cannot be the ultimate goal, as Black being makes clear. The noncitizen presence contradicts normative claims about democracy and universal participation. This limitation expresses itself through waning state funding,[1] the regulation of everyday noncitizen political expression, including noncitizen participation in public protest, and also through the constraints noncitizens face when they take part publicly in the arts.[2]

In analyzing *democratization as exclusion* and also as *exclusionary incorporation* (see Partridge 2012),[3] this chapter examines the extent to which states imagine and insist on preconditions for participation. From the perspective of those constantly held under suspicion, that democratic participation always seems limited.

My investigation in this chapter thus centers on what has happened in Germany since post-Word War II *democratization,* a historical top-down process meant to teach people how to participate in *actually existing* democracy.[4] In Germany, democratization relied on America and Allied (American, British, and French) occupation. After Nazi perpetration, Americans and their partners argued that Germany would need to be both de-Nazified and democratized. American-led de-Nazification seemed largely symbolic, in the sense that it relied on executing Nazis as well as military occupation, but neither the violence of execution nor the force linked to occupation could rout out the pervasiveness of the broad adoption of Nazi ideology.

The American occupiers, though, thought of democratization as a technique that could be applied broadly, be built into education, and secured by military occupation. This form of engagement, however, was filled with inherent contradiction. Americans "democratized" Germany just as they enforced segregation in the Army and in the southern US States through Jim Crow, and more subtly in the North, Midwest, and West through redlining, restrictive housing covenants, pay differentiation, school and employment discrimination, and systematic forms of death, slow death, and dispossession.[5]

Democratization thus always worked as a bifurcated process where some could and would become citizens, whereas others would never achieve this status in any complete sense. The hope, in fact, worked and continues to work as another form of regulation, including self-comportment that would try to fit in and not challenge the existing system and its hierarchies too much. On the other hand, in comparison to the United States, for the occupiers, Black occupation felt like liberation.

As historian Maria Höhn notes: "[I]n the depictions of the influential African-American press, the heartland of Aryanism was converted into a haven of equality and freedom for black soldiers" (2008, 623). As I argue in chapter 2, some of this sense of freedom had to do with the fact that African Americans were now militarily and socially occupying Germany. Höhn recalls: "A September 1946 blurb in the *Chicago Defender* advertising an upcoming feature story on black soldiers in Germany in *Ebony* stated boldly, 'Paradox in Race Relations. In Berlin . . . One time citadel of Race Hatred . . . Negro GIs Are Living in a New World of Social Equality'" (623). Even before the war, scholars such as W. E. B DuBois recount the simultaneous experience of witnessing anti-Semitism in Berlin while nevertheless freely engaging with German women as a Black man.[6] Höhn notes that *Ebony*

> contrasted the experience in Germany with the reality of black life in the U.S. *Ebony* informed its readers that the 'Negroes are finding more friendship, more respect, and more equality than they would back home—either

in Dixie or on Broadway.' With an obvious jab at the situation of African Americans in the U.S., *Ebony* concluded that, 'many of the Negro GIs . . . find that democracy has more meaning on Wilhelmstrasse than on Beale Street in Memphis" (623–24).[7]

In other words, the American top-down approach to democratization came with contradictions, revealing a power hierarchy, including a racial hierarchy, embedded in the term and actual practice of democratization itself.[8]

This chapter thus explores the effects of the post–Cold War German nation-state taking over these rigid top down forms of democratization, which have necessarily regularly excluded noncitizen participation. It is significant, here, that the Cold War ended as a victory for the West German state. That state's form of democracy and democratization (one that it had learned from the Americans and was free to implement after American and Allied occupation ended) could then self-righteously overtake the East German state, migrant, and postmigrant forms of governance and social life.

This form of democratization continued to be linked both to a "no war of aggression approach," given the Nazis' war-mongering expansion through Europe, although this stance keeps getting softened and modified as NATO, often led by the United States, demands both funding and intervention, as well as a strict interpretation about how to prevent anti-Semitism. If a key tenet of postwar West German democracy was to "Never again" repeat a Nazi Holocaust, then, especially after American occupation and following the 1968 generation protest[9] and insistence on holding their elders (the Nazi generation) accountable, it would be left up to West German institutions to now teach East Germans, and later migrants and postmigrants, even if they were not always recognized as such, how to remember. This form of democratization, like the American form, represents a top-down strategy, which also both imagines and articulates a form of moral superiority, with establishment West Germans imagining themselves as the ones best positioned to teach their East German, immigrant, and postmigrant counterparts both how to remember the past and how to be democratic. The claiming of the teaching role is linked to the more explicit forms of violence that erupted after the Berlin Wall fell, with East German neo-Nazis as the most visible perpetrators of attacks against so-called foreigners. On the other hand, Muslim men find themselves persistently portrayed in popular media accounts and in federal government policy as violent articulators of patriarchy and potential "terror," including against Jewish people. Mainstream interpreters and analysts continually see both neo-Nazis and Muslim men as anti-Semitic.

ADDITIONAL BACKGROUND

After German policy makers established family reunification as state policy in the early 1970s as the primary means for the families of former "guest workers" to immigrate to Germany, migrant and postmigrant youth became a major presence in German schools and on news media landscapes (see also Chin 2007). Alongside these presences, immediately after 1989, mainstream West German media portrayed East Germans as not yet trained in democracy and potential violent perpetrators of anti-Semitism. The East German state had emphasized and memorialized anti-Fascist victims of Nazi-perpetration. The West German state imagined itself as needing to educate both groups about the dangers of perpetration and need for particular (East German, migrant, and postmigrant, with a particular emphasis on Muslim) forms of accountability.

These interpretations of the then-present need for *democratization*, which persists with an emphasis on Muslim immigrants and their descendants, became the central mainstream images of East Germans and so-called migrants (often actually dependents of migrants and not migrants themselves), alongside images of the secret police and the East German governmental apparatus, which the mainstream West German media and politicians compared to Nazi fascism. In this context, it became difficult for East Germans or migrants to make political claims without also somehow appearing to be not yet worthy of participation, because mainstream policy makers regarded them as not yet democratic. West Germans, then, took up roles to self-righteously teach East Germans, migrants, and postmigrants democracy, which included, as Daphne Berdahl (1999) has pointed out, promoting the post-Wall consumption frenzy, and regulating East Germans, migrants, and postmigrants as those who had failed to account for their Nazi past—or genocidal Turkish past *vis-à-vis* the Armenians—or anti-Semitic Muslim past, respectively. But since East Germans were also acknowledged as Germans, there was the possibility of ultimate rehabilitation, redemption, and mainstream incorporation. For this to happen, however, East Germans had to express their belief in the new post-Wall order—that is, consumption, economic efficiency, and privatization.

The West German governing regime, however, did not imagine this possibility in the same way for noncitizens. (I would argue further that noncitizenship, itself, as I define it here, marks the impossibility of universal address or participation. Democratization for these groups means persistent regulation.) Many activists and others have spoken to me about the turn away from multiculturalism just when the Wall was falling. At most, one would have access to what I have termed exclusionary incorporation (see Partridge 2012 and above), where the emphasis moved from multiculturalism to integration. I understand multiculturalism as a form of incorporation, but also as a problematic term, because it often assumes and defines cultural difference as a rigid distinction without necessarily taking power relations into account. Integration ultimately means the acceptance of the exclusionary part of the incorporation. Both multiculturalism and integration leave White supremacist logics intact. The post–Cold War governance established both as norms. Integration, at least for those perceived as foreign, happens largely through West German-led *democratization*. This, then, relies on massive social, economic, and political investment from youth work to the public schools, which almost all children and youth attend in Germany—homeschooling is illegal, and private Muslim schools are rare.

Mainstream media representations of migrants and postmigrants during this era focused on the repression of Turkish women, including restriction of movement, young brides, honor killings, and the practice of women wearing a headscarf from a young age. Again, the normative society sees these acts as problematic "cultural differences," whereas they understand *democracy*, brought about in these instances through *democratization*, as superior. After September 11, 2001, as scholars such as Yasemine Yildiz (2009) have pointed out, what the same mainstream saw as a "Turkish problem" became a Muslim problem in its imagination. In opinion pieces in the major newspapers, on television, in government policy and in public school pedagogy deliberations, major swaths of the normative population assumed that Muslim migrants harbored anti-Semitic beliefs. Integrating migrant and postmigrant residents into the democracy meant educating "them" against anti-Semitism, sexism, "intolerance," and gang violence.

"Exclusionary incorporation" operates as this form of pedagogy, intended to integrate migrants into Germany, but on limited terms, that is, ones that also make it difficult for them to talk about their own marginalization. Even if juridical citizenship seemed possible for new migrants, this form of citizenship, as what Etienne Balibar (1991) might call culturally racist inclusion, remained. Noncitizens would be incorporated into the nation to the extent that they could be tolerated and persistently reminded of their "inferiority," or, as I have argued in *Hypersexuality and Headscarves* (2012), live up to exoticized, and often hypersexualized, national fantasies, which include things like removing the headscarf so that everyday Germans can see and experience the Other.

To train young people in democracy, the federal government invested funding in youth programing, targeting both neo-Nazis and immigrants (often construed as "young male Muslim migrants")—although again, what separated the neo-Nazis from the migrants and postmigrants was their potential to become normalized citizens. This is, in part, demonstrated by the fact that young neo-Nazis have had their own political party in parliament, first the NPD and then the AfD (Alternative for Germany), a populist openly anti-Muslim and anti-Black party. While one can link this German phenomenon to a broader European rising of a populist right, a trend that pro-Europeans have been attempting to manage, with former Chancellor Angela Merkel in the lead, the trend persists in Germany, across Europe, and beyond (with the United States as a major ideological contributor). This is, in fact, a more visible form of how incorporation works. In either case, the acceptance of inclusion means an acceptance of the implicit and sometimes explicit hierarchies that go along with citizenship, and the production and re-production of noncitizens.

While I would like to make an argument for why participation that would include those who define themselves as neo-Nazis should also be taken seriously, disrupting the top-down administration of democratizing programs, I am focused here on the contrast between democratization of neo-Nazi versus so-called migrant (including refugee) and postmigrant youth. A 2008 brochure representing a federal government program linked to an event that I attended with the leader of the program that led to the Auschwitz visit with primarily Turkish/Turkish-German and Palestinian/Palestinian-German youth (see chapter 4), describes then-existing programs as well as the criteria necessary to obtain seed money administered through state and local initiatives. Speaking to the plan to *democratize* both potential neo-Nazis and Muslim "migrants," the Federal Ministry for Family, Seniors, Women, and Youth[10] notes:

> The central point is to link all of the local social researchers to develop strategies for democracy.
> Every local action plan will receive, in addition, a yearly subvention of 100,000 Euros.
> Local coordination points will administer the subvention funds. Individual projects can receive up to 20,000 Euros of support.[11]

The document goes on: "The fight against right wing extremism, anti-Semitism and Xenophobie will be strengthened where the fight must be led: in the local districts." [12]

Throughout this document and the actual practice of funding, one clearly sees the ways in which the federal ministry and the projects they and their local administrators fund focus primarily on East German Neo-Nazis and "Migrant" youth or those they identify as youth "with migration backgrounds." (I have been using the term postmigrant as the term that has come to reflect the ways in which children of those seen as descendants of non-Germans have, in some contexts, come to identify themselves.)[13]

Again, these forms of intervention are the concrete measures the German state undertakes to implement its top down systematic process of *democratization*. In focusing on anti-Semitism, alongside "tolerance" and "diversity," with anti-Semitism and violence prevention appearing as the common nodes for intervention between right-wing youth and "migrants." Throughout the document, there is also a subtle emphasis on Islam. *Democratization* also comes to be linked to the politics of *Never Again*, in particular, putting the mainstream (center-right/center-left) German government in charge of what it would take to create eligible participants in democracy. Again, even this eligibility comes with limitations, depending on how one is ultimately situated *vis a vis* normative citizenship. The teaching role that the state takes

DEMOCRATIZATION AS EXCLUSION?   103

on clearly creates a hierarchy of participation, re-emphasizing the production of noncitizens in the process.

In *Memory and Forgetting in the Post-Holocaust Era: The Ethics of Never Again,* Alejandro Baer and Natan Sznaider argue that "Never Again means never again in general but also in particular: never again Holocaust and genocide, never again communism and other dictatorships, never again apartheid, never again colonialism. Thus Never Again connects universal principles with particular concerns. The ethics of Never Again means also that besides fear there lies hope" (2016, 1). In the German case, which, in this instance, seems to follow the Israeli one, "Never Again" refers to the Nazi-led Holocaust, in particular, and the murder of over six million Jewish people. In spite of the distinction between their integration and the particularity of the German State interpretation of "Never Again," Baer and Sznaider make an important point when they argue that "The logic of Never Again tells those who use it that an event is already over; that the past, the catastrophe, is already past. By embracing the Never Again paradigm, social actors construct a new temporal framework that represents the past and the present as radically different and antagonistic. However, while the catastrophe is placed behind us, it is situated in the future as well as a ghastly possibility" (4). I would go further, to argue that this possibility can never be exactly the same and that while there is a preventative effect of a "Never Again" pronouncement that can work as a form of accountability, it does not prevent the repetition of targeted mass murder.

Furthermore, in the German practice of *democratization* one sees the responsibility for future (and contemporary) repetition being placed on some groups more than others, as evidenced in the particular modes of state intervention we have seen. In these instances, it seems that the German state holding itself accountable to "never again" repeat anything like Nazi genocide, inasmuch as this also becomes a targeted teaching role, risks the danger of this claim becoming a kind of moral superiority substantiated by the state's making it through another year, then decade, then century of not having orchestrated mass murder. The implicit and explicit proclamations about its success in achieving its goal of "never again" positions that state to both claim success and, from its perspective, to have the moral authority, even moral necessity, to teach others who might do something like it, if left to their own devices. It is not that one shouldn't remember or pronounce "never again," but that pronouncement is complicated by the hierarchy of its application and monumentality of its memory. The other problem, as I have already expressed, is that inasmuch as the enormity of this form of perpetration is not matched, the German state lets itself off the hook for other, seemingly less enormous forms of atrocity, including those it might have committed, or definitely did commit, in the past.

Furthermore, *democratizing* states who claim that the catastrophe is over have enormous difficulty thinking beyond the particular iterations of that catastrophe, even when they, themselves, take on new roles of perpetration.[14] In *Illuminations*, Benjamin (1969) notes:

> To articulate the past historically does not mean to recognize it 'the way it really was' (Ranke). It means to seize hold of a memory as it flashes up at a moment of danger. . . . Only the historian will have the gift of fanning the spark of hope in the past who is firmly convinced that even the dead will not be safe from the enemy if he wins.

Here, the enemy might be all of those who try to speak for the dead in their interpretation for what their death, here, in the case of mass murder, might mean and for whom and how it should be important. The question might be for whom should "never again" stand and who should have a right to participate in the conversation?

Baer and Sznaider remember:

> On April 19, 1945, only a few days after American troops had entered the Buchenwald concentration camp, thousands of survivors gathered at its *Appellplatz* and took the following oath:
> 'We will not stop fighting until the last perpetrator is brought before the judges of the people! Our watchword is the destruction of Nazism from its roots. Building a new world of peace and freedom is our goal. This is our responsibility to our murdered comrades and their relatives' (2016, 9).

There might be East German versus West German interpretations of *Never Again*, in which the East version is focused on the murder of communists and anti-Facists and the West German version is focused on the mass murder of Jewish people. In the West German interpretation of

history, the one that ultimately wins,[15] Never Again emphasizes the particularity of Holocaust as linked to Jewish death via genocide.

Baer and Sznaider (2016) ultimately conclude: "The Holocaust has tran-
scended the framework of Jewish and anti-fascist partisan memory and has
been universalized" (11). I would argue that exactly the opposite has become
true, which is precisely my argument about the need for the emergence of
Blackness as a universal claim. Comparison of one's contemporary experience to the Nazi-led Holocaust is taboo. Attempts to make the Holocaust
transcend its particular history get read as anti-Semitic. Claiming Blackness,
though, seems to stand in as a different kind of possibility *vis a vis* citizenship and in relation to the German and European history. Again, Adelson's
language of touch and Rothberg's understanding of the multi-directionality
of memory are important as other ways to think about not forgetting and
not repeating. They are also more helpful in thinking through collective
struggle.

I think, though, that Baer and Sznaider get it wrong in their conclusion
that "Present-day Germany's Never Again, which is universal ('Never
again war'), stands in contrast to the Israeli state's Never Again, which
is particular '"Never again victims!')" (2016, 13). In fact, German geopolitical legitimacy depends on being aligned with the Israeli state, at least
in the accounting of Never Again mass murder of Jewish People and definitely not again in Germany. The discussion around the 2019 resignation
of the then-head of the Berlin Jewish Museum emphasizes this point.
Deutsche Welle (2019) reports:

> Berlin's Jewish Museum said its director, Peter Schäfer, had resigned Friday
> to 'prevent further damage' to the city's drawcard that attracts 700,000 visi-
> tors annually and describes itself as a 'place for reflection' on Jewish history
> and culture, migration and diversity in Germany.

In addition to an incident concerning the Boycott, Divestment, and Sanctions
(BDS) movement (see below), some critics of the museum believed that its
exhibit "Welcome to Jerusalem" favored Palestinian points of view. This controversy eventually led to then-Israeli Prime Minister Benjamin Netanyahu
requesting that then-Chancellor Merkel shut down the exhibit.

On the same day as the *Deutsche Welle* report, the *New York Times*
reported that the Berlin Jewish Museum's director had resigned from his

position after he was criticized for coming too close to the Boycott, Divestment and Sactions movement, meant to protest against Israeli policies but "which was recently designated as anti-Semitic by the German Parliament" (Eddy 2019a). The *Times* referenced, in particular, the then-director's Twitter post: "The post promoted an article from a German daily that cited an open letter signed by 240 Jewish and Israeli scholars." The letter, the *Times* reports, came out before the then-new German parliamentary condemnation. In it, "scholars urged lawmakers not to sign the resolution declaring the boycott, divestment and sanctions movement, known as B.D.S., anti-Semitic." Finally, the *New York Times* piece reported the special German sensitivity to the BDS movement, "where responsibility for Israel's right to exist is a cornerstone of foreign policy, and where calls to boycott the Jewish state carry historical associations with the Nazis." The *Times* piece also recalls criticism around Schäfer having invited a Palestinian scholar to give a talk at the museum and having given a "personal tour [of the museum] to the cultural director of the Iranian Embassy."

Here, memory cannot escape geopolitics. Even if the Jewish Museum emphasizes that it is not a Holocaust Museum, but a museum of the historical Jewish presence in Germany and Europe, Holocaust memory remains as a central dimension of how memory of a German-Jewish presence works. Even if Germany has taken on a democratizing role, other institutions and other nation-states still hold it accountable to the specificity of how and why democratization emerged as a technique in the first place. In this sense, the seeming risks of a failed process are not just local, but also transnational.

DEFUNDING AS TECHNIQUE

The stakes of *democratization* and *democratic participation* in relation to Holocaust memory and anti-Semitism are not only targeted towards individuals but also institutions and linked to the threat of defunding. This includes the defunding of organizations that have been established to attend to the artistic expression and the social, financial, and psychological needs of Black people and People of Color (POCs). In Germany, many artistic and cultural organizations primarily operate through state funding, not through private foundations or donations. From the perspective of someone who favors the kind of support that social welfare states can offer, this seems like a good thing. On the other hand, it also means that state institutions have a lot of say in how and what gets funded or defunded. This puts artists and organizations that want to share social critiques of the state or society in a precarious place.

It is worth noting that "the state" is not simply a top-down entity, but organized in terms of many different entities that receive and redistribute funds. There is national, local, city, and regional funding, and even state-administered and funded foundations. There is social welfare funding, youth funding, and funding for the arts. In Germany, there are also federally administered grants that, depending on the initiatives of the political parties in charge, will determine overarching directions for funding initiatives.

In terms of artistic and other cultural organizations, it seems important to note that there are state funded theaters with permanent ensembles. Then there are youth centers and other kinds of artistic bodies that have to constantly rely on grant funding. Much of this funding is from the city or city-state. But there are also pots of money that come from institutions like the European Union. This may allow primarily Black and POC organizations to get around national or local funding political and financial initiatives and limits, but the sources are not always consistent. The kinds of theaters that I worked with could not rely on an annual budget that they could simply renew. Distinctions exist between theaters that have varying relationships with the funders. These relationships also work as forms of regulation, often tied to political party connections and the risks that those in the city-state parliament decide or refuse to make.

If accusations such as anti-Semitism against a funded organization appear in the news, then the politician risks their own political future if a line of funding can be traced to them. In this sense, taking risks means taking risks not only *vis a vis* the audience, but also *vis a vis* the state funders, *vis a vis* the voters, and even *vis a vis* the perception of other national, international, and transnational organizations and audiences who want to hold state funders accountable. Risk, from the perspective of the state funders, is also deeply connected to artistic interpretation. And that interpretation is directly connected to who is making the artistic claim, and, of course, the kind of claim they are making. Finally, those claims are tied to the issues that most move the claimants. From the perspective of the politician, then, the immediate solution to controversy, particularly as it concerns migrant, postmigrant, or Muslim artists, is defunding.

The point of these artistic institutions is not profit. The theaters with which I was involved did not rely on their box offices to sustain their existence. They relied on state funding in the extended sense I have already described. One incident, as exemplified by the experience of the "theater in crisis" (see below), might help to make this point.

In the summer of 2016, I participated in a special international American Modern Language Association meeting in Düsseldorf, Germany. I worried a bit about the title of our panel—"Holocaust Memory in Europe and the Exclusion of Racial Minorities." Should "Holocaust Memory" and "Racial Minorities" be so easily juxtaposed? Who were the "racial minorities" and what did it mean to say that they were being excluded from Holocaust memory? To what extent would European and German Jewry be included in this "racial minority" categorization?

The previous chapter takes seriously monumental memory and the politics of contemporary race and racism. It addresses the complexities of what Michael Rothberg calls multidirectional memory and what Leslie Adelson calls touching tales (see above and previous chapter), in which the point is to think about touch both in terms of overlapping histories and in terms of the ways in which people might be moved (or touched—*berührt*) by each other's stories. Touch is, in many ways, opposed to comparison. Touch should be able to bring experiences in connection with each other, both rationally and sensorially. In Rothberg's account, it should be possible to think of the Shoah and colonial perpetration at the same time. As noted in the previous chapter, memory, as Rothberg argues, is not a zero-sum game. Recounting one atrocity does not blot out the space for recalling another. Following Adelson's argument, and my interpretation, if people are not touched by the recalling, then, to some extent, the recounting of the history's horror has failed.

The reality of memory and racialized Others in Europe is more complex than the facile juxtaposition of Holocaust memory and the exclusion of racial minorities. In terms of the Nazi-orchestrated Holocaust memory,

Germany is, of course, at the epicenter. It takes responsibility not only for national memory, but for European memory, and even the world's memory as articulated through the naming of its federally funded "Memorial to the Murdered Jews of Europe," its Jewish Museum, or its Humboldt Forum, rebuilt as the City Palace (Stadtschloss), a site that, in its re-inauguration, houses colonial collections that many have argued would be better returned to their original locations.

While rapidly aging out of the generation of perpetration, Germany still holds the moral aura of Holocaust accountability, which has increasingly turned into a teaching role (see above), educating not only Europe but even the world in its own formulation of "never again" as state-mandated policy.[16] In this sense, Holocaust memory works not as a discourse of total exclusion from a national citizenship that necessarily mandates remembering, but includes incorporation, in schools, in museums, in television roundtables, in long newspaper and magazine articles, in the national film industry, and in funding for special youth projects that particularly target migrant and postmigrant youth for visits to Auschwitz or Israel, as seen in the last chapter. And at least until the 2015/2016 public New Year's Eve party in Cologne, when Muslim men from North Africa were accused of raping White German women (see Werthschulte 2017), "refugees," including Muslim refugees from Syria, "[were] welcome" in Germany. Here too, Germany saw itself as taking on a responsibility that should have been more globally distributed. If others wouldn't do it, Germany would. While I am quite critical of the current arrangement, even then, its chancellor, in collaboration with the EU, organized billions of dollars to go to Turkey to process refugees there before sending many fewer to Germany. And in spite of a more skeptical approach to refugees after the so-called "Summer of Migration" in 2015, programs of incorporation continued, and refugees remained living in temporary housing in the countries of their desired destinations, even if not in apartments or houses, or in the exact cities they had originally set as their goals.

Given this context, scholars must nevertheless attend to the pretense of moral superiority demonstrated, in part, through the supposed national mastery of an antiracist, feminist, and refugee politics. In this logic, Europeans and mainstream German institutions imagine themselves as morally superior, in the sense that they see Europeanness as standing up for the freedom and protection of women and women's rights and standing against racist perpetration. Fighting against anti-Semitism and neo-Nazi articulations have become the particular realms of antiracism that have become (as a result of German and European history) the focus of governmental and pedagogical interventions. The terms of European and German antiracism and top-down feminism are established through the negative example of the "Other." Combined, they help to establish the grounds for a broader moral authority. It is not that the German mainstream wants to condemn the refugee outright. But the refugee's political participation risks falling into a moral trap.

Holocaust Memory and a Refugee Theater in Crisis

My research moved into the arena of a public debate in Germany when I learned that two German sisters who had underwritten the launch of a refugee theater had been accused of anti-Semitism. This immediately led to the public defunding of the group, which was on the verge of being awarded 100,000 euros to support their theater work.

I had spent the summer of 2015 working with many of the group's members on the film project *Filming the Future from Berlin: Noncitizen Perspectives*. I experienced it as one of my best teaching experiences ever, more impactful and more engaged than my regular job at the university, as the group could immediately link the otherwise abstract concept of noncitizenship to their everyday lives and discuss what that meant in both abstract and embodied dimensions. Even though I was leery of the taint of anti-Semitism, I went to the meetings that the theater put together to challenge the charge and the group's defunding, so that I could find out how this charge had come about. I was struck by the accusation, launched primarily by the American Jewish Committee's Berlin office, that two of the founding members had been instrumentalizing (using) the refugees, that the two sisters had participated in pro-Hezbollah demonstrations in Berlin, in which their father was the leader and, ultimately, that these protests included both anti-Israel and anti-Semitic slogans.

At first the sisters denied raising money for Hezbollah or other anti-Israeli organizations. They said that they were irregular participants. It turned out, however, that their father was a key organizer of the event.

Then, under a misleading heading, "Berlin government allegedly supports Hezbollah activists through refugee project," an Israeli newspaper reported 2016 that "there are 250 active Hezbollah members in the capital" (Weinthal 2016). The article goes on to report on "video and photographs" of the two sisters helping out at the rallies, while one wore "earrings with the Hezbollah logo." Switching abruptly to the theater group co-founded by the sisters, the article asserts, "The RCI [Refugee Club Impulse] is slated to receive 100,000 Euros from the Berlin government for refugee work. Public taxpayer funds have been furnished to the RCI for a number of years." The stakes of this paper's reporting are revealed when Berlin city senator Benedikt Lux is quoted as saying that there "is a danger that the project [RCI] funds will be used for anti-Semitic forces." The article then concludes with a suggestive report about *Commerzbank*'s provision several of "anti-Israel" (that is, pro-BDS) bank accounts. Here, the paper links the theater to what it sees as a dangerous pattern. German funds and institutions are supporting anti-Israel institutions and policy.

However, the *Jerusalem Post* investigation did not include interviews with Refugee Club Impulse members, nor did it justify the linking of the theater group to an anti-Semitic force. The sisters were clearly involved in activities that more directly connected to anti-Israel support, but how does this involvement relate to the theater group? While no one ever established that any German state funds went via the theater to Hezbollah, the two sisters ultimately resigned, and the 100,000 Euro prize for the theater got cancelled. German politicians did not want to be seen supporting anti-Semitism, which a number of institutions in Europe also define as being against the state of Israel.

The German press also lodged complaints against other theater members, including the founding artistic director. *Deutschland Radio*, the national radio broadcaster, reported:

> Even in the first instance of the jury deliberation of the [city-state] Senates own Culture Project, GmbH did not want to hear critique. In March, they awarded a 100,000 grant to Refugee Club Impulse RCI. Only after the intervention of the American Jewish Committee and after the first press reports did the most recent advisory committee reverse the decision at the last minute. Today, one wants a better check on which work with and from refugees is receiving financial support; the vice head of the Culture Project

GmbH, Torsten Wöhlert, says: 'Of course, we have a red line. That concerns the question of anti-Semitism, the position in relation to the state of Israel, and the relationship to xenophobia, [and] gender equality. These are the cultural conflicts that are coming to us. This is a learning process for us, as a cultural funding organization. This is the first time that we have had to contend [with these issues] with these kinds of project grants.'[17]

Had the American Jewish Committee (AJC) not intervened at the last minute, the RCI theater project would have received a major sum. After the scandal, Deidre Berger from the Berlin AJC office asked that Berlin Senate[18] pay more attention to refugee politics:

> It's also very important that the theme of Anti-Semitism is on the Agenda as it concerns refugees. This is especially important, because the refugees come from countries where anti-Semitic stereotypes are very widespread and there is a lot of hate against Israel. And now these refugees are coming to Germany, where anti-Semitism is frowned upon by the society of laws, and where there is a strong connection to Israel. How can we communicate this? This is the most important aspect: How can we convey democratic values and help the refugees understand that there is no place today for anti-Semitism in Germany? (Klatt 2016, my translation).

Here, even if Germany seemed to be slightly relaxing its *democratizing* role, the AJC's Berlin office was calling it to account. Problematically, however, it assumed a kind of *a priori* (or what Catlin 2022 calls "onto-logical") anti-Semitism. The two sisters (and their father, Jürgen Grassmann) who participated in the protest were not refugees. They and their father came from Germany. That fact, however, gets elided in order to focus on the suspicion of anti-Semitism without proof directly linked to the actions of the refugees themselves.

While the founding artistic director had made statements about Israel in the past, including the call for a "cultural intifada" (Klatt 2016), none of these actions or statements could be applied to the refugee actors in the theater. The theater's funding also could not be linked to anti-Semtism or Hezobollah funding. Even after the sisters resigned, however, the actors were told to prove that they were not anti-Semitic and even to write a statement supporting the right of Israel to exist.

Finally, again, even after the sisters resigned, in addition to the a priori anti-Semitism suspicion, claims emerged suggesting the instrumentalization of the refugee theater participants. The mainstream media and politicians did not give them credit for being artists in their own right. Their rhetoric marked them "merely" as "refugees," in effect, not yet fully ready for full participation in democracy. Of course, the "need" for *democratization*, in the first place, foreclosed Muslim migrant participation. Here, *democratization*'s endgame remains unclear. No one called to debate the charges in the press. Politicians and the mainstream media held them under suspicion, even after the sisters resigned, and then the Senate defunded them. The nomination for the 100,000 Euro grant reflected the power of their art. But this power, in the end, did not count. The Senate and the mainstream media ultimately refused them as political or artistic actors.

Their Global Day Against Racism participation, in which the refugee theater group took a lead organizing role, led to the instrumentalization charge and the initial AJC investigation. At the protest a Boycott, Divestment, and Sanctions (BDS) group had participated, even taken over, according to one of the theater group's leaders. It was later that I found out about the charges against the two sisters and founders in the German press. After going to the first meeting, I was asked to come to the others to support the group. One of the members asked me to help make a fund-raising film after it was clear that they wouldn't receive any more money from the state; the Berlin city-state Senate wanted to distance itself from any hint of anti-Semitism, as did the German group that had made the original nomination for the 100,000-Euro prize. Eventually, the two founding members resigned, but it seemed to be too late. Theater after theater distanced themselves from the refugee theater. Redemption seemed impossible, as did a more public debate. A clear path for future funding remained unclear.

Instrumentalization seemed an even more damning charge than anti-Semitism, viewing the refugees as pawns of competing agendas concerning Israeli politics (assuming that they could not speak for themselves). The press accounts did not include their voices. Could they be instrumentalized? After coming across all of those borders, were they so naive? In the meetings I attended, the instrumentalization charged never emerged in discussion. It would divide the leaders, who spoke of this as a self-organized theater, comprised primarily of the refugees who provided their experiences and artistic labor. And yet, the leaders who remained after the two founding members left were still people I trusted. I saw the power of their work and the space they had created. Even though we had sometimes had our own disagreements about politics and directions, I still found the theater to be an important space. The theater group had been together for over three years. For many, it had paved the introduction, the path, into Germany. It had allowed for another kind of mutual recognition, beyond pity. It provided the space for articulating things that might not otherwise, could not otherwise, be said in public. It allowed for a kind of truth telling that not only broke through the fourth wall, but made the kind of experimentation possible in the theater a part of their everyday lives. The theater had too much to offer for it to be dismantled in this way. But what strategies would they use to fight for their survival?

Here, the discussion of anti-Semitism and moral superiority enter the picture via implicit discourses of perpetration and atonement, and the discussion of anti-Semitism as an ongoing threat, with new immigrants suspected as a potential source.

On the Ground/In the Theater

The rehearsal was packed. There was no evidence of the withdrawal of funding. It was life as usual, except there was a huge hole in the ceiling. Through the cracks, one could see up to the next floor. My friend joked that we were in Syria and someone had bombed the theater rehearsal space.

At the end of the rehearsal, the friend who had asked me to help make a fund-raising film to support the theater after defunding kept saying: "*Es tut mir Leid, dass Du um sonst gekommen bist*" ("I'm sorry that you came for nothing"), which made me think that he was sorry that I came, even though we barely spoke about the film that he would be making. But, it turned out, he also meant it literally. He was sorry that I came "*um sonst*" (for free), that is even though I wasn't getting paid. In this sense, he was referring to his own work as well. He wasn't getting paid either.

At the S Bahn (regional train) station on the way home, my friend talked about the accusations that one of the Europeans was getting paid, even though most of the refugees were not. From our perspective, he went on, it's just hard to understand why Europeans would do this work for free. In fact, most of them were not. They were existing on grant money, usually via state funding, but that was still more than the refugees were receiving.

Before we'd left the building, the theater director wanted to do a cheer in which everyone put their hand in the middle and said something together. Should it be *"Zusammen bis zum Tod"* ("Together until death")? Everyone, except for my friend, agreed. He said, *"Das ist eine Luge,* it's a lie. I never should have said this phrase." He was referring to the group's willingness (perhaps out of necessity) to sacrifice—distance themselves from—the two women who had been accused of anti-Semitism. One of the newspaper accounts showed a young man holding a sign at one of the demonstrations in which one of the former organizers had marched; it was clearly anti-Semitic. She had brought my friend into the organization. Without her, he wouldn't be there. She was responsible for changing his life and trajectory in Germany. But if anti-Semitism is like pedophilia, as the theater director had said, then there will be no opportunity for redemption for her. In the end, solidarity seemed impossible. And the taint of the accusation of being instrumentalized had affected the entire group. The long-term prospects for the funding of their art remained unclear.

CONCLUSION: POLITICS AND INCORPORATION

The question that I have raised throughout this chapter concerns the extent to which refugees and postmigrants can participate in planning the future of the nation-state and Europe as well as their positions within it. To what extent do processes of *democratization* push them out? Humanitarian interventions on their behalf, even the initial 2015 "refugee welcome," as others have argued (see Ticktin 2011), often preclude political participation, in the sense that politics exceeds the conditions under which their incorporation gets imagined and planned.

Nevertheless, particularly in the German context, theater has become a particularly active realm for refugee participation. It is an arena in which the broader public is called to think through the so-called "crisis," usually on normative directors' terms, which often includes the terms of established theater houses. In my research, refugee actors spoke of being paid only 70 euros or less for a performance, while established directors and actors received an income on which one could maintain a middle class lifestyle. In this sense, refugees found themselves treated more like props than artists. The theater that I observed was a rare instance in which refugees were telling their own stories from their own perspectives. And yet, the instrumentalization charge and the accusation of anti-Semitism (largely connected to their German hosts), led to their seemingly permanent defunding. The charge of anti-Semitism, of course, made participation, linked to the project of German democracy, even more difficult.

In the late winter of 2016, at a weekly meeting organized by refugees themselves at an important Berlin-based cultural institution, a Black man in the audience, speaking in French, commented on the upcoming "Global Day Against Racism," the event that precipitated the charge of anti-Semitism against the theater group. The man observed, "Many people fear that if they join the demonstration, they will face deportation." His friend, he told the meeting, did not know about the demonstration. "Many people are isolated in refugee camps." He asked about the security of the refugees at the demonstration. The main organizer responded, "We also have the problem that some refugee camps don't allow our posters. This is the problem with my refugee camp. I have tried three times." In a show of solidarity, a White German organizer added: "There will be a legal team with legal support."

The event had an innocuous name that pointed more to performance and theater than to politics. And yet, the legal team could not protect the refugee theater group, one of the co-organizers of the event, against the moral charge of anti-Semitism. A BDS group was also at the demonstration, promoting the Palestinian cause alongside the boycott of and divestment from Israel. While the refugee group did not participate directly in this action, the BDS group's participation as a coalition partner led to the initial investigation by the American Jewish Committee. This event led to the political outing of the two co-founders and the defunding of the group, a group that had almost earned a sanctioned space for democratic participation. Their democratic participation, however, ultimately seemed akin to the failure of the phrase that my friend ultimately regretted uttering: "Together until death." Trumping participation, *democratization* would act as the overarching project that would condemn them.

PART III Noncitizen Futures

6 The Rehearsal Is the Revolution

"INSURRECTIONARY IMAGINATION"

Rehearsing Black politics becomes a key node for re-articulating the self and the everyday realities of who one, as part of a collective, might become.

The above observation emerges from research based in postmigrant, Black, and POC[1] theaters (or spaces in theaters) based on the following set of initial questions: Given the relative lack of care and protection for Black people in everyday White Europeanized life, what other kinds of possibilities for living might emerge? What role might Blackness play in shaping these possibilities? Can one disarticulate the kind of Blackness that is hailed by the normative subject from the kind of Blackness that Black people themselves might want to produce? What kinds of spaces and what kinds of power are required?

It cannot be an accident that the research that led to this book led me to spend so much time in postmigrant/Black/POC Berlin theaters. In American contexts, where many people are regularly working two or three jobs, theater might seem like a luxury. If one is to think seriously about systematic change, though, the arts more broadly, and theater, in particular, should be thought of, even in the United States, as a kind of necessity. And as I will show in this chapter, the rehearsal might become the main site of possibility for practicing and thus realizing a new social life.

INSURRECTIONARY IMAGINATION

In an interview with the artistic director of the Youth Theater Bureau (now Theater X) about what it was trying to achieve, he chuckled and then pointed out (in German): "It's the rehearsed revolution. It is the rehearsal for the revolution. . . . It's the practice hours. It's not the dress rehearsal. It's actually before that. It's the rehearsals. . . . It is a place where theater is happening. And theater *is* . . . the laboratory for insurrectionary imagination."

It is critical to understand the importance of the rehearsal in order to think through the relationship between theater, creative imagination, and the possibility for a politics based on social change, in this case, a politics based on claiming Blackness. The theater production that I rehearsed with and followed over more than six months in person (and much longer remotely) emphasized both improvisation and the contemporary relevance of Black Power. The staged performance was not the main point. The main point was rehearsal. The rehearsal space was a known, familiar, relatively comfortable space that allowed for experimentation.[2] A play that used improvisation and historical investigation to focus on Blackness in the United States and Germany allowed the actors to learn about what it could mean to combine their everyday experiences with what it has historically meant to be Black in different contexts, in different time periods, and as differentially gendered subjects. The rehearsal space became the space that allowed the actors to practice for everyday life, to turn everyday life into practice, while then also practicing for the staged performance. The experimentation that took place in the safer space of the rehearsal allowed the actors to develop the skills for the necessarily revolutionary imagination. The rehearsal as an everyday revolutionary practice is what would ultimately lead to the revolution, not as a sudden break, but as planned methodical social transformation.

FUNDING

Of course funding is an issue, but the theaters where I spent most of my time, and particularly the Youth Theater Bureau Berlin, were used to getting very little funding (see previous chapter). They were also used to linking their theater acts to participation in demonstrations. In the Youth Theater Bureau, which relied on external funding for youth programming, the same people were there even after five years. Some had already aged out of "youth" status. Some had never been there as "youth." For many, the theater became the center of their lives, even if they had jobs, were in secondary school, or were working their way through the academy. The theater as a collective, self-governed, self-initiated space has also been critical to its longevity and impact (compared to the many theaters with established annual public funding). The Youth Theater Bureau / Theater X does receive some state funding, but it must regularly apply for public grants to operate. Even municipal youth centers with once regular funding sources have turned to more irregular grant funding as broader political initiatives and agendas change (see, for example, chapter 3).

An anti-racism group in Berlin-Kreuzberg where I spent a lot of my time in the 1990s also once existed in a similar way, but the building where they met was bought and renovated, and they eventually had to move out. Their model was to refuse all state funding in order to not have their agendas controlled or managed. They relied on ABM (*Arbeitsbeschaffungsmaßnahme*) positions, positions organized by state institutions to pay people without work.[3] They had work, but they were not reliant on capitalist logics. As former chancellor Gerhard Schroeder, a Social Democrat and Angela Merkel's predecessor, pushed through "reform," this possibility disappeared. Many of those who were part of the original anti-racism initiative ultimately had also to rely on grant funding and turn to the state. Philanthropic organizations do not have the same kind of importance or impact as they do in the United States. Most of the funding is public funding.

As one of the co-founders and the artistic director of Youth Theater Bureau, often put it, "Even if we are not citizens, we should demand resources from the state. They are also our resources."[4] As we saw in the previous chapter, they took this funding even while critiquing policies they did not like. Sometimes they underwent sanctions, but they persisted nevertheless. They got the right to the space owned by the city, part of the church structure where they met. This space was at risk of being privatized and sold off, but (partially as a result of their work in the theater, their existence as a collective, and their organizing) they were able to effectively fight off this move. Eventually, they secured funds to renovate.

In the years that I frequented this space, the community was able to use its status in a church building—despite many or most members being Marxists, Muslim, or not religious—to effectively create a sanctuary to protect refugees at risk for deportation.

Art, then, was not just aesthetics in an ephemeral sense. It was a way of life. For those considering how to use this kind of space, one that demands resources from the state in which it resides, including not only the German federal state, but also the European supra-state, and the Berlin city-state, I observed the practices that I analyze in terms of the following kinds of logics:

1) Why should we just enter a work economy that is barely there for us anyway?
2) A basic income is a great idea, but we cannot wait.
3) Let's be unproductive collectively.

These kinds of logics can lead to what one might then call an "Insurrectionary Imagination."

EVERYDAY LIFE IN THE THEATER

The rehearsal space of the insurrectionary theater is important as a space that attempts to not be top-down. The pronouncement that it is not top-down becomes a means for holding those who proclaim their leadership to be held accountable to those who are younger and have less experience. Sometimes this leads to tensions in terms of the direction, but, at the very least, older, more experienced people attempting to lead have to make a case for the ideas they are working to promote. No director in this theater can tell people to wait and sweat under hot lights, to stand still, afraid to move, as *he* realizes *his* vision. Instead, in many instances, I found the artistic director calling people on their cell phones, reminding them that they were late to rehearsal. Once it got going, rehearsal was regularly quite powerful. Actors used improvisation to relate their own experience to the material they rehearsed. There was no formal script, but a direction based on characters drawn from the US Civil Rights and Black Power movements. Workshops and trainings endeavored to offer more about events, institutions, and real people personified in these characters. Sometimes, the artistic director brought in music from the era and the movements to expose the actors to the feelings and the sounds of previous times focused on revolutionary imaginations.

The rehearsal space in the Youth Theater Bureau worked as a creative space, a collective and pleasurable space. People were serious and playing around at the same time. The commitment to the theater went beyond fear or the dream of becoming famous. The stakes centered around the possibilities not only of surviving, but thriving under conditions that would otherwise expose one to constant threat. The rehearsal space changed the power dynamics of live theater; it demanded participation. No one was allowed to simply observe and watch.

NO BLACKFACE

Given the risk of appropriation, in the theater especially, but also in everyday life, it is important to distinguish between claiming Blackness as a means of political mobilization and putting on blackface as a form of appropriation and mockery.

I spent most of my initial time in the Youth Theater Bureau working on the play *Schwarzkopf BRD* (*Black Hair in Germany*). Just before leaving Berlin after an initial performance, I made a short film about the production for the *Kiezmonatsschau* (The Neighborhood News Show) at a self-proclaimed postmigrant theater. In the film, I asked one of the key actors, Jamil, to describe the play, beginning with the title. He responded in German:

> JAMIL: *Schwarzkopf BRD:* Who's the victim here?
>
> ME: Why that title?
>
> JAMIL: We're all black heads [that is, have black hair].[5] And, 'Who is the victim here?' because it is often said that we always claim victimhood. And we want to show that we are not victims, that we also do things, that we resist, that we fight.

The actors are primarily People of Color in the German sense. They have "black hair," which leads people to see them as "foreign." Even though

most German adults do not have blond hair, White Germans define themselves in this way.

In a central scene in the play, this actor and the one who played Angela
Davis stood on stage yelling repeatedly: "No blackface! No blackface!"
But how does Black claim-making work in relation to this pronouncement? In the same period, hot discussions about blackface emerged
in and around the major Berlin theater houses (that is, those with well-
paid regular ensembles and regular state funding) in the press and
amongst activists, because they were regularly using blackface. Major
resistance also emerged,[6] but what did blackface have to do with this
play? In this case, mobilizing Blackness required distinguishing between
those who appropriate Blackness and make it grotesque, ultimately to
become White (see Roediger 2002; Rogin 1996) or re-emphasize their
Whiteness, and those who mobilize Blackness as a means for making
social change.

One cannot get away from phenotype here, but the significance of phenotype depends on the context. One does need to remember and constantly remind oneself about the historical and contemporary persistence
of the vilification of particular forms of Blackness. Universalizing claims
to Blackness, however, in order to assert a connection to Black people,
must insist on the connection between the particular circumstances and
their broader application both via the production of Blackened subjects
(see Ong 1996, 2003),[7] in relation to Black people, and via Blackness as
the means for making social change.

This connection is what allows for a more linked struggle, which must
nevertheless be aware of the potential for its own hierarchies, colorisms,
and racisms. On the other hand, the tools of Black articulation can be used
as an effective resource (see J. Brown 1998 and the introduction), even for
those who might not otherwise be seen or see themselves as Black.
Centering Blackness in this form provides another possibility for being.
Its rehearsal here, including its re-imagination, is necessary for realizing
the possibilities for its most effective performance.[8] This includes critiquing blackface and also enacting Blackness as part of a simultaneous process of self-fashioning and social protest. In order not to be appropriation,
though, it must be linked directly and consistently to the struggles of
Black people.

Referencing the historical context of Black presentation, the Berlin actors continue:

JAMIL: Why did we connect this piece to 1968?

ANGELA DAVIS ACTOR: Because of the Black Panthers.

ANOTHER WOMAN: Because it is a very important date in history, and everyone has a particular feeling associated with it. And we wanted to bring this feeling into the piece.

JAMIL: Exactly, and we also, maybe, want to found our own party in the piece, or maybe in general (in real life)— *Schwarzkopf* Party, or something like that. [He smiles.] And the Black Panthers were. . . . They were the heirs of Malcolm X. They took to heart what Malcolm X said and they worked to realize it. They didn't just give in. Whatever skin color, whether man or woman, they didn't just take it; they fought. And we want to show that there are people that are still doing that.[9]

He might have added that "We are practicing, to learn how to do that too." Forming the political party was a serious endeavor, not just an exercise.

My short film includes clips from the staged performance of this early version of the play: "We are making history today. Do you remember 1968?" The four on stage, two women, two men, raised their fists and turned their backs to the audience, a testament to the power of protest at the 1968 Olympics in Mexico City. Whether or not Blackness is universal, they were making a claim to its usefulness here, even its necessity as a tool for everyday survival.

WHY *KULTÜR AUF?* WHY OPEN A CULTURE UP?

In thinking about theater and culture in Germany, one is immediately confronted with the distinction between "high" and everyday art, "high" and everyday culture.[10] At the major theater event that I describe below, where *Schwarzkopf BRD* had its major premiere, one of the representatives from the Youth Theater Bureau asked the participants from a range of theaters, including major German/Berlin theater houses and local youth clubs, whether or not everyone could be an artist, and whether or not one had to be trained to be one. Participants stood in a large room, and the exercise leader instructed everyone to move to the left or the right of the room depending on whether or not they agreed with a series of claims. If they were unsure, they received the instruction to stay in the middle. When she asked whether or not one needed to have formal training to be an artist, the theater pedagogue for Berlin's most prominent theater house moved demonstratively in the direction of "Yes!" In contrast, those from the Youth Theater Bureau all moved in the opposite direction; they overwhelmingly thought that everyone could be, or already was, an artist. Furthermore, they made it clear that they did not need to be paid for their work in order to be an artist. The woman who led the exercise was in training to become a kindergarten teacher, but she spent all of her free time in the Youth Theater Bureau. Was she not an artist?[11]

The stakes of participating in "high" versus everyday culture[12] include how much funding one will ultimately receive. Berlin's budget rivals that of the National Endowment for the Arts in the United States. Furthermore, "the arts," in Germany, get much more funding than activities state funders and decision makers deem "social work," including art categorized under the rubric of "migrant" youth work. On the whole Germany, and those who visit as tourists, recognize the importance of "high art," and thus pay its practitioners accordingly in addition to offering "high art" artists long-term job security, particularly in the theater.

If one takes the point about "insurrectionary imagination" seriously, though, then one should note with Isa Fremeaux that, "The real seeds for revolutionary changes can grow in artistic practices." Fremeaux is a co-founder of the Laboratory for Insurrectionary Imagination. In an interview with her and her co-founder, the interviewer notes, "[T]hey don't want to make political art, what they do want is to make politics artistic.... Their way of working is not 'showing,' but transforming'" (Fremeaux and Jordan 2018). As we have seen, a key actor from the Youth Theater Bureau links the production of the play to the formation of a political party outside of the theater. From my perspective, though, the line between art and formal politics is necessarily blurred, as is the distinction between artistic and political mobilization. It seems to me that one needs to be doing both simultaneously.

Art is not merely there to serve the politics. While politics is art, art is also politics. The stakes become what both do to and for noncitizen bodies.

At the Youth Theater Bureau, transformation happened through the act of practicing new selves. The staged performance could attract new participants, but being in the audience, alone, would not be enough. As John Jordan, the other co-founder of the Laboratory for Insurrectionary Imagination, notes:

> In 1758, philosopher Jean Jacques Rousseau, in his letter to Madame d'Alembert, had written about theatre and said, 'In giving our tears to these fictions, we have satisfied all the rights of humanity without having to give away anything more of ourselves.' What he was saying was that we were letting the audience experience a kind of public virtue and ignoring it in their everyday life. So they would cry over the unfolding drama and the theatre and the crisis that was on stage and then build all their emotional armour so that they could leave the theatre and go back to life as normal. We do the same, we go to see a show about the end of our civilisation and we return home to do business as usual (Fremeaux and Jordan 2018).

On several occasions, I heard the artistic director of Youth Theater Bureau saying that art will not replace the revolution. But is art not necessary for social change? In the theaters I observed, art seemed to create a stage for the possibility of being new selves. This meant something other than consuming art as part of a passive audience. Again, I would like to emphasize, here, the rehearsal as opposed to the staged performance, that is, the more subtle, everyday form of the revolution, that necessarily begins with a revolutionary imagination.

Jordan's argument concludes:

> We very much agree with Steven Duncan, who says politics is not primarily about reasonable thinking and rational choices, it's an affair of fantasy and desire. People are rarely moved to action, support or even consent by realistic proposals, they are motivated by dreams of what could be. This is where we think that artists can have a real important role, in what are the dreams of what could be (Fremeaux and Jordan 2018).

As opposed to only dreaming, I think it is critical to both rehearse and enact what could be now. This is what I observed happening in the Youth Theater Bureau. It did not mean that everything in the world around them necessarily changed, but inasmuch as they also participated in demonstrations and made political claims, some of those things changed too. It was also possible for the actors (read in the multiple senses of the word's meaning, from those who ultimately ended up on stage to those who were primarily writing grants) to think simultaneously about change in the theater, change in the collective, change in Berlin, and change in the world. They also developed transnational networks and made sure that I, for example, kept coming back for our collaborative film project.

BLACKNESS AS MOBILITY: UNDOING THE FIXING

If Blackness is often produced as static and dangerous, or exotic and hypersexual, how does one turn it into a vehicle for social change? In writing about the process of being "fixed," Frantz Fanon (1969, 109) offers an example from his own experience: "I came into the world imbued with the will to find a meaning in things, my spirit filled with the desire to attain to the source of the world, and then I found that I was an object in the midst of other objects. . . . The Other fixes me with his gaze, his gestures and attitude, the same way you fix a preparation with a dye." The passage begins with the words that simultaneously "recognize" and "fix": "'Dirty nigger!' Or simply, 'Look, a Negro!'"

In a different example offered by Judith Butler (1993, 121), it is the police who "recognize" and fix, initiating "the call or address by which a subject becomes socially constituted. There is the policeman, the one who not only represents the law but whose address 'Hey you!' has the effect of binding the law to the one who is hailed." There is, of course, also the police person who shoots the Black figure (here, seen as object or menace) and asks questions later. While Butler attends to the gendered constitution of fixing, Fanon (1969, 91) reminds the reader of the racial dimensions, recalling a young White girl confronted with the mere presence of a Black man/thing (see Wilderson 2020): "Maman, look, a Negro; I'm scared!."

For Youth Theater Bureau, the rehearsal space became the most important space because it regularly offered the possibility to undo fixing. It helped to mobilize Blackness as a possible position from which one would no longer feel stuck. It became performative, enacting change.

Blackness as produced in these theaters also created a different possibility for hailing a future self.

Memories and Articulations of Blackness

"Interpellation" (Althusser 2006,[13] cited by Butler 1993) suggests the ways in which the body already speaks for itself from the perspective of those who see and ultimately name it. The physiognomy works as a sign, performing on its own even when it is not trying. The performance carries a history that cannot be easily manipulated by the person who lives within that skin. But within the Youth Theater Bureau one finds other ways to enact new selves.

While theater might not be an obvious site for the reconstitution of noncitizens, it is important to note that theater (including postmigrant, Black, and POC theater) becomes possible as a result of making demands on the welfare state—and thus on asserting noncitizen enactments. Particularly in the rehearsal space, artistic performance becomes crucial to sustaining noncitizen life and creating possibilities for it to thrive. It offers the actor an (at least temporary) possibility to unfix. This unfixing can become permanent if the performance is ultimately successful, or at least if one is able to spend enough of one's time in the theater, in the rehearsal space.

In contradistinction to the theater space, the artistic director of Youth Theater Bureau said that the schools in Berlin/Germany were failing the youth; he said that students were learning in the theater what they couldn't learn in their schools. He kept emphasizing gender, race, and class.

WHO IS THE AUDIENCE?

The broader German public already recognizes theater as a place where citizenship is being learned and articulated. For the Youth Theater Bureau and other postmigrant, POC, and Black theaters, the audience might be beside the point. On the other hand, the staged performance might lead to the next grant. In thinking through and re-enacting Blackness, one also realizes that citizenship (on the current terms) will not be adequate. We need something more.

Youth Theater Bureau was not documentary theater, even though "high theater" establishment figures frequently suggested this, taking away from the creativity and hard work actually involved. This was art in a space of experimentation. Even though they referenced these roles, they had not lived as slaves, sharecroppers, or Black Panthers in everyday life, but they sought to see how these experiences related to their own. They also inherited the globalized and capitalist legacy that produced those positions. This was a legacy not only of class, but also of sexuality, dis/ability, debility,[14] gender, and race. Race, after all, worked as the critical distinction, making chattel slavery in the Americas possible.

The Fourth Wall Is Not the Central Issue

Brecht identified the problem in the performance stage as the separation between the stage and the audience. This relationship, however, changes when the audience learns that it has the potential to join the cast in their everyday theatrical practice. This seems a particularly important realization for those audience members who are also noncitizens. For those not already on stage, the staged performance becomes the path towards joining the rehearsal space.

In the rehearsal space, rules followed that disallowed anyone from maintaining their distance from the acting, improvisation, and necessary experimentation. This refusal, on which the artistic director insisted, meant that new participants could not remain as they were when they first entered the space. While greeted with warmth, they also had to learn to find space and themselves in the performance. This led to new forms for articulation, even in other spaces, including predominantly White spaces outside the theater.

From this perspective, at first, audience participation emerges as a central problematic. In my first experiences at the *Haus der Kulturen der Welt* (where *Schwarzkopf BRD* also had its major premiere), I began to realize that many of the audience members were also already participating or potential performers. Here, performance referenced not just those acting in the staged performance but also those capable of enacting and those who require performative acts to shift the very grounds of being in the world, because otherwise they suffer death, slow death, deportation, dispossession, and defeat.

Youth Theater Bureau Berlin: Experiencing the Rehearsal Space

Today, the artistic director made me perform.

I had to play the good teacher who teaches about Black Power.

I also had to give the first speech about what we should do, how we should rise up.

[In the play,] I talk about the quiet revolution, in order not to attract the attention of the police.

In the piece [though], one young woman (the new one) responded that we should get the attention of the police in order to get the attention of the people.

Do you think that they believe that the teacher should be at the same high level?

Improv is hard. I am not as good at it as they are, but the artistic director always tells me to participate. He says that they should interview me so that I can be part of the piece. He tells the youth that I have interviewed him and others, that they should turn the weapon back around on me before I leave.

Yesterday, a mother whose kids want to participate in the theater says that her husband wants to come to the Iftar tomorrow to see what it is like. The artistic director says, "Yes, of course, but the youth also have veto power. Sometimes they want to be alone, among themselves."

Another "Postmigrant" Theater (After the Performance)

The theater is more than a safe space; it is a space that builds you up. It is a space that trains people. It not only makes it possible to have a voice; it helps to construct that voice and to make it visible.

I thought that it was just a neighborhood theater, but in the workshop the next day, I noticed that people were from überall *(everywhere).*

There was a woman who is originally from Turkey, but she lives in London now. She works to pay her rent, but she is an actress. She told me that she prefers Berlin.

Another person had only been in Berlin for a few weeks. One participant has lived here since March. In contrast, others define themselves as gebürtige Berliner *(Berliners by birth).*

MIND THE TRAP: CRASHING "HIGH" CULTURE

Demonstrating the links between theater, performance, experimentation, and the politics of social change, members of the Youth Theater Bureau and others crashed a theater conference at one of the major Berlin and German theater houses and made their own demands. They took over the lectern:

Dear Public,

Welcome to MIND THE TRAP! As we, as people with the labels "young people, people with migrant backgrounds from non-Western countries, people with disabilities and people with limited incomes," looked at the flyer, I mean the leaflet, from "MIND THE GAP!," we found it comforting and cute that the organizers noticed that there are entrance barriers. It was an ambitious attempt to change something. From our vantage point, however, we noticed major traps. For this reason, we, a coalition of critical cultural producers, did not just want to be the recipients. You did not only not invite us. We came anyway. We came in order to lend you a helping hand, to give you free tutoring. One could even call it development aid. . .

We were surprised to learn that the term "high culture" still exists. Apparently, particular people have been equipped with the resources from the so-called "high culture." They have climbed so high that, meanwhile, they can look down from a huge distance and in the process have ended up at a cultural distance that is so far away that they cannot find their way back. We asked ourselves, why there are no People of Color speaking here, no people with the actual practical experience of living with limited incomes, no experts with disabilities, etc. At the end of the day, the people who have experienced marginalization have not been invited here as experts. The monocultural Biotope is again talking about us to keep itself alive. We asked ourselves, why a conference that is supposed to address entrance barriers, costs 40 Euros. Why isn't there a sign language interpreter? Why isn't there translation into other languages? Why isn't daycare being offered? We asked ourselves, why youth, about whom this conference has been organized, are not able to become participants because this conference is happening at a time at which most youth are, for the most part, in school.

And we asked ourselves why discrimination against people at cultural institutions as a result of racism, sexism, classism, and ableism, etc. is not being named explicitly. Case after case, as you see, ladies and gentlemen, there is a big surge. To make it easier to participate in the society of the twenty-first century, we have reflected on how we can produce a more accessible offering.

We have developed an alternative conference and titled it "MIND THE TRAP!" Ours will include experts, who are, unfortunately, missing from the current conference, but who are nevertheless plentiful. We have even taken the time to create a list of speakers who could have been invited to your conference. Anyone who would like to know more about this intervention is invited tomorrow at 2 PM to come to hear our position statement and press conference in front of the *Deutsches Theater* (German Theater).

You not only did not invite us, we are going again and wish you a lot of fun as you talk about us and not with us. We leave you alone to your parallel society.

With best wishes,

*The Collective "MIND
THE TRAP!"*[15]

Just as they had come, the group who stormed into the theater conference, handing out flyers and taking control of the lectern, left. They also left the group of professionals a bit stunned. I observed signs of receptiveness and feelings of guilt. The MC invited the interveners to stay, but the sentiment seems to have come too late. It appeared as an afterthought.

Here, one sees a context in which the rehearsals lead to the event and, in this case, the event is not the staged performance, but the intervention into a theater conference with all the key (recognized) figures of "high art." They miss the point, though, of what art is and can do. They thus fall into their own trap, one that their elevated nation of "culture" has produced for itself.

The Space of the Theater and the Space of Politics

How does one make the rehearsal space more like everyday life? The rehearsal space became a revolutionary space, but it also needed to engage everyday life. The struggle was to keep the space and the collective approach to theater. The importance of a place for people who don't have a place or who are dispossessed. Again, the fact that the space was connected to a church meant that it could also be used as a sanctuary. The space is located in the center of the city in a gentrifying/working class/migrant/postmigrant neighborhood. Most of the people in the theater have been displaced within Berlin. Even if they started in the same neighborhood, they now have to come to the theater, for the most part, from other districts, from far away, from outside the center. Speculation has led to their displacement and even threatened to displace the theater until they fought to keep the space and prevent it from being sold off—and they won. The theater collective was strengthened by the fact that they had struggled together to sustain the space.

Longevity is sustained through modes of establishing accountability, making the theater into a safer space. Two moments demonstrate this point: 1) The artistic director asks a woman asked to leave the theater after she makes racist remarks, alluding to the "danger" of areas inhabited by Muslim men; and 2) the artistic director tells a parent that they can come to the rehearsal, "but the youth have a veto" (see above). These efforts protect the people within the space and the possibility for experimentation.

CHANGE THE SYSTEM—*FILMING THE FUTURE FROM BERLIN: AFRICAN PERSPECTIVES*

When he first came to Berlin, one of the key characters in the play *Schwarzkopf BRD,* Mamadou (see preface), a young man from West Africa, was soft-spoken, until the theater made him loud. He asked me the kinds of questions that would lead to the situation outlined in my article on street bureaucrats and club scenes after the fall of the Berlin Wall (see Partridge 2008, 2012). There, I showed how White German women gain bureaucratic discretionary power in their willingness or unwillingness to marry African men who exist in Germany as noncitizens, usually with no other way to legally stay other than marriage, or, as Mamadou suggests in his first film, under even more constrained and contingent conditions, by fathering a German child. If he had followed the path I outlined there, that would have led to him relying on a White German partner to decide whether or not he met her criteria for whether or not he could stay (as a documented immigrant) in the country. In other words, he would have to know whether or not she was willing to marry him.

Later, theater became the means for his initial psychological if not physical survival. You could see his will strengthening the whole time. He eventually took on a lead role in the play. He became an actor (politically, in the rehearsal, and even on stage). In an intermediate period, though, when I returned to Berlin, I often saw him at the train station in a spot where some were selling drugs. I was a bit embarrassed, because it was the train station near where we lived, where my daughter took the U Bahn (metro) to school. It didn't seem dangerous, but I was worried about the association of "Blackness" or "Africanness" with drug dealing.

I acknowledged Mamadou every time I saw him at the train station. And he acknowledged me, slapping that familiar five. Once, the people who were standing there with him also tried to acknowledge me in the same way, but he got angry. "You don't know him!" He was distancing them from me. He knew, I think, that I was a professor and wanted to maintain a sense of respectability amid what others might see as nefarious activity. I think that he also wanted to maintain a sense of his own future self that wouldn't have to rely on an income that involved standing at the bottom of the U Bahn station stairs where African "Black" masculinity was supposed to suggest a product on offer without having to say directly what that offer was. (I never saw actual drugs, but my daughter, at some point, said that it was obvious.)

In any event, years later, when we were doing the *Filming the Future from Berlin: African Perspectives* project at Theater X, I was determined to get him to make a film about his experiences at the train station and what he, in that same period, spoke of as "going to work" in the park, a park which some Berlin antiracist activists defended in terms of the right to "deal" without police interference. Tellingly, he titled his film "Change the System."

The film begins with him walking toward the *Ausländerbehörde* (Foreigners Registration Office), then cuts to him in front of a black backdrop (on stage). He is also dressed in black:

> 'Do you feel how someone lives illegally in the country? Do you know how that is painful, how that is hard?'
> 'You don't even know. You've got no idea.'

In the next scene, he has made it to the *Ausländerbehörde*. He stands in front of the state-commissioned "multicultural" graffiti that pictures men with beards, women with headscarves, kids playing, and the symbols of Berlin, with his head bowed and the raised and clenched fist of Black Power. His fist then melds into the peace sign.

He switches to German: "Why is it so complicated for me or for the other people from Africa? Why is it so complicated for the people from Africa to *arrive* in the German society?" The camera pans up to the graffiti image of the famous TV Tower and the words: "Welcome in Berlin."

He then interviews people at the same site. One woman has fled from a war in Sierra Leone. She says that she doesn't have any alternative, so, "Even if the Germans put me on the floor, I prefer it than to die in my country. . . . You see," she goes on, "they use their democ . . ."—she switches to the term "bureaucracy," but the slip is not lost on the audience—"to suppress human beings, the Germans. I like the Germans. . . . But the people have to look at what they are doing. Their racism suppresses the innocent one. And they don't allow the foreigners, so they can't know, so they [the Germans] can use their power."

The film then cuts to a double image of the filmmaker onstage. He is both the immigrant and the bureaucrat deciding his case: "Dammit. Why do I have to go back to Dortmund," the "asylum seeker" on the right side of the screen says. "You have to go right away," the bureaucrat on the left side of the screen responds. "Otherwise, you won't get anything. We won't be able to help you."

The film cuts again, back to a scene in front of the *Ausländerbehörde*. The filmmaker interviews another man from Sub-Saharan Africa: "Actually, I've been here for five years. Not only [does] a person have to get a woman. Or [does] a person have to get a wife, or a child, before he have [*sic*] to leave." He goes on, referencing the title of the series: "The future is tomorrow, you know, because we have only three days, I think. . . . Yesterday, which is gone, and today, which we have. And tomorrow, if God permits, which we are going to have. You understand? And tomorrow is the future. So you know, if you have tomorrow, you have a good future. I think I have a good future." The filmmaker responds: "You mean you have to fight for it from today." The man shakes his head. Filmmaker: "To prepare for tomorrow." The man agrees: "Yesterday, I make sure I fight it today, so that tomorrow will be a good future."

In the next scene, Mamadou talks about the theater group, which supported him and helped him to find a place to stay. Then, the filmmaker appears again with a double image of himself. He is now playing a director from one of the major theater houses in Berlin: "It's not so easy to work with us without an official work permit. This is a major theater. You know what I mean? We can work with you, but not 'officially.' We can't do it officially, but you will get money from us. We can't do it 'one hundred percent.' But we can try to do something. Do you know what I mean?" (Mamadou did, in fact, appear as an actor with one of the major Berlin theaters, but he had to play the role of the silenced refugee, and they only gave him the minimal amount of 35 Euros per night, while the other actors received their regular salaries as longstanding members of the major ensemble.)

The next scene, a monologue, follows:

> If someone wants to go to school, why don't [you] just let the person go to school? If someone wants to learn a job, why not just let the person learn a job? Don't stay there, sitting at your office with your own computer telling people: 'Oh, you're not allowed to. You're not allowed to.' What am I going to do afterwards?
>
> 'Young boy, let me tell you something, if you want to stay here in Germany, just try to marry, or make children.' Then I was like, 'Damn, I'm definitely not ready to have children right now. I'm definitely not ready to get married. So what should I do. Should I do something that I'm not planning for?' I'm trying to go the education way. I want to go to school first.

Next scene: The filmmaker is again on the left and right of the screen. On the left, he is sitting in a chair. On the right, he is holding a binder with papers and walking into the room.

MAN WITH THE FILE: Hey Herr [Mr.]. . . . '

THE LAWYER CUTS TO
    THE CHASE: I just wanted to tell you the truth. I really would like to help you, but the main point is that for most people from Africa to stay here in Germany, they either have to have a baby or marry someone.
       The man in the chair looks away, turning away from the lawyer's advice.

LAWYER: That's the fastest way. To stay here.

Outside in Berlin, Mamadou interviews a "White" German woman with two apparent "African-German" children. She talks about a discussion with her partner, who asked her to marry him. She thought, "Maybe he just needs papers." She asked him: "Do you need documents, to marry me?"

MOTHER: Because I never wanted to be married, not with him, and not with anyone else. . . . And he was completely disappointed. And we had a big fight. Because he didn't need any documents. He loved me and wanted to marry me.

FILMMAKER: Exactly.

MOTHER: I loved him and wanted him to stay with me and the child.

FILMMAKER, GESTURING TO THE CHILDREN: How are you going to treat them, as. . . .

MOTHER: I think that they are German like me and you.

FILMMAKER: I'm still. I'm still not. . . .

He doesn't allow her to fudge the difficulty of citizenship and associated risks of deportation, insisting that he is "not," even when she objects.

In the next scene, the filmmaker plays both himself and a former girlfriend:

GIRLFRIEND (IN GERMAN): I don't know that I want to marry. In my head, I think that you just want to use me.

FILMMAKER (ALSO IN GERMAN): I don't understand this, because. . . .

GIRLFRIEND: So, I'm sorry.

FILMMAKER: I don't want to marry you just for the papers. I like you. I want to have a relationship with you.

GIRLFRIEND: Don't take it so personally. I like to tell the truth.

FILMMAKER: I don't like this at all. I want to have a real relationship. Don't think about the 'papers.'

GIRLFRIEND: I know, but think about it. We've been together for a long time.

FILMMAKER: This doesn't make any sense.

The film cuts to Mamadou in front of an *Imbis* (fast food station) with a picture of food: "Chicken pocket. . . ." The camera zooms in to a young man with a New York Yankees baseball cap, also from West Africa, speaking: "For seven years, I don't have any papers. I only stay here in Berlin. I cannot travel. I cannot do nothing. I just stay here until, one day I find my love in a club. I get girlfriend there. Then, we have child together. Even my child is here. I can show you." He holds up a picture of his child, the sleep screen on his iPad. "Ohhh," the camerawoman coos. "The mother is here." He shows a picture of the mother and toddler kissing each other.

FILMMAKER: Are you guys still together with the Momma?

YOUNG MAN: No, we don't live together.
The filmmaker makes a gesture to the camera, as if to say, "See, I told you." He speaks directly to the camera:

FILMMAKER: You see? You see the point?

YOUNG MAN: I have my child only on Wednesdays. I be with him. Then, after that, it's finished. He goes with his mom. Then, I'm living lonely.

CAMERA WOMAN: How do you see your future?

YOUNG MAN: Only difficult, I think. The future.

He shakes his head, as if to say there is none or that it is very uncertain.

CAMERA WOMAN: And his future?

YOUNG MAN: Her [*sic*] future. Yeah. For him, he has luck. He was born here. He have this document. You know, he has a German passport. But me, I don't have it. I have my own passport. Zambia. So, even I don't know yet.

FILMMAKER: It's not that we're against the woman, we're not against the children. . . . We're against the system. Change the system!

In the next scene, Mamadou sits alone in a chair in front of a black backdrop. "Afterwards," he says, "I be in the street. Living. Hanging around with friends. Okay? I went to the bad places in the city. Yeah, and like going to the park. Having the friends who know about a little bit of weed. And they tell me, 'Okay, if you got no papers, no nothing, why do you sit like that? Why do you trying to cover your hands, stay like this, always acting as an old person, as a handicap. Are you handicap?' I said, 'No.' 'Come on, just chill. Do what you gotta do. Make your own money. Try to survive.'"

Now, Mamadou is playing himself and a drug dealer. He sits on the left, and the drug dealer paces on the right of the screen.

FILMMAKER: I don't really understand why you. Tell me about things different than going to Görlitzer Park and doing that kind of stuff.

DEALER: Want to get some weed?

FILMMAKER: All that stuff is the illegal way. I don't want to do that. I don't want to be in the street and selling weed. It's not my thing. It's not my game.

DEALER: Go away man.

FILMMAKER: I want to learn something. It's really important for my future. That's what I'm looking for.

DEALER (SHOOING WITH HIS HAND): Simply go away.

FILMMAKER: You understand what I'm looking for?

DEALER: This is my place? What are you thinking?

FILMMAKER: I can't learn in the street. No one's going to learn in the street.

DEALER: I don't understand. What are you looking for here? Why are you sitting here the whole time, man? Go away. This is my place, man. I'm the king here.

The film cuts back to Mamadou by himself, sitting in a chair with a black background. "It's like I'm living in this world, but it's like I'm still in jail," he says to the camera. "I'm not allowed to do nothing. I'm not allowed to go to another city. But now, this last year, they tried to change it. You stay as an immigrant in Germany, now you're allowed to move to different cities. But all those things is horrible. How long can a human being live in a country that they are not allowed to move?" Street art appears on screen at this point: "How long is now?" The scene cuts back to the filmmaker: "I just want to let people know, we have to be against this system. They have to change something. We have to attack the system."

Ultimately, Mamadou's role in the theater led to his ability to stay in Berlin. When the state wanted to move him to another city, Youth Theater Bureau members made a case that he had established a life and artistic career in Berlin. While he had to leave briefly, he was ultimately able to come back and stay in Berlin. At the present time, he still lives there, and is still acting and making films. He has done all of this without getting married or having a child. He ultimately embodies the figure that he plays on stage; even though he has had to go through a rough period in between, he comes back and forthrightly asserts: "Change the system!"

Rehearsing the Film

Acting in film and hailing one's future self means taking on the position of the one who hails as a means of mastering, but then also ultimately undoing that position. One doesn't have to return to the original. The art, itself, is enough.

What we don't see on film is the multiple takes and days that went into learning to play that part, the work on remembering and thinking about what playing that part and coming to that position might entail. In order to make them persuasive, as the actor does, he has to really delve into the Other's psyche. Delving into that psyche means that the power position of the hailer is somewhat diminished. He can, at least temporarily, master the situation. It is, after all, his stage. This doesn't happen all on its own. The theater director pushes him. I, taking a place behind the camera, push him too. "It was almost right, but can you do it again?" Every day, he comes back with exactly the same clothes so that the scene can look like what we filmed the previous day. Ultimately, we get it, just in time for the premiere screening. The audience also gets something out of the performance. But Mamadou has already gotten much of what he needs through the very act of the rehearsal. Two years later, when we make the next film, "Dear Society," Mamadou is a totally different person. He has grown even further as a social analyst. He takes on a more forceful role in directing the scenes. He tells us where to film him and already knows what kind of acting will work.

CONCLUSION

The stakes of the rehearsal and subsequent performances of a re-articulated Blackness are better understood when one sees the otherwise deleterious effects of everyday racism. One sees friends, colleagues, and acquaintances being undone.

Even without a state on which one might otherwise rely (at least via the fantasy of protection), rehearsing Blackness becomes a means for re-articulating the self and transforming the everyday realities of who one might otherwise become. The anchor (see Fanon, cited in Hall 1990), here, is clearly not the nation-state, but the migrant/postmigrant/POC/Black rehearsal space, a much better possibility for becoming now.

We need institutions, we even need to make demands on nation-states for resources, but we cannot support the borders and killing and death mills they promote. The theater might be the best place for experimenting with possibility. The rehearsal is revolutionary, but perhaps not the ultimate revolution. It might, however, be the best place from which to start. The rehearsal allows us to get to the immediacy of the need for change now, while also thinking through and acting on longterm arrangements. It is focused on the immediate space while also creating the means to intervene in others. The rehearsal of insurrectionary imagination might ultimately lead to major social change, that is, if it can be taken seriously and replicated often.

7 Articulating a Noncitizen Politics

NATION-STATE PITY VERSUS BLACK POSSIBILITY

While it will not be obvious at first, the argument in this chapter also grows out of the theater. It draws on the work of the members of the refugee theater collective who participated, during the so-called "summer of migration" (2015), in our "Filming the Future from Berlin: Noncitizen Perspectives" project. Here, refugee[1] artists, mostly from Syria, made the primary contributions. For these and other noncitizens, politics necessarily required other means and even, perhaps, a different audience. Pity, as a top down form of recognition, would not be enough for social change.

MOVING FROM SYRIA TO BLACKNESS

In order to address concerns over potential appropriation when thinking about the universality of a politics based on Blackness it is important to think through the politics of what I will call *actually existing solidarity* as well as the politics of pity. The 2015 "refugee crisis" becomes an important moment that allows one to see how these politics play out. For the purposes of this analysis, in this chapter I will move slightly away from thinking about Blackness, in particular, before returning to it again in this chapter's and in the book's conclusion. Ultimately, attention to Blackness remains critical, as it operates ontologically both as the lacunae of both citizenship and humanitarian exceptionalism. Even if those traveling via the Mediterranean from Africa to Europe are primarily African and not yet Black in their political articulation, the case for the legitimacy of their arrival gets differentiated from those European states and European mainstream media deem *real* (and not economic) refugees. Most African immigrants in Europe find themselves contrasted politically and socially with those whose cases get evaluated as humanitarian *par excellence*. In the summer of 2015, this meant those fleeing war in Syria. The analytical paradigm that I will highlight in this chapter, the politics of *suffering with*, gets to the original intent of solidarity and pity, but refocuses attention on those who experience the original suffering. This refocused attention also demands that the analyst and activist reconfigure their approach to who should lead and who should follow, keeping in mind that the original sufferer knows best.

In the late summer and early autumn of 2015, Germany received a great deal of global credit for accepting so many refugees, with numbers approaching one million. In 2016, continuing into 2017, as the world seemed to turn toward nationalist populism as a solution to fears of globalization and global migration, and at a time when many fewer migrants actually made it to Germany, its then-Chancellor, Angela Merkel, gained major credit across the world for standing up against an exclusionary sentiment. One should not forget the results of that extended moment of welcome. Real people benefited from the possibility of living and staying in Germany. Still, one needs to ask: under what conditions? When one looks more closely at the forms of incorporation that took place during this time marked by "Refugees Welcome" initiatives, one should consider both the extent to which these forms of incorporation operated as both exclusionary (see Partridge 2012) and exceptional forms. One needs to look systematically at who got left out of the so-called *Willkommenskultur* (culture of welcome) and who persistently finds little to no space within it.

It becomes critical to think through the ways in which forms of incorporation in that summer and autumn might have established the conditions for future partial (if not total) exclusion, making it subsequently much more difficult to immigrate as a Black, Indigenous or POC refugee or migrant. Of course, refusing to welcome People of Color is not explicitly stated as part of German or European policy, but POC countries find themselves much more stringently regulated, particularly as it concerns the possibilities for their citizens to migrate to Europe. This remains true even for those experiencing constant war, including those who were initially welcomed.

For some time, and particularly after the fall of the Berlin Wall, it became clear that Germany, and Berlin in particular, worked as important destinations for those wanting to flee seeming impossibility elsewhere, from more conservative environments in southern Germany to war in Syria. In the summer of 2015, the consequences of war heated up as people sought refuge throughout Europe. While not initially welcomed with open arms, as the autumn approached, refugees encountered "Refugees Welcome" signs across the country, due, in part, to what one might call a politics of pity. The much-publicized photograph of a boy's lifeless body found on the shores of Turkey on his journey to Greece became a turning point. On a route that typically led to Germany, the boy, Alan Kurdi, died and his body washed up. The German chancellor subsequently expressed her willingness to accept responsibility for those fleeing war, with a policy more open to refugees than any other European country.[2]

This chapter examines the possibility for a noncitizen politics against the backdrop of pity. It examines further the extent to which pity is necessary for the initial welcome, but also how pity differentiates the citizen from the noncitizen "guest." Hospitality, as I will show, sustains the hierarchical position of the citizen in this relationship. Even while he, she, or they welcome, he, she, or they also sustain a morally superior position in a relationship in which reciprocity seems impossible. The memory of the lost child is quickly overwhelmed by the good of the subsequent policy shift and the many refugees who do, in fact, come. For those who arrive, there is not a chance to return the gift of the post-sacrifice welcome. Even if it could be returned, the enormity of the offer of refuge cannot be matched. The refugee is then left in the position of needing to be eternally grateful. Moreover, the logic of hospitality dictates, as one of my German host fathers once told me, that "the fish starts to stink after three days." While guests find themselves initially welcomed, the duration of stay could easily change the relationship—one that is not built on equality, but on a host/guest dynamic.

In the last part of this chapter, it will become clear that while solidarity might initially seem capable of saving the day, in the sense that solidarity implies a mutuality that does not exist in the host/guest relationship, the *actual practice of solidarity* makes mutual understanding difficult. The host/guest relationship persists. Europeans do not generally imagine themselves as having a responsibility for the crisis, at least that part concerning the lives of those outside Europe, beyond the emotional states of pity and compassion. The historical and contemporary links between European culpability and war or economic disaster in Syria or Sub-Saharan Africa are constantly cut, largely escaping notice in the popular imaginary.

FILMING THE FUTURE FROM BERLIN: TOWARD A REFUGEE/NONCITIZEN POLITICS

In that summer of intense migration that ultimately led to the (temporary) culture of welcome, I was conducting research on noncitizen perspectives on *Filming the Future from Berlin,* for the film project bearing this name. Most of the participants were refugees from Syria, including one Palestinian refugee who had previously lived in Syria. He had to carry papers to show that he was from Syria but not Syrian, and thus was without a passport.

The first iteration of *Filming the Future from Berlin: Noncitizen Perspectives* took place over one month in July 2015. In addition to the people from Syria—who included three Kurdish participants—three students from Canada/Spain, the United States, and the United Kingdom took part. Participants also included three young people from Berlin, who one might also call noncitizens, in the sense that their immediate and extended family members came from Pakistan, Turkey, and India, in addition, in two of these cases, to their having one German parent. The majority were members of the Youth Theater Bureau or had some association with it. In one film that emerged from the 2015 project, the non-German artistic director and activist, Ahmed Shah, who had also helped accompany and guide the films, concludes:

Give us our rights. Hannah Arendt talks about the right to have rights. . . .[3] It's a wide thing. It's not just a question of refugees. It's a question of fighting, of collectivity, of helping each other. Sometimes you're weak. Sometimes you're strong. Together. . . . We have to do it together.

Here, he gestures toward solidarity, a concept that I will address later in this chapter. The other point, however, is about politics. What kind of politics can refugees or noncitizens articulate when the mainstream media and politicians view them as guests? What right does the refugee/noncitizen have to make demands on the state that offers him or her refuge? In what context can one establish these demands as rights? Amid pity and crisis, the extent to which refugees can become political actors in the places in which they arrive to claim asylum leads one to ask to what extent these politics require solidarity and, on the other hand, to what degree that solidarity is always already caught up in asymmetrical relations of power.

In the spring of 2016, Chancellor Merkel stood behind relaxing agreements that had allowed open borders within Europe, but that had also restricted noncitizen movement. The agreements had declared that refugees must claim their need for asylum at their first European point of entry. This politics, a reflection of the Helmut Kohl era—that included (re) unification and the related national fervor—insulated Germany. That insulation seemed particularly significant in the wake of EU enlargement in 2004, as it left the responsibility for regulating refugees coming to Europe to Mediterranean countries such as Italy, Greece, and Spain, while simultaneously advocating freedom of movement for those recognized as (implicitly, White) Europeans. In the post-Cold War moment, after the Iron Curtain, freedom of movement seemed to stand as an important achievement, a demonstration of the Enlightenment *freedom* ideal,[4] then also caught up in the anticommunist push toward the capitalist appropriation of the Enlightenment term. As I have noted elsewhere:

Reference to foreign (and particularly African) migration in contemporary Germany is often a reference to an asylum law that the national legislature changed in accordance with EU norms in 1993. These changes occurred amid increasing discussion about the social and economic costs of unification, in which the financial and social support for East Germans and for ethnic German migrants from other parts of Eastern Europe was leveraged against the state's ability to support those thought of as unnatural, economic refugees. The legislation created many more restrictions for the latter, requiring, for example, that refugees leave Germany if the state deems that the situation from which they fled is again safe. Refugees who first land in neighboring countries deemed to be 'safe third countries are excluded from the right to political asylum' in Germany (Donle and Kather 1993). These include all countries on Germany's borders. The possibilities for asylum within Germany thus have become much more limited. 'By 1993, about eighty per cent of all applications for political asylum within the EC [European Community] had been filed in Germany. More than ninety per cent of these applications were finally rejected as unfounded' (Donle and Kather 1993). At the beginning of the twenty-first century, the number of successful applicants has dropped even further. According to a UN High Commissioner for Refugees report from April 2001, asylum seekers have seen a steady decline in the number of cases the German government officially recognizes or that are filed at all. The numbers went from 23,470 out of 127,940 applicants in 1995 to 10,260 out of 95,110 applicants in 1999 (Hovy 2001) (Partridge 2012, 78).

In 2015, with her initial turn toward welcoming refugees, Chancellor Merkel signaled a new era, which reinvoked Enlightenment values as tied also to their Christian roots. Germany could lead through moral authority, showing that it had learned from its past and, as a result, could take on the moral responsibility that seemed to be absent almost everywhere else, with the exception of those countries that were Syria's immediate neighbors, where most refugees from the Syrian war were still residing.

Amidst what seemed to be a magnanimous approach, an additional problem emerged: pity. With pity and what had come to be called a refugee crisis—a crisis that seemed to be more about the crisis of Enlightenment universality as opposed to the reality of differentiation between Europe and its Others—Merkel seemed to claim, in her magnanimous act, an air of moral legitimacy. This claiming worked against the backdrop and memory of freedom claims that led to the Berlin Wall's destruction, alongside the devastating memories of Third Reich-led genocide, refuge denial and its consequences. Moral legitimacy and moral superiority become part of the same project, here, in the sense that the one hosting the refugee becomes able, on the surface, to offer more than the refugee will ever be able to give back. Of course, the host never fully grasps what the refugee does have to offer. The discourse (including the practice) of pity allows one to see how the differentiation between Europeans, refugees, and other noncitizens takes place. This is demonstrated, in part, through the seeming impossibility of a noncitizen politics (with an emphasis on local political participation) that could be articulated by the newly arrived refugees themselves, even if their own crisis in and flight from Syria had emerged as a result of their initial political assertions via the Arab Spring.

This is not to say that Merkel did not believe in what she was doing or that she was intentionally instrumentalizing refugees in order to gain a morally superior position. In thinking about a politics of moral superiority, intent is not nearly as important as an analysis of the effect of the host/guest dynamic. Even if one does not intend to establish one's position as morally superior, this is the kind of relationship that persistently emerges. While solidarity (i.e. solidarity with the newly arrived refugees in Europe) may appear as the morally legitimate counter to pity, even solidarity seems to differentiate. But before showing how, I would first like to think through the articulations of pity and its counter.

AGAINST PITY: *FILMING THE FUTURE FROM BERLIN*

Based on a related initiative that I started in 2014 in Detroit, in the summer of 2015, I began this film project in Berlin with two Berlin-based artists. We wanted to make short films about the future from the perspectives of noncitizens in the cultural and political capital of one of the world's favorite countries.[5]

We initially left the term "noncitizen" open, and "the future" as the stakes for a politics that had yet to emerge. The future would be filmed *from* (as opposed to *of* or *about*) Berlin, because noncitizenship was the subject, and many noncitizens do not intend to stay in this city forever. But Berlin, as a postindustrial city with major public financing for the arts and a history of unaccounted-for, not yet re-privatized, property, offered distinct possibilities for living, creating, and imagining futures. So we—refugees, postmigrants, a youth theater artistic director, a filmmaker, and an anthropologist—met every weekday for one month. Our project to make a collection of short films for a broader public also became an opportunity to see how noncitizens imagined their futures from the vantage point of Berlin, and how they would contribute to a politics of reshaping them.

Pity No More

In the ensuing discussions, one young participant from the Kurdish region of Syria decided to make his film a pronouncement against pity. He had been in Berlin for two years and the authorities had recently recognized his asylum case. He wore thick, black-rimmed glasses, had a sarcastic smile, and constantly referred to himself playfully as a *scheiß Flüchtling* (shit refugee). He hated pity and was making fun of the way people saw him, turning that image into a flattened caricature so blatantly ridiculous that it could not be believed. Through the persistent performance of the caricature, he was also showing that he was not a desperate refugee, but a reflective artist. The attention to the caricature as a caricature ultimately created the possibility for him to emerge as a new self.

In response to his argument against pity, another participant from southern Germany (with a German mother and South Asian father) said that he also wanted to make a film about pity, but from the other side. He wanted to extol pity as a laudable Christian value. The artistic director intervened, telling him that pity was hierarchical, that it put the pitied person beneath he or she who was pitying. "But," the young man retorted, "pity can be good." He went further, saying that White men also deserve pity; however, in the final screening at a packed cinema in the district of Berlin-Kreuzberg, the audience refused this move. Through its laughter, the audience demonstrated that it could only read the White German male's call to pity him as ironic. In spite of the filmmaker's intent, the audience read his film as a meta-commentary against pity. The White German male characters were too robust, too confident, too self-assured. The film spent a great deal of time going to sites where the filmmaker assumed that he could find an understanding of Christian pity. He went to White German priests, to White German male social welfare activists, and to the artistic director from the theater from which many of the filmmakers came:

> ARTISTIC DIRECTOR: I say not 'thank you very much, that you're giving us a little place on the edge of existence, outside your city.' [You] don't recognize us. We are the naked humans.

We are the invisible people. We are not allowed to
work and all of these kind of things. We have to say:
'Thank you'? And then get pity? Because you think
... someone is pitiful? It's also *Ekel*. It's also disgust.

FILMMAKER (NARRATING): Pity seems to reaffirm hierarchies and inequalities
between citizens and noncitizens on an emotional
level, all while being very friendly, helpful, and
polite. Citizens underline their superior position,
questioning pity to noncitizens, by helping through
pity. Is pity different from the German word *Mitleid*
(literally, 'to suffer with' someone)? Do Christians
have a different perspective on pity?

In response to a question about whether or not he as a White German has
been the recipient of pity, responding to the filmmaker's query, one man
notes that at some point in his life he likely has, but he cannot recall any
recent experiences. He goes on to argue that society is not oriented toward
pity, and especially not for White men. "Pity is reserved for small cute ani-
mals, small children, Blacks, and women. Men are, in principle, excluded."
It is at this point that the audience in the Kreuzberg-Berlin theater, in
association with his call to be pitied, broke out into laughter. His call to be
pitied conveyed arrogance, and missed the point.

From here, the filmmaker goes on to talk to religious thinkers and
authorities. A minister of a church who has committed to living a year in
poverty tells him, "One identifies Jesus' association with suffering (one
part of the German word, *Mitleid*) and argues that, in the suffering, he is
encountering God." The minister, though, does not say how one should
address this suffering in contemporary life, but he does say that Jesus, in
identifying himself with suffering people, said: "I was hungry, and you gave
me something to eat. I was a stranger, and you gave me a place to sleep."

The filmmaker then goes to a religious institution, apparently also in
Berlin, and asks "What role does pity play in your everyday life? What role
does it play for you as a priest?"

PRIEST: I would say that pity is not a relevant category for me. Maybe it's because
this is a university community. There is a privileged target group. It's
actually my responsibility to show people how much wealth they have in

their lives. My praxis is marked by the fact that the people have the problem that they have too many possibilities as opposed to too few.

In the same room, another participant in the conversation says that he does encounter pity and refers immediately to refugees. He says that he sees his role as trying to reduce the suffering (again, referencing part of the German word *Mitleid*).

> PRIEST: Recently, I had contact with a refugee who said that he needed urgent legal advice. Then I felt pity (*Mitleid*) for a person who has come from a foreign country, who doesn't properly speak the German language, who is overwhelmed by his engagements with the German authorities. I could understand that this was a situation of suffering. I tried to help a bit. I am a lawyer. . . . I didn't just stay with the question of pity. I also tried to reduce the suffering a little bit. Maybe that is a positive meaning of pity, not just to look from above at the pitied, but to stand on the side of the suffering, and to try to bring him out of his suffering.
>
> FILMMAKER (OFFSCREEN): In the end, the question is the same for citizens and noncitizens. How can we get beyond pity?[6]

The question does not seem to be one of "identifying with the poor," as another religious figure in the film suggests, but to live as a poor person oneself: "With faith as the background, pity would probably fall away," the priest (who does not encounter pity) says. "Then I would most likely turn to the category of rights." The film concludes with this category. "Give us our rights," the artistic director of the youth theater demands.

CHANCELLOR MERKEL EXPRESSES PITY

Over the same summer, in a televised conversation with Chancellor Merkel, a Palestinian teenager, Sahwil, speaking perfect, fluent, native German, told the Chancellor her story: "We had a hard time recently, because we were close to being deported." The girl spoke in a shaky voice, hesitantly, seemingly on the verge of tears, as if she would rather not tell the story. But it was also clear that she wanted to use this opportunity to plead her case, not just for herself, but for her entire family. Merkel interrupted: "[You were told] you should go back to Lebanon?" Sahwil answered, "Yes, exactly." The footage that shaped how the public perceived this event then cut to another moment in the conversation:

MERKEL: I understand this. Umm . . . However, umm . . . [she hesitated slightly]. I must now also . . . umm—and sometimes politics is hard so, when you're standing in front of me, and you're a very pleasant (*sympatisch*) girl, but you know, in the Palestinian refugee camps in Lebanon there are thousands and thousands. And if we now say, 'You can all come, you can all come from Africa, you could all come'—we just can't achieve this.[7]

And we are in the situation, and the only answer we have is: don't let it take too long until these things are decided. But some people will have to go back.

The video clip then cut to an awkward pause, before Merkel walked over to the young girl, who had started to cry, and said, "*Ach komm.*" In English, one might say, "Oh, don't worry." The camera then went to a wider shot that showed the host and the audience of schoolchildren, including the girl, as Merkel approached her.

MERKEL:	But you did that really well [as if to congratulate a child on a recital performance, even though it was not successful].
[THE HOST JUMPS IN]:	I don't think that this has anything to do with 'doing it well.' It's a distressing situation.
MERKEL [RETORTING]:	I know it's a distressing situation.
[MERKEL TELLS THE GIRL]:	I still want to touch you once. Because I—because we don't want to bring you all in such a situation. Also, because it's difficult for you. And because you have depicted the situation many, many others can get into. Yes?[8]

At the moment when Chancellor Merkel walked over and awkwardly stroked the girl's arm, as if to say, "don't worry," she did not offer a legal remedy. However, perhaps as a result of her tears, the girl had the potential benefit of the exception. In addition to the tears, "medical care for Reem Sahwil, who has cerebral palsy and a shortened Achilles tendon, is among the reasons her family wants to stay in Germany" (Coburn 2015). After this incident, her family received a temporary residence permit until 2017.[9] Is it the Chancellor's awkward pity that led to Sahwil's temporary relief?

While potential pity rules one day, the threat of "terror" rules another. Even as Germany agreed to take in hundreds of thousands of Syrian refugees, it was speeding up the legal frameworks for the deportation of others. Just after the three-year-old dead Syrian child (Alan Kurdi)'s body washed up on the shore of Turkey, his boat having capsized on the way to entering the EU in Greece (see Parkinson and George-Cosh 2015), the mainstream German public again displayed an outpouring of German pity, guilt, and compassion (on compassion, see also Ticktin 2011; Fassin 2012). Both compassion and guilt, while suggesting at least temporary social hierarchies through feeling, are nevertheless of a different order than pity. Pity immediately signals the social alienation of the pitied person.

Many young people from Syria participated in our film project. All had had relatively privileged educations and most came from the middle class. One had originally applied for political asylum, but did not get his case recognized until he switched to an application for *humanitarian* asylum. Pity worked for the specific (Syrian) case, but not, as a general rule, for Afghanis, Pakistanis, Palestinians, Bosnians, or "Africans." Neither pity nor compassion nor guilt work for those judged conscious or calculating, as demonstrated by the response to those deemed "economic migrants." On the other hand, in taking in so many refugees, Germany seemed to show that it had learned from the past and that it could claim moral superiority, a term that points simultaneously to the virtues and the problematic hierarchy associated with this morality as articulated most prominently through pity (Partridge 2015). Germany's asylum policy is a direct result of its working to find a new national (and global) direction after its Nazi-led Holocaust. As a financial and political leader within the European Union, it is at a point at which it can teach the world (including the United States) how it should be acting. But what would constitute solidarity in this context? Is solidarity even enough?

PITY AND HOSPITALITY

Regarding hospitality, one of the refugee filmmakers from Syria spoke about staying in a friend's house. At some point, he also stayed in our apartment. He spoke about being asked to sleep on a mattress on the floor of his German friend's place, as if that friend were doing him a favor by offering him a place to sleep on the floor. He felt insulted and spoke about all the property his family owned in Syria. In speaking about hospitality, he noted that if a family friend came to his house and refused the initial offer of tea and he didn't offer again, or even if he only offered two more times, that family friend would leave and tell people that he came to his house and he did not even give him anything to drink. On the one hand, a good host treats the guest with honor. On the other hand, when that guest is pitied, sleeping on the floor seems good enough. Even after asking someone to sleep on the floor, the host who pities expects gratitude. Eventually, even this gratitude might not be enough. As Merkel insisted, "Some will have to go back."

The Christian examples of the Good Samaritan and St. Martin are illustrative. Here, the Christian form of incorporation offers a distinct form that reaches out to strangers as those to be pitied. One should not, however, ignore the speech of the stranger in response to this pity. It is important to listen to the pitied beyond the imagination of the thoughts of the person who pities in both the Good Samaritan or the St. Martin stories.

SEXUAL VIOLENCE: A TURNING POINT?

Before turning to solidarity, I will continue to theorize the relationship between pity, hospitality, and noncitizenship, where noncitizenship is defined in terms of social, legal, political, and/or economic non-belonging. "You live in the country, but it doesn't belong to you," as one of the refugee filmmakers in the *Future Cities* project put it. Others linked it to being homesick, not being able to go home or not having rights: "You hold the citizenship, but you still feel homesick" or "You can't have your values valued."

Amidst pity and noncitizenship, it is important to think about how sexual violence served as a turning point. The "refugee crisis," some have argued, was caused less by the number of people coming to Germany and more by the question of how to respond. It was, in this sense, a crisis of rich, predominantly White, Christian, state-sponsored morality, a crisis that Chancellor Merkel initially seemed to overcome with her "welcome culture." It became a crisis because European practices of Christian morality dictated against refusing people who clearly needed refuge. But some members of the Bavarian regional sister party of Merkel's own Christian Democratic Union (CDU) began to revolt, as did new members and voters of the Alternative for Germany (AfD) party, a more nationalistic group who argued that refugees were getting too many of the state's resources and the national government's compassion. Here, one might recall the film that initially wanted to make a case for pity, and the White German man's claim that White men generally are not the recipients.

As part of what emerged next, sexual assault ruptured the possibility even for pity, as a discussion about it became part of a generalized discussion about refugees, even if it was not refugees who were primarily involved in the assaults at the 2015/2016 New Year's Eve celebration in Cologne (see Kosnick 2019). Mainstream journalists and suspicious politicians read these attacks as the result of the culture of hospitality—*Willkommenskultur*—and the other side of compassion, with major discussions about refugees and North Africans attacking German women. Conservative activists claimed the mantle of feminism and condemned "their" culture of sexual violence, simultaneously sparking fear in large segments of the population, even leading, for example, to a temporary ban on male refugees at a public swimming pool in Bornheim, a small town not far from Cologne in North Rhine-Westphalia. The other side of pity emerges as the turn that happens after sexual violence, in which the refugee and "his culture" are seen as the culprit. Pity requires a kind of helplessness that is undermined by the perpetration of violence that mainstream politicians and German media outlets then generalized, in this case, as violence perpetrated by North Africans, but also with a persistent suspicion about refugees.

Inevitably, Merkel shifted in order to maintain her own political future, and the differentiation between refugees—"good" versus "bad," Syrian versus other, humanitarian versus economic—intensified. Amidst this shift, activists and others known for their antiracist positions in the past suddenly began writing and giving interviews in the popular press that publicized that they were now also afraid.[10] Refugees are guilty before they arrive. Compassion is undermined by fear, and while the formal political discussion focuses on German interests, the noncitizen wonders in which kind of politics she/he/they needs to participate. Who will be accountable to him or her or them and to his or her or their interests beyond voluntary compassion or sudden condemnation?

MAKING DEMANDS IN SPITE OF PITY: SPEAKING THROUGH FILM

In one scene in the *Filming the Future from Berlin: Noncitizen Perspectives* film against pity, the noncitizen filmmaker is confronted with trying to find housing for his friend. "What are you doing?" the artistic director who is helping him with the project asks him offscreen. "I'm trying to help a refugee." The artistic director goes further: "You know we're trying to make a film, right?" The filmmaker: "I know, but I won't leave him like I did yesterday." (One night, when we were editing the films in the theater collective's space, his friend slept on the floor in the next room.) "He has no place to sleep." In the meantime, the asylum hostel worker searches for housing online. "Sold out," she reads from the website. The friend has vouchers from the welfare office for 50 euros to get housing. Since all of the shelters are already full, he has to look to the private housing market.

The filmmaker's conversation with the artistic director continues: "For me, I don't help. I do it all the time. And I don't have to say that, 'I am helping' and all this shit.'" "I am helping," the filmmaker mimics, imitating the ideal helper, pointing to the fact that he is not doing it to get moral credit. His motivation, he suggests, goes beyond pity. He goes on: "But I must do [it], for me." It is an obligation, not an act of charity. His reasoning suggests the opposite of the contemporary reading of pity. "For me, I was also in this situation," he says, recalling. "I can feel him, I can understand what the refugees suffer, because I'm also a refugee. But in the beginning, it's difficult and different, not like now." His search for housing for the newly arrived refugee is an obligation that is distinct from the regular contemporary reading of the Good Samaritan form of compassion, but perhaps more like the story of the minister who had taken the, at least temporary, vow of poverty: "I was suffering and you gave me food." The newly arrived refugee looking for housing is a version of himself.

The fact that refugees would have to rely on pity to get housing, even though they had a cash-equivalent voucher, revealed the dehumanizing effect of the refugees' treatment. Even money was not enough to secure housing. In this case, the refugee was not even entitled to (paid-for) hospitality. The hospitality/pity link is a mode of incorporation. Without it, one might not find a place to live at all. On the other hand, needing to resort to mercy is not an empowering position. William Blake's poem "The Human Abstract" (cited in the film; see Blake and Bloom 1982) explores these paradoxes:

> Pity would be no more,
> If we did not make somebody Poor;
> And Mercy no more could be
> If all were as happy as we.

Pity, in the form critiqued here, de-historicizes. It hides the relationship between Europe and those to be pitied. It does not demand accountability. At the very least, though, solidarity takes the relationship out of the realm of a voluntary emotion and puts it into the arena of political practice. In practice, though, solidarity acts like (this articulation of) pity. It does not necessarily eviscerate hierarchy. Institutions to support the accountability of those who claim to be in solidarity are now largely absent. On the other hand, when the filmmaker says that he wants to help his friend, that he must, there seems to be a moral imperative that is based not on hierarchy, but on the experience of having been in the same situation (of retrospectively suffering with), and knowing what that is like. The knowing (in German, *Betroffenheit*, that is, having been affected by the same situation) is critical. In my analysis of Holocaust memory (see chapter 4), I use the work of Leslie Adelson (2005) to think about what she calls touching tales, that is, the ways in which historical experiences of racism and genocide provide links (see also Rothberg 2009), which is not to say that experiences are the same, but they can (and do) produce connections (what one might think of as a mode of *suffering with*). Perhaps these sorts of connections are what one should require for a more efficacious articulation of political connection and potential collaboration.

SOLIDARITY

Amidst these shifting politics, in theory, solidarity works as a constant for those opposed to the dehumanization of refugees, but what does solidarity mean in practice? Is it, as a University of Michigan graduate student suggested at a public screening of *Pity No More* (Kello 2015), similar to pity in the sense that it differentiates between the one who offers solidarity and the one who receives it? To what extent can the refugee be in solidarity with the normative white German citizen who decides whether or not to accept his or her claim to asylum, who is never accused of being, by nature, a sexual predator? In *Pity No More* (Kello 2015), the protagonist expresses solidarity with a new acquaintance who has recently arrived from Syria and who also seeks to claim asylum, but it is hard to see what he would mean if he said that he was in solidarity with the border agent.[11] Less obvious than the symbolic distance between the refugee and the border agent is that between the pro-asylum activist and the refugee.

Writing about the dynamics between her role as an anthropologist, her role as a shelter director, and her connection to the young women who lived in the shelter in her ethnography, *Shapeshifters: Black Girls and the Choreography of Citizenship*, Aimee Cox notes:

> The social spaces that we created together were rife with power differentials. There were many things I was not. I was not homeless, not a girl, not born and raised in Detroit, not an hourly staff member, and not a parent. There were other things that I was. I was a PhD student, a program director with the power to hire and fire, and a middle-class Black woman. The things that I was and was not, the labels that preceded me, and the ways in which these labels were attached to privilege mattered in every context for how I was both seen and able to see. It also mattered that I was often able to witness and write about struggles that did not necessarily affect me outside of my own political investments and commitments to these girls and women (2015, 33).

In a different context, Fiona Wright (2016, 132) refers to "a kind of solidarity that enacts its own violence." Alexander Koensler (2016, 352) writes about "the difficulty of enacting solidarity in practice without new boundaries or misunderstandings resurfacing in unexpected ways." While solidarity appears to suggest equality, in fact it inevitably means hierarchy. One advocates a politics of solidarity, and yet the conditions of the German pro-asylum/anti-border activist and the recently arrived refugee are not the same. The means for enacting social change are not equal. If the refugee and the German activist disagree about the best political strategy, the German activist has an advantage, sometimes without realizing it, and may unwittingly enforce his/her/their own will over the refugee's own desire. The pro-asylum activist might be willing to take certain steps, but not others.

In the summer of 2014, some African refugees occupying a Berlin-Kreuzberg school threatened suicide. Here, "African" operates as a broad category that differentiates too little among Africans, but nevertheless reflects the European differentiation between "legitimate" and "illegitimate" migrants, often via the category of economic versus humanitarian or politically persecuted refugees. Furthermore, in the German context, it is well known among activists and asylum camp workers that Africans whose asylum cases have yet to be decided are unlikely to get the right to stay in Berlin. One asylum hostel worker in Berlin told me that I would not find any Africans in the hostel she managed, as a result of this national placement policy. In the protest at the square in Kreuzberg, the refugees (who notably were not from one single country in Africa) used occupation as a means of achieving their ends, protesting against the German asylum policy and the legal regime that refused to allow them to live in the parts of Germany or in the parts of Europe they chose. In this instance, solidarity only seemed to go so far. The existential questions and the potentially necessary political means were not the same for everyone. This suggests the need to think more rigorously about the possibility of a noncitizen politics.

NONCITIZEN POLITICS: POSSIBILITIES AND LIMITS

In his account of politics, philosopher Giorgio Agamben (1998) refers back to the literature of the ancient Greeks to differentiate between what Aristotle called "bare life" and "political life." Bare life is, according to Agamben's reading, life that can be killed but not sacrificed. For him, this distinction leads all the way to Auschwitz, and the lives of those who would be murdered as a matter of state policy. In *Casualties of Care*, Miriam Ticktin refers to bare life as the "universal suffering body best exemplified by the sick body, or by the racialized, sexually violated body" (2011, 4). Under French humanitarianism, the incorporation of bare life is the exception to the rule of deportability (see de Genova and Peutz 2010), in the sense that French law incorporates bare life only to the extent that these bodies will likely die if deported. They have no right to stay in France other than the fact that the French are compassionate and have developed a humanitarian exception. They get differentiated from political life in the sense that political bodies have rights, like the right to work, the right to get an education, and the right to stay forever in France. Ticktin (2011) calls the form of care that incorporates bodies through the humanitarian exception a "politics of care [that] is a form of antipolitics" (5, see also Ferguson 1994). It is not the result of noncitizen activism, but a humanitarian exception that allows the almost dead (or suffering) bodies to stay because they do not have access to appropriate care in their home countries.

In an earlier piece, Ticktin (2006, 35) argues:

> Although both human rights and humanitarianism are complexly constituted transnational institutions, practices, and discursive regimes, in a broad sense, human-rights institutions are largely grounded in law, constructed to further legal claims, responsibility, and accountability, whereas humanitarianism is more about the ethical and moral imperative to bring relief to those suffering and to save lives.

Agamben's discussion of bare life connects the ancient Greek concept both to the death camp and to the refugee camp, where the refugee does not yet have full rights while his or her case is being decided. Agamben's analysis, though, tells us little about the political practices and imaginations of those imprisoned in the camp. Even Ticktin's hope for human rights as more grounded in law is obscured by the lack of accountability that state institutions have *vis-à-vis* the unrecognized refugee as he or she or they wait for asylum. The nation-state is too imperfect an institution to enforce universal rights. As Agamben points out, even in states which claim to offer universal rights, the rights of the citizen are still distinct from "the rights of man."[12] The state enforces the citizen's rights, not "man's" rights. Solidarity is too unstable as a universal legal or social category, as can be seen in the case of actually existing socialism (see Partridge 2012, Verdery

1996). The socialist brothers and sisters who came as contract workers or students to the German Democratic Republic (East Germany) were nonetheless distinct from the national members of the republic.

Noncitizenship is the juncture at which we need to be theorizing the political because it immediately points to the problematic distinction between the "universal human" and the citizen. "Human rights," as a concept, suggests that no human life is truly bare. There is always the potential to invoke rights claims, at least for "humans," if not for those seen as "things." The gap between human rights and universal rights is reflected in the position of the noncitizen, for whom no sovereign entity necessarily claims responsibility.

One of the *Filming the Future from Berlin* films depicts, through fictionalized reenactment, the refugee (playing a version of himself) who, after months of waiting, ultimately changed his case from political to humanitarian asylum (see also above). He recalls the period before he made the switch. In his film, the fictionalized character travels by train from the town he has been assigned while he waits for the state's decision. Even though he has made frequent inquiries by telephone and in person with local authorities, he ultimately decides to travel to the center processing his original claim in order to find out his case's status. He has received ambivalent messages; he has even heard that some of his documentation might be missing. The scene begins at the asylum officer's office. He knocks politely and she barely opens the door. Even before she opens it, we can see him primping. She then opens the door slightly, just to take his ID before closing it again. He is forced to wait. The officer comes back (after spending some time on Facebook) with no additional information other than that he will have to wait. He then starts talking about brandy and asking what kind she likes most. While she initially engages him in this discussion, and even smiles slightly, the conversation quickly turns, and she abruptly closes the door in his face. "I know what you are trying to do!," she says. The title of the film, *Please Take My Money* (Hakami 2015), makes the point. In one scene, the refugee speaks to the audience, as if they can make the decision: "You're getting paid to do this job, so why can't I just give you a little more to get you to do your job a little faster?"

The extent to which the refugee acts as more than a simple vehicle to highlight the politics of morality, crisis, and fear seems striking in this film and in *Pity No More*. The audience sees intervening discussions that one does not normally hear if one is not already a noncitizen or, at the very least, not already involved in the daily lives of noncitizens. Gratitude, expressed by those who might get asylum, is not the end of the story. In the summer's discussions, many noncitizens expressed discomfort with the fact that they were constantly expected to say thank you, even when the help that they had received came through pity, and not through mutual recognition. A more equitable relationship would have recognized the refugee's expression of political demands: "I want to stay, but under these specific conditions. . . ." Those offering the help imagined themselves as being in solidarity with the more recently migrated, but important aspects of mutual respect went missing. This discrepancy suggests the necessity for a noncitizen politics.

In this sense, the theorization of a noncitizen politics demands expansion. The analyst and the activist need to think further about the degree to which the noncitizen's disrespect for national borders itself works as political expression, even if it first appears merely as desperation. In our conversations during the film project, many spoke of their experiences and strategies for crossing borders, recounting the Turkish border as the most difficult crossing point. In other discussions about the border and the recent migrations from Syria and elsewhere in the world, colleagues, activists, and refugees suggest that Europe cannot actually enforce its borders. If people are determined to come, they will get in; depending on European policy, though, more or fewer will die trying, a circumstance also *apropos* to the the situation in the United States (see de Léon 2015).

Mainstream politicians and journalists express, at times, their desire to deport, but deportation will prove impossible on a mass scale, not least because of the memory of Nazi-inspired European genocide. This remains the case even when the threat to imminently deport is no longer announced. People's lives will, of course, become more precarious (de Genova and Peutz 2010), but they will not all, ultimately, leave. In addition to the insistence on coming in, the refusal to leave Europe is also an expression of a noncitizen politics, in which one does not necessarily appeal to a political representative like the German Chancellor, because one does not belong to institutional networks in which that participation finds recognition as a right. This is true even of human rights, because they consist of only minimum standards with no guarantees, with no sovereign who is institutionally committed to be appealed to or to protect them, him, or her. On the other hand, if one looks carefully at how Chancellor Merkel and German voters responded to the refugee crisis between the summer of 2015 and the spring of 2016, the movement politics of refugees, who chose to come to Germany via Turkey and Greece or from North Africa via the Mediterranean, suggests that this is, in fact, politics—that these movements do have effects on national elections and geopolitical relations.

By "welcoming refugees" in the summer of 2015, Germany seemed to be taking a moral high ground that would shame even its former (post–Second World War, democracy-teaching) occupiers, who were, in spite of war and their participation in it, unwilling to take in many refugees, even those living within civil war. But in the late winter of 2015 and spring of 2016, in part because of internal pressure from a more anti-immigrant wing of her own party and voter support for the more stubbornly racist right, the German chancellor was forced to pursue political survival, to change her position. On the other hand, even though she was not representing refugees, their presence in Germany forced her to find a political solution at the beginning of the summer of 2015. At first, she adjusted, via a politics/anti-politics of pity, in favor of welcoming. Then, through a politics of political representation that painted refugees as sexually violent Muslim men (the other side of a pity politics that relies on voluntary compassion, which then turns to disgust), she adjusted again. But to what extent can one openly organize around noncitizenship and a politics that refuses border regimes, but nevertheless appeals to nation state-based welfare?

CONCLUSION

As recalled in chapter 4, in the late winter of 2016, at a weekly meeting organized by refugees at an important Berlin-based cultural institution, a Black audience member, speaking in French, commented on the upcoming "Global Day Against Racism." "Many people fear that if they join the demonstration, they will face deportation," he said. His friend, he told the meeting, did not know about the demonstration. "Many people are isolated in refugee camps." He also asked about the security of the refugees at the demonstration. A West African man, active in organizing undocu-mented migrants, added: "You don't hear the voice of the refugees. Most of the refugees are traumatized and they stay in the camps." Once again, the possibilities for noncitizen politics become significantly reduced through the forms of "care" to which they seem most likely to gain access.

If moral superiority was the initial story, then Germany was losing it in the spring of 2016, as the European Union (under Merkel's leadership, many in the German and international press were arguing) formed an agreement with Turkey to return migrants from Greece, and Germany made family reunification more difficult for those who had already arrived in the country. With so many new restrictions and oppositions to their entry, it seemed that many more people would die in the Mediterranean or elsewhere en route. Money (at least money to travel to Germany) seemed to be less of a problem than the fact that European and American governments fail to facilitate flights for Syrians, Iraqis, Kurds, or Palestinians from countries torn apart by war.

A class analysis cannot attend to some of the racial tensions that are the result of global trends in migrations, war, and the associated geopolitics. German Social Democratic politicians have written some of the most rac-ist political interventionist texts in recent memory (see Sarrazin 2010; Buschkowsky 2012), and the Red-Green coalition, led by Gerhard Schröder between 1998 and 2005, seemed to be more about compromis-ing the rights of migrants/noncitizens than reformulating the discussion. In refusing to speak more often and more explicitly about racialized exclu-sion in everyday life, even Cem Özdemir, the former Turkish-German co-head of the Green Party (and later the Minster of Agriculture), has empha-sized the more explicit racism of the populist right, as opposed to the normalized quality of systemic racism.

Merkel put her own political future at stake by opening things up. She shifted on issues of immigration and asylum in ways that one would not have anticipated if one had assumed that right versus left was an ideal guide for understanding contemporary life. Her Christian commitments to compassion and her experience of growing up on the more restricted side of the Berlin Wall led her to see contradictions in the rigidity of for-tress Europe. Then again, the other side of pity and compassion is the quick turn toward hatred and resentment, because compassion is not a right. It acts as a voluntary sentiment, and who deserves compassion becomes a matter of interpretation. Furthermore, the pitied person might lose all of the compassion if they do not seem grateful enough, and especially if they (usually he) is suspected of being a rapist. The humanitarian beginnings of more open borders make the politics more difficult—even if refugees have to spend and risk a lot more to walk as opposed to fly to Europe. But a social movement in Europe organized by the refugees themselves will emerge. It is already asserting itself in the theater. These kinds of movements have happened before, so why not again? Even if things begin with compassion, a more robust politics must still emerge. A politics of pity, in its contemporary hierarchical form, is problematic from the start, that is, unless pity, solidarity, and compassion start again to mean *suffering,* and then organizing, *with.*

Conclusion

FROM CLAIMING BLACKNESS TO BLACK LIBERATION

If anything is universal, it is anti-Blackness. But this book has focused on Blackness as a universal claim. Why does one claim Blackness and with what effect? It is certainly not to experience life as a thing (Wilderson 2020), but to think, work, and live through the agency of Black power.

Germany symbolizes a particular case, in the sense that a previous iteration of its government orchestrated mass murder. The Allies negated a central punishment, a divided nation-state, after forty-five years; the newly unified country, then, emerged as a locus of apparent liberation. But immediately those who on the outside of normative Germanness experienced massive violence, alongside the systemic racism they already faced. Nationalist actors attacked Vietnamese homes in newly "liberated" small towns. Former East German contract workers and foreign students from Mozambique and Angola had to hide in their rooms while neo-Nazis took over the streets (see also Partridge 2012). In this same period, those on the right wing burned down Turkish-German homes (BBC 2018). I lived in West Germany from 1989–1990 and saw graffiti all over my small town exclaiming "Ausländer raus" (Foreigners get out!) and "Turks get out!" Once, my classmates started yelling at two men with dark curly hair walking down the street in the middle of the town, telling them to leave. Notably, my own Blackness did not seem to them to pose the same threat. Part of the appeal of American Blackness is its more universal attraction and occupying presence. One is weighed down by the burden of injustice it takes on, while simultaneously having some sympathy and often identification with the effort to undo the world its articulation seeks to overcome.

Between 2000 and 2007, the National Socialist Underground committed a series of anti-Turkish/anti-Greek/anti-police murders that, it turns out, the German state worked to cover up (see *Focus* 2018; *DW.com* 2022). They had paid a committed Neo-Nazi informant. Instead of investigating to find the real culprits, the mainstream press initially blamed an alleged Turkish-German "Döner Mafia."

Many moments of racialized and racist violence go unnoticed by the mainstream. These include moments when a White German teacher challenges a Turkish-German woman about wearing her headscarf, when an English teacher insists on reading the German N-word in a literary exercise, when Palestinian-German youth get called violent, when Jewish-German youth are assumed not to be German. Amidst the history of mass murder, these and other everyday experiences disappear into the background. While one hundred thousand Germans marched in 2020 in favor of Black Life after the murder of George Floyd, most likely saw that violence as an American issue. The Initiative of Blacks in Germany[1] also gained more prominence, but, according to the artistic director of Theater X (previously known as Youth Theater Bureau), other protestors and sympathizers in the advocacy for Black Life told Arab- and Turkish-German youth were that the struggle for Black Life was not their own.

Nevertheless, Blackness emerges as a universal claim, because it effectively contends with deeply embedded Enlightenment contradictions in Europe, the United States, and many other parts of the world. It interrogates claims of liberation from the perspective of those who have yet to experience real freedom, those never addressed in the original liberatory pronouncement. Again, Locke advocated freedom while holding stock in slavery. Rousseau wrote about liberation while failing to mention the French *Code Noir*. The French advocated universal freedom while enslaving Haitians. Hegel promoted a concept of universality while seeing Africa as inferior.[2]

Black Power in in the theater space, the space of intentional perform-ance, practice, and rearticulation, though, offers alternative strategies in the fight for liberation. Youth Theater Bureau learned with and re-enacted Black power as a way of practicing and equipping oneself for everyday life, particularly life as experienced through contemporary racisms. Black power offered tools. Black power as articulated in Youth Theater Bureau offers a more accountable path towards liberation. It is not from the posi-tion of the Enlightenment, but from the position of Blackness that we all might become truly free, necessarily against the constraints of what bell hooks (2014) calls "imperialist, white supremacist, capitalist [add transphobic and heterosexist] patriarchy" and what Puar (2017) calls "debilitation."

Sovereignty, meaning, in this case, the ways in which Black people often experience *democracy* (that is, as White supremacist sovereignty/democracy), continues to take Black people for a loop.[3] Sovereignty, also as state sovereignty, implemented through the power to kill, the power to enforce borders, the power to declare states of emergency, and even the power to enforce a democracy that actually produces minoritzed, racial-ized, differentially gendered, sexed, economically disadvantaged, debili-tated, and Black populations (see also Puar 2017; Foucault 1990, 1991; Agamben 1998; and Schmitt 2006 [1922]). What one does not only about top-down sovereignty, but also about more insidious, everyday forms of regulation will ultimately suggest the means for collective, neces-sarily also Black, flourishing. Exclusionary incorporation means that we will not thrive under contemporary conditions. Blackness, though, offers a position from which to articulate a politics that not only analyzes the contradictions in liberal democracy, human rights, and contemporary claims that we are all (potentially) free. Unfortunately, we have not uni-versally achieved liberation. Most of us are not even on the right path. If Blackness is ultimately successful as a universal claim, though, it will con-tinue to demand accountability while undoing the universal demand, inasmuch as that demand is also a form of oppression. That is why this book centers on the universal claim and leaves the outcome undeter-mined, while nevertheless focusing on the importance of everyday prac-tice, including insurrectionary imagination as rehearsed in the theater and then in everyday life.

Blackness remains embedded in Enlightenment universality and the experiences and histories that follow. To the extent that we continue to be oppressed, we need to find new experiences now; the "guarantees" for citizens and of universal rights were not originally for us, and if some ephemeral element of citizenship for Black actors does appear to exist, this will only ever be as an exception. In other words, as Mamadou suggests in his film, we need a new system.

OPTIMISM VS. PESSIMISM

In *Cruel Optimism* (2011), Lauren Berlant writes about the "attrition of fantasy," but for whom was that fantasy "of the good life" ever imaginable? Inasmuch as Blackness is, by definition, always an exception to the norm, recognizing the effects of sovereignty, and not just "biopower" or "governmentality" will be crucial to liberation. "Not being governed quite so much" (Foucault 1997) will not be adequate when "care" is not at the center of how Blackness gets incorporated or regulated.

On the other hand, even if Black people regularly face slow and premature death (Puar 2017; Gilmore 2007), necropolitics (Mbembe 2003)[4] will not be an adequate means for analyzing the position of those who live within nation-states or other places that also allow them access to resources. Strategizing around potential death might get in the way of making use of the more limited but available resources that one needs to fund the rehearsals and ultimately change the system.

This is also where a need for pessimism seems relevant (Wilderson 2020; Hartman 2019, 1997; Sexton 2010, among others). Optimism is cruel (Berlant 2011) in the sense that inclusion under regimes of *democracy* and *democratization* actually mean the impossibility of flourishing. One has to accept a version of one's own inferiority in order to "thrive" under contemporary regimes of citizenship. And this inferiority is not the same for everyone. If one does not pay special attention to intersectional Blackness here, then one misses the point (see also Crenshaw 1989, 1991; Ferguson 2004; Puar 2012, 2017).[5]

In this book, I have used the persistent presence and production of noncitizens to mark the production and reproduction of the impossibility of flourishing within the current system. It is also critical to note that Blackness is distinct from noncitizenship, in the sense that noncitizens can also be anti-Black. They can make claims to Blackness and neverthe-less participate in the production of Black people, as those they will expose to anti-Blackness.

As I noted in the previous chapter, solidarity cannot do enough to get one out of this problematic. *Suffering with* as a means of political alliance seems to be the only way. This requires being accountable to Black people. That is, as one of my students recently noted in a different context, it should not be happening about us without us.[6] Anti-Blackness is perva-sive. One should assume, as opposed to having to prove, its existence. Any claims to Blackness, therefore, should be linked to a discussion about anti-Blackness with Black people. Those Black people should not be incorpo-rated and then discarded. (Inasmuch as it is anti-Black, such incorpora-tion will always be exclusionary.) To change the system, everyone must systematically attend to anti-Blackness, including in their own practices, meaning that Black people will have the means and capacity to clearly assert their own needs, claims, and desires as people do not only borrow Blackness, but live it.

While the Youth Theater Bureau did not consist only of Black actors, it was important, there, that mobilizing Blackness became a possibility for everyone. Nevertheless, in every context in which one is making Black claims, one also needs to attend to the micro-politics, the everyday asser-tions, of anti-Blackness, those both subtle and obvious. If the rehearsal is the revolution, that discussion can also happen and be enacted in the rehearsal space, but insofar as those rehearsals are making Black claims, they must also be held accountable to Black people. The claims should not, in effect, be anti-Black. With that said, claims to Blackness have become universal, because the production of Blackness is so pervasive, even if this production happens along graduated lines (see also Ong 2003), that is, based on skin color, proximity to Africanness and other fac-tors, the mainstream will see one as more or less Black. Some will, there-fore, have more and others, systematically, less privilege, depending, in part, on their proximity to Blackness.

In the end, I do not want to tell people what to do or how to enact the future, but I do think that liberation needs to be at the center. This liberation, too, must be accountable to Black people. In writing about the end of socialism in eastern Europe, Katherine Verdery (1996) once argued, "What comes next is anyone's guess." With the fall of the Berlin Wall, she wasn't sure what kind of political regime would dominate the world, what would happen after the end of the Cold War. Could new social paradigms, new ways of living ethically together, emerge under these conditions? If so, they have not emerged yet. I would argue that we cannot leave things up to chance: that Black people, colonized people, and noncitizens all need to be intentional about the direction. They (we) cannot afford to leave the future up to chance. We could all take to the streets now, but we need local critical organizations with transnational links to help formulate, practice, and enact our new tactics. Thinking through Blackness also means thinking beyond "the human" and "human rights" or even "the body" or "the body politic" as the grounds for that emergence. In the meantime, we'll be rehearsing in spaces we design to cultivate ourselves and our insurrectionary imaginations.

Key Terms and Sites

BLACKNESS

In this book Blackness should be thought in relation to occupation (that is, military occupation after the First and Second World Wars—emphasizing a shift after the First World War, where Black French occupying troops were largely viewed as rapists, to the end of the Second World War, where occupying Black troops in what became West Germany (and West Berlin) were viewed in more sympathetic terms—for example, as draft dodgers or deserters who needed to be protected and hidden in the protest against the Vietnam War (in Muhammed Ali's telling: "No Viet Kong ever called me a Ni**er"), and also because of their segregation in the initial phases of occupation (after the Second World War). Black people were separate from the occupying American mainstream. They didn't have the same access to rights and were also seen as more generous to their German (occupied) counterparts. This is not to say that there was not any anti-Black sentiment, but there was a different kind of possibility for affiliation and connection. This was also demonstrated in the German response to the Civil Rights Movement and Black Lives Matter.

In this book, it will also be important to note the role Holocaust memory plays in relation to Blackness. Historically, when one speaks of racism in Germany, the Holocaust (that is, genocide, particularly the mass murder of European Jewry) has been at the center. Amidst this culture of memory, Blackness has also sustained a presence that doesn't attempt or appear to attempt to deny this history.

In this sense, Blackness can be seen as another site of racist perpetration. It is one that does not attempt to make equivalences with the Shoah, partially because its origins are seen as different. Even with the recent turn towards the demand that Germany also account for its colonial history, Blackness has sustained a different kind of place (which has allowed for the associated atrocities to be recognized and remembered without accusations of Holocaust denial). This, however, is not the case when Arab and Turkish or Arab-German and Turkish-German subjects make claims to experiences of racism. In these cases, at least in the mainstream, they then come to be seen as deniers. When they claim racism, the mainstream public, politicians, media analysts, and schoolteachers see them as making equivalences between their experience and what happened to Jewish Europeans during the Nazi era. Because there has not been the experience of mass murder and loss, this claim then gets read as denial. Blackness, however, offers a different kind of referent. Even this equivalence remains tenuous, but it nevertheless has become possible. Beyond state recognition, it creates a possibility not only for managing, but also thriving in everyday life.

A third arena in which this book takes on claims to Blackness is in relation to noncitizen politics and refugee/noncitizen futures. These articulations of Blackness are still emerging, but they are also part of what I observed in and outside of the theater. Of course, many noncitizens are also of African descent, but I would argue that their Blackness becomes evident in White space, in this case Europe. This is the point of the opening anecdote about being injured as the African subject enters German nation-space (see preface).

While it might not be obvious at first, Blackness remains open as a site of political articulation, even for the most recent immigrants (including refugees) who may not yet have a direct connection to the history of Blackness as it gets read in Germany. Of course, globally circulating Black culture continues to offer an arena of connection. Its political mobilization, though, must be thought consciously in order to be politically efficacious. Again, the theater, as will become evident in this book, plays an important role.

In this sense, I argue that occupation becomes a global phenomenon that no longer requires a physical (occupying) presence. On the other hand, the global circulation is often accompanied by empire (see von Eschen 2004), but often the empire loses control and the counter-message finds new arenas of circulation. One can see continuity here between the immediate postwar period and the present if one follows US State Department policy. Now with other forms of circulation, some of this policy is outside of State Department hands, as can be seen via the solidarity protests concerning the 2020 murder of George Floyd where the groups marching also took up their own particular versions of the cause, such as police brutality in France, or anti-Black racism in Finland. I return to some of these latter points in the conclusion.

Additionally, throughout this book, it is important to note that Blackness is variously gendered and a constant site of struggle in its differentiated articulation.

NONCITIZEN

In addition to Blackness, in this text, noncitizenship is another key analytic. From my perspective, noncitizenship includes those who have formal membership but who are nevertheless excluded from the potential of ever becoming normative White Germans. For noncitizens, there is a constant reminder that they can never become "normal." This doesn't mean that normality is desirable, but it does mean that access to resources and social, political, and economic possibilities have become differentiated and unequal.

POST-MIGRANT

The everyday experience of not being seen as a citizen also takes its toll. Blackness offers possibility not primarily via a new politics of recognition, but as a means of mutual recognition, offering each other a different kind of framework. Mutual acknowledgment is critical here, particularly in a context in which the basics offered by a rich welfare state (even if minimal) are already standard if not guaranteed. Beyond this, Blackness, via a modified anti-heteronormative feminist-informed Black power, means that one learns also how to make demands on state and other resources even if one is not a citizen or not perceived as such. Because one does not subscribe to the nation-state, one no longer needs to make demands on this basis. One does, however, recognize that the resources also belong to her/him/them. The collective of mutual recognition is also central here. Recognition is not once and for all, but a process that allows for persistent transformation. It might create its own (unfortunate) outsides, and this is a serious problem, but it attempts to be loyal.

THE NATION-STATE

In this account, I take seriously the role of the nation-state as a location of resources and a site of sovereign power, but I also want to think through the importance of transnational actors and transnational possibility. I also take seriously the presence and articulations of the supra-state—for example, in the form of Europe. This book works to think, though, more systematically about possibility beyond the nation-state while acknowledging its presence, its enforcement of borders, as well as its potential to redistribute resources.

HOLOCAUST MEMORY

As noted above, in this book, Holocaust memory plays an important role in understanding contemporary life. This will be most evident in my analysis of its monumentality and the charge of its denial (see chapter 3).

ISLAM

An analysis of Islam is not the main point of the book, even if many of the people about whom I am writing have been raised as Muslim (some still practicing, others not). Some were Christian, others atheist, although this was not the main topic of discussion. While some readers might want me to think more about the connections to the practice of Islam (this is clearly a factor in the network of identifications—for example, with Muhammad Ali and Malcolm X), my research did not take place in mosques and I did not observe people praying in the theater, although there were sometimes discussions about the most appropriate ways of representing Islam. There were also outside accusations about being anti-Semitic, which were likely linked to perceptions of the theater as a Muslim place.

Again, referencing Blackness references a different kind of possibility which, importantly, is not the same as denying Islam.

THEATER

As alluded to above, my research for this book took place primarily in two "post-migrant" theaters, where the primary contributors were People of Color, including those of Turkish, Arab, Kurdish, and African descent. There were also members from the Balkans and White Germans.

Joining the theaters was relatively easy. One, the one I refer primarily to as Youth Theater Bureau and sometimes as Theater X, had a long-term sustained membership, whereas the other theater was more project-based in terms of participation. It also had a definite and sustained leadership that shifted after I left.

What are the conditions of possibility for joining the theater? What does "scaling up" mean in this context? What about those who cannot make it in this theater setting?

Again, for those who might assume otherwise, it is important to note that the theaters were mostly secular. The founding artistic directors for both theaters had Marxist orientations, although the everyday implications of these orientations was different.

Both of the theaters make demands on and rely on state funding. They see it both as a necessity and as a right.

Notes

1. My translation (from German to English). I think of this wounding in relation to what Wendy Brown (1995) calls "injury," but Blackness seems to be more of a kind of undoing, or, perhaps, a necessary undoing of the world in order to be of another kind of place.

2. All names in this text are pseudonyms, with the exception of public figures.

3. Shoah refers to the specific mass murder of those the Nazis defined as Jews during the Second World War in Germany, and Europe more broadly.

4. I put the term "immigrants" in quotes, because many are, in fact, not immigrants, but the children or grandchildren of immigrants—or just those who appear to the normative and normalizing public as not phenotypically German—that is, those without blond hair.

5. In Germany, mainline Protestant and Catholic churches are often owned by their municipalities and receive funding collected by the bureaucratic state.

6. See also Hartman 1997, Buck-Morss 2000, and Wilderson 2020.

INTRODUCTION

1. At the start of a seminar on "Blackness and Universality," I asked graduate students how they understood the relationship between Blackness and Universality. At

some point, one of the students circled back and asked the question quoted here. The original questions on the course syllabus were as follows: "How do we think Blackness and Universality together? Can they be combined? Is Blackness always outside of the universal? Is that its very definition? If this is the case, how can one think about politics and Blackness together? If it is not the case, how does one explain the global persistence of anti-Blackness? Or is it anti-Blackness that is universal?"

2. Blackness cannot and should not be thought of as separate from gender, sexuality, (dis)ability, capacities (see Puar 2017), political/economic possibility, or place. It is necessary, in fact, to consider Blackness in relationship to multiple, interlinking positions together (see Hull, Bell-Scott, and Smith 1982; Combahee River Collective 1986; Crenshaw 1989, 1991; Puar 2012). Also see the "key terms" at the end of this book for more discussion.

3. Here, "Turkish, Arab, Turkish-, and Arab-Germans" includes minoritized populations within the countries primarily viewed by normative Germans as Turkish or Arab.

CHAPTER 1

1. What I would call *Black resources* are different from what Brown calls "diasporic resources," in the sense that Black resources exceed any one diaspora or group.

2. "In Locke's view, the origin of slavery, like the origin of liberty and property, was entirely outside the social contract" (PSWC, 119). Locke's philosophical argument tempered the universality of equality in the state of nature with the necessity of consent before a social contract could be undertaken, thereby excluding, explicitly, children and idiots from the contract and by inference others who were uneducated or uneducable. See Mehta 1990, cited in Buck-Morss 2000, 827n17. In Buck-Morss's text, PSWC refers to David Brion Davis's *The Problem of Slavery in Western Culture* (1966).

3. On intersectionality see Combahee River Collective 1986; Crenshaw 1989, 1991; Ferguson 2004.

4. See Partridge (2012) for an analysis of "exclusionary incorporation."

5. In *Homo Sacer* (1998, 105), Giorgio Agamben outlines the limits of citizenship as follows: "In the system of the nation-state, the so-called sacred and inalienable rights of man show themselves to lack every protection and reality at the moment in which they can no longer take the form of rights belonging to citizens of a state. If one considers the matter, this is in fact implicit in the ambiguity of the very title of the French Declaration of the Rights of Man and Citizen, of 1789. In the phrase *La declaration des droits de l'homme et du citoyen*, it is not clear whether the two terms *homme* and *citoyen* name two autonomous beings or

instead form a unitary system in which the first is always already included in the second. And if the latter is the case, the kind of relation that exists between *homme* and *citoyen* still remains unclear. From this perspective, Burke's *boutade* according to which he preferred his 'Rights of an Englishman' to the inalienable rights of man acquires an unsuspected profundity."

Following Wilderson (2020), I would argue that "the human" also needs to be put into question. Even if Black people think of themselves as human, their historical and contemporary treatment constantly proves otherwise. Being "human" offers no guarantees of protection, not to mention thriving. We need something else. Beginning with Blackness is one possibility of thinking that something else into existence. Here, I do recognize the possibility of pluriversal approaches (Mignolo 2007), including Indigenous ones—with the additional recognition that Black can also be Indigenous—but I am focusing on Black possibility here. Part of the reason for this focus has to do with the fact that people are globally articulating Blackness in a way that it would be more difficult to do as an Indigenous person (particularly because those who are mobile have more difficulty claiming indigineity where they are local [see Selasi 2014]). It is also important to note what my recent graduate seminar members pointed out as the universality of anti-Blackness. I would argue that Blackness does not need to be everywhere as a lived experience in order to be universal as a necessary expression of those who are constantly being left out and excepted. The modern, Eurocentric, Enlightenment conceptualization of democracy seems to be built on a necessary blindness to slavery, rape, murder, and dispossession (Combahee River Collective 1986; Buck-Morss 2000).

6. In *Buddha is Hiding* (2003), Ong argues that immigrant incorporation into the United States should be read in terms of a Black/White bipolarity. Here, she thinks about the blackening of Cambodian immigrants versus the whitening of East Asian immigrants in their incorporation into American life. She attaches these processes of incorporation to an existing (historical rule) of "ethnic succession" (3). In this book, I argue that one needs to understand the global dynamics of a related form of incorporation, inasmuch as racial elements of enlightenment thinking have been globalized. Of course, many forms of colorism also preceded the Enlightenment and are prevalent outside of Europe. In any case, as suggested in the introduction, inasmuch as anti-Blackness seems to be universal, so does Blackness.

7. According to Ong (1999, 3), "David Harvey identifies flexibility as the modus operandi of late capitalism." She examines the ways in which wealthy Hong Kong residents, for example, use their capital to gain access to multiple passports in order not to be subject to the risks of having only one. By contrast, "Whereas the movements of capital have stimulated immigrant strategies of mobility, many poor Americans are unable to respond in quite the same way and are instead 'staying put' or 'being stuck' in place." Here, she also cites Williams 1993.

8. In *Afropessimism* (2020), Wilderson refers to Jared Sexton's (2010) differentiation between "citizen, noncitizen, and anticitizen," which assumes differentiation between "noncitizen" and "anticitizen." Sexton argues that anticitizenship is linked to Blackness. Both Wilderson and Sexton see Blackness as being outside the possibility of citizenship. I also see citizenship as always lacking, and always lacking for Black people, in particular (among others). While Blackness stands in, for me, for the impossibilties inherent in citizenship, I want to think with the broader category of noncitizenship in order to also see how, why, and in what circumstances those perceived as non-Black are also accessing Blackness. This possibility, even after one obtains formal membership is defined against (in opposition to) Blackness (see also Ong 2003).

9. According to Saidiya Hartman (2006, 5), "The very term 'slavery' derived from the word 'Slav,' because Eastern Europeans were the slaves of the medieval world. At the beginning of modernity, slavery declined in Europe as it expanded in Africa. . . . The Iberians can be credited, according to one historian, 'for restricting bondage, for the first time in history to peoples of African descent.'" Of course, the notion that the "Eastern Europeans were the slaves of the medieval world" is problematic in its formulation. From whose perspective were Eastern Europeans slaves? Who remained within and who was wholly outside of this formation? Where did Eastern Europe begin and where did it end? Hartman's broader point is to trace the history of the term and to think concretely about how it got attached to Blackness. See also Kopp (2012) on Polishnesss and Blackness.

10. "The gaping hole of history and knowledge that Afro-futurism fills with fantasy and the multiverse embraces the greatest power a story can hold by reinstituting the ultimate hero's journey.

"When Dr. Quantum was asked about the lessons of possible time travel and his scientific discoveries, he said, 'The past is being created as much as the future. Once you get yourself into the position of creating the past, present, and future, rather than just being a victim of the past you become a magician. . . .'" (Womack 2013, 155).

11. See Amy Goodman, The Freedom Struggle in 2020: Angela Davis on Protests, Defunding Police & Toppling Racist Statues, *Democracy Now*, December 31, 2002, https://www.democracynow.org/2020/12/31/the_freedom_struggle_in_2020_angela, accessed January 1, 2020.

12. In *Habeas Viscus* (2014, 2), Alexander Weheliye notes: "Building on Hortense Spillers's distinction between body and flesh and the writ of habeas corpus, I use the phrase *habeas viscus*—'You shall have the flesh'—on the one hand to signal how violent political domination activates a fleshly surplus that simultaneously sustains and disfigures said brutality, and, on the other hand, to reclaim the atrocity of flesh as a pivotal arena for the politics emanating from different traditions of the oppressed. The flesh, rather than displacing bare life or civil

death, excavates the social (after) life of these categories: it represents a racializing assemblage of subjection that can never annihilate the lines of flight, freedom dreams, practices of liberation, and possibilities of worlds. Nonetheless, genres of the human I discuss in *Habeas Viscus* ought not to be understood within the lexicons of resistance and agency, because, as explanatory tools, these concepts have a tendency to blind us, whether through strenuous denials or exalted celebrations of their existence, to the manifold occurrences of freedom in zones of indistiction. . . . How might we go about thinking and living enfleshment otherwise so as to usher in different genres of the human, and how might we accomplish this tax through the critical project of black studies?" Recognizing the limits of "humanity" as an analytical or legal category, the current book works to think politics and possibility through Blackness.

CHAPTER 2

1. As Heide Fehrenbach (2005, 65) finds: "In a survey conducted in the early 1950s, German social workers queried German women to determine why they become involved with Black troops. (Tellingly, this question was not posed to women who fraternized with White troops.) On the basis of interviews with 552 women, social workers concluded that for 56 percent 'material benefits were decisive': 'For the women themselves, it was naturally a great inducement to satisfy their hunger with American canned foods, and, in addition, obtain tasty treats, cigarettes, silk stockings and money from their colored boyfriends.' However, such incentives were not the only motivation, as social workers found. Of the remaining 44 percent of women polled, 27 percent responded that they had chosen African American lovers on the basis of affection or love, and 17 percent said they were motivated by sexual curiosity, carnal desire, or 'simply the wish not to be outdone by their friends who already had negro boyfriends.'"

2. Even in the arena of consumer goods, "canned food" is enhanced by a desire that exceeds the function of eating to avoid hunger. It is clear to me that fiction film is just as critical to daily life as other forms of sociocultural production and critique.

3. This is a term that refers to Germany's economic miracle after the Second World War. Like "Miss" in English, *"Fräulein"* is a somewhat antiquated term that refers to an unmarried woman.

CHAPTER 3

1. As Butler (1993, 122) notes, "In Althusser's notion of interpellation, it is the police who initiate the call or address by which a subject becomes socially

constituted. There is the policeman, the one who not only represents the law but whose address 'Hey you!' has the effect of binding the law to the one who is hailed."

2. While historian Timothy S. Brown (2006) has written about the process of "(African) Americanization and Hip Hop in Germany," importantly pointing out the mass appeal of the genre (also among White Germans), I am interested here in the longer trajectory of the relevance of Blackness to political mobilization in unanticipated locations. Following Ayse Çalgar (1998), I am also interested in the degree to which the promotion of the global connections to Blackness at times take on official state forms, such as in the work of social workers at youth centers in Berlin (see also Bennett 1999 for the connection between state-sponsored youth centers and the promotion of hip-hop). In a 2009 tour of his neighborhood, Neco Celik pointed out that American officials had actively participated in the programming of his youth center, where he grew up and ultimately became a media pedagogue.

3. Of course, the desire for African American men and Africa are linked, as can be seen in the example of Leni Riefenstahl's visual shift from Jesse Owens to *The Nuba*.

4. "Althusser conjectures this 'hailing' or 'interpellation' as a unilateral act, as the power and force of the law to compel fear at the same time that it offers recognition at an expense" (Butler 1993, 122). The cost of recognition is a result of the fact that the one being hailed/interpellated is simultaneously being identified as one who has trespassed—i.e., violated the law. Butler asks later: "Are there are [*sic*] other ways of being addressed and constituted by the law, ways of being occupied and occupying the law, that disarticulate the power of punishment from the power of recognition?" This is a critical point underlying the politics of occupation. Under conditions of African American occupation, the performance of Black Americanness opens up the possibilities for others to be recognized and not punished for not living up to previous ideals of Germanness. Occupation changes the conditions of enforcement while still referencing a politics of recognition, by the military police in Massaquoi's case—the fact that he is hailed does not lead to punishment but to a transformation of his status—to German women who now openly desire and ultimately recognize African men in spaces and contexts made possible, in part, as a result of African American occupation.

5. In popular discourse, Kreuzberg became shorthand for Turkish-German urban life, or, more crassly, the problematically named "Turkish ghetto." On the other hand, one should note that since Celik's youth, this position has changed significantly. Kreuzberg, once on the edge of West Berlin, is now in the center of the unified city. Since the fall of the Wall, it has rapidly become one of the most popular districts for hip students and partygoers, in addition to remaining a long-term mecca for 1968-generation bohemians, anarchist house squatters (at least until most were forced out and removed or forced to buy their build-

ings), and other cosmopolitans, now including real estate speculators and urban professionals.

6. This was part of one of the two original postal codes. The postal code 36 still signifies the "rawer," more radical side of Kreuzberg.

7. In the German context, one can link "African Americanness" to recognizability not only via the history of occupation, but also via its link to "urban culture" in contrast to "rural Anatolia," seen as a space of tradition, and linked (in the popular German imagination) to women wearing headscarves, charges of anti-Semitism, etc.

8. Gemünden (1998, vii) notes that Americanization comes in part through a culture of opposition: "As Theodor W. Adorno once remarked, 'It is scarcely an exaggeration to say that a contemporary consciousness that has not appreciated the American experience, even in opposition, has something reactionary about it.' Though Adorno did not know Frank Zappa, he may well have been thinking about him when he made this out-of-character statement, because it captures Zappa's obstinate, oppositional, and irreducible music."

9. See also Kanak Attak 1998; Heine 2016. According to Heine, Kanak originally referred to the Hawaiian term for human but has since come to reference British, French, and German terms for people in the South Pacific. While it has at times meant foreigner in Germany, it now refers in a derogatory way to Turkish and Arab Germans, in particular.

10. Arslan is another Turkish-German director who has received funding to make films about his neighborhood, what Mennel (2002b) (problematically) analyzes under the rubric of a transnational "ghetto" aesthetic.

11. It seems important to note that the forms of Blackness here are often linked to commercial success, whereas Blackness more broadly conceived offers a wider range of possibility. Again, it is important to distinguish Blackness as a possibility and Blackness as alimit. Activists and artists such as Angela Davis, Muhammad Ali, and Malcolm X are exciting referents, precisely because they push normative and normalizing boundaries. Finally, even while commercial success might be important to many media makers in Germany, the fact that the major funds for filmmaking and film study come from state-backed institutions also suggests other means towards Black ends, which, one might argue, are also linked to a universal claim.

12. Aihwa Ong (2003) points out that for Southeast Asian immigrants to the United States, there is not this same possibility, as they are more likely to become Black(ened) amidst the Black/White polarization linked to Americanized incorporation.

13. The Free University's website states: "A protest meeting was organized in the West part of the city as the University Unter den Linden withdrew the admission of three students on political grounds. On December 4, 1948, active students and professors with support from Berlin politicians and the

American occupation power founded the Free University" (Freie Universität Berlin, n.d.)

14. Again, one should note the relationship of the Free University to Cold War politics and the American occupation.

CHAPTER 4

1. One of Allen Pred's interventions was to note that the various forms and targets of racism are multiple (see Pred 2000).

2. Again, I know that these categories are a problematic gloss. They also include those who are often excluded from these national, racial, and linguistic imaginaries such as people who are or descend from Kurdish people and regions, descendants of Berbers, and many others. In calling the students "German" in this context, I am less concerned with their official legal status or whether or not they identify as German—most do not, at least not in an unqualified sense—but with the fact that they have either been born in or socialized in Germany.

3. In reporting about a Turkish-German guide (Ufuk Topkara), then at the Jewish Museum in Berlin, and his young Turkish-German visitors, the *Frankfurter Allgemeine Zeitung* gave an account of a visit to the Museum by a class from a school where 96 percent of the students had parents "who were not born in Germany": "Only eight students have come. A girl from an Arab family simply did not show up this morning. 'One can absolutely assume that her absence is on purpose,' the teacher Elke Menzel says. 'And sometimes I also assume this.' Menzel was also not sure that Zafer would come today. But now he is sitting next to the other fifth graders on a bench on the ground by the Jewish Museum in Berlin. 'Do I also have to go with the class? I'm not a Jew at all,' Zafer had asked in class a couple of days before. He was required to go" (*Frankfurter Allgemeine Zeitung* 2008b). In a piece on the Jewish Museum, the *Deutsche Welle* and *Qantara* quote Topkara: "The teachers often tell us that the children say to them: 'Why should I go to the Jewish Museum? I have nothing to do with the Holocaust!'" (Deutsche Welle and Qantara.de 2008).

4. This part of the original Reichstag structure had been preserved by the British architect of the modernized reconstruction to commemorate the Soviet victory against the Nazis.

5. For more on the relationships between Holocaust memorialization, memory, and touch, see Adelson (2005).

6. In "Between Anti-Semitism and Islamophobia: Some Thoughts on the New Europe," Matti Bunzl (2005) is careful to distinguish between contemporary and previous (nineteenth-century) anti-Semitisms. He also wants to demonstrate a break between anti-Semitism and what he calls Islamophobia. In a response to the piece, Dominic Boyer (2005) points out that the legitimacy of the European

Union is, in part, based on the prevention of future holocausts. In this chapter, I am not arguing for an analytical continuity between the genocidal logic of the Nazi era and contemporary racisms (see Pred 2000), but for an analytical and political connection between the politics of Holocaust memorialization and anti-racist politics now. At the same time, we should acknowledge that anti-racism is only a starting point for what should ultimately be policies that promote the flourishing of those who experience the effects of racism on a nearly daily basis. This call is driven, in part, by what I have observed, from 1995 through the present, as a refusal to name racism as such in mainstream politics, unless it mimics forms previously recognized by the White mainstream. This refusal to name the problem is combined with a finger-pointing mentality that blames racialized Others for their "refusal to integrate." As anyone who follows contemporary European politics knows, this is not a distinctly German problem.

7. As Bruce Mannheim has pointed out (personal communication), the German novel has its own important place, and monumental status, in German history. Reading backward from my argument about the monumentality of Holocaust memory, the book becomes something like a portable monument, sustaining a sense of "Germanness" even without a state. In the case of the Holocaust Memorial, its location within the nation-state and its fixity are both critical to understanding the ways in which the terms of belonging, and ideas of homeland, have now shifted. Buried there are not actual people, but rather nationalist and European memories.

8. According to the *Frankfurter Allgemeine Zeitung* (2001), "Historian Peter Schöttler initiated the protest and within a few days a number of historians and colleagues in cultural studies have joined him. They are asking for 'an immediate stop to this absurd campaign that gives the impression that the Berlin Memorial is first and foremost oriented against deniers, when, in reality it is supposed to serve the memory of the victims of the Holocaust.' The signatories include Holocaust researchers such as Christopher Browning, Saul Friedländer, and Hans Mommse, academics including Carlo Ginzburg, Richard J. Evans, and Judith Butler, Gary Smith from the American Academy, Reinhard Rürup from the foundation 'Topography of the Terror,' the sociologist Heinz Bude, and the author Marlene Steeruwit."

9. While Eisenman himself resists interpreting the Memorial, on a March 2009 visit, and in an earlier conversation with an official Holocaust Memorial guide after a presentation of Irit Dekel's ethnographic work on the Memorial (see also Dekel 2009), I was struck that the guide referred directly to the memorializing function of the stelae, which, he pointed out, referenced ancient Greek practices of honoring the dead. It was apparent that he did not want to leave interpretation open to chance with a group of visitors in their twenties from the nearby city of Magdeburg. Magdeburg has been the site of dramatic neo-Nazi attacks. When the guide spoke independently with the group's chaperone and

asked if some of them were right-wing, the latter said that he was not sure, but that it was possible. When the guide showed a picture from another nearby memorial, of a dining room table with a fallen chair, and spoke about Gestapo raids of Jewish homes, I noticed two of the young men laughing.

10. "Wir wolten ihnen [die Besucher] also nicht vorschreiben, was sie denken sollen, sondern ihnen das Nachdenken ermörglichen."

11. The answer to the Frequently Asked Questions continues: "However, the Foundation also has the task of acknowledging and preserving the memory of all victims of National Socialism. This also involves building memorials to the Sinti and Roma and to homosexual victims, which the Federal Government has already decided upon" (*Stiftung Denkmal* 2008). These additional memorials have now been constructed in Berlin.

12. This can be seen, for example, in the debate about the role of Germany's military (noncombatant) participation in Afghanistan and the German call for a NATO air strike that ended up killing nearly one hundred Afghanis (Eddy 2021).

13. While a counter-monument movement (see Young 1993) and even Eisenman himself try to get beyond the problem of monumentality and call for ongoing reflection, these counter-movements have not been successful in the same way in producing a national discussion about memory, responsibility, and atonement (see Till 2005).

14. This was a parliamentary agreement that reduced the possibility of asylum in Germany. While it did not eliminate asylum, it made entry by airplane with evidence of foreign government persecution one of the only ways in which one could be recognized as a refugee in Germany. An exception was the refugee welcome policy that was initially part of a mass movement until it was largely abandoned; see chapter 7, where I explore the problematics of a politics based on pity.

15. In mainstream German media accounts and in the mainstream public imagination, Germans imagine a distinction between Germanness and Jewishness.

16. Michael Rothberg's (2019) discussion of "implication" or "implicated subjects" is an important addition to this discussion, inasmuch as at it attends to those who are implicated even if they did not participate directly in historical or contemporary atrocities. Implication, however, is also distinct from my focus on perpetration here, which remains a persistent issue.

17. Part of the innovation of this most recent articulation of memorialization itself is that it honors the murdered Jews of Europe, not only of Germany. In the Information Center, one sees that the largest number of murdered Jews were actually Polish. Furthermore, one sees that the concentration and extermination camps were aggregated in Eastern Europe while memorialization has taken place primarily in Western Europe (as an audio tour of the information center points out). One wonders if there is an implicit point about the "progress" of Western Europe in pointing to the frequency of its contemporary sites of memorialization.

18. Michael Rothberg (2019, 1) defines "implicated subjects" as follows: "Implicated subjects occupy positions aligned with power and privilege without being themselves direct agents of harm; they contribute to, inhabit, inherit, or benefit from regimes of domination but do not originate or control such regimes. An implicated subject is neither a victim nor a perpetrator, but rather a participant in 'histories and social formations that generate the positions of victim and perpetrator, and yet in which most people do not occupy such clear-cut roles.'"

19. The controversy around the question about "Whether or not the Jewish Museum is really Jewish" has complicated questions around whether or not non-Jewish figures could lead the Museum and the Museum's relationship to those who openly have an ambivilant stance in relation to Israeli policy (see Eddy 2019b).

20. It is important to note that the Jewishness of the Jewish museum was put into question in 2019, when the non-Jewish director ultimately resigned over a social media post that he sent out referencing Jewish Israeli support for the Boycott, Divestment, Sanctions movement in regards to Israel. The *New York Times* wrote about the incident as follows: "'Enough is enough. The Jewish Museum appears to be completely out of control,' the head of the Central Council of Jews in Germany, Josef Schuster, wrote in a response published on Tuesday. He went on to question whether it was still 'appropriate' to call the museum 'Jewish,' and said the council no longer trusted the institution" (Eddy 2019a).

21. According to Rothberg, "The model of multidirectional memory posits collective memory as partially disengaged from exclusive versions of cultural identity and acknowledges how remembrance both cuts across and binds together diverse spatial, temporal, and cultural sites" (2009, 11).

22. Tzvetan Todorov has argued, "It is often right to want to erect a monument to the past in order not to forget, in order to preserve the memory. But it is even better that it become at the same time an instrument to help us think and live better in the present" (2001, 19).

23. Again, the example of the Turkish-German guide at the Jewish Museum offers a counterexample, but it is an unusual case. It is clearly not the norm in the German classroom, where most teachers are much older than their pupils and are very unlikely to be Turkish-German.

24. These are my translations of a conversation that took place in German.

25. This claim seems similar to Michael Rothberg's assertion that "Comparisons, analogies, and other multidirectional invocations are an inevitable part of the struggle for justice" (2009, 29). Against memory as a zero-sum game or as necessarily universal, he suggests the possibility of "multidirectional memory" (on Rothberg see also note 18; on memorialization, note 17). See also Gryglewski 2009.

26. The woman insisted on speaking with me in English. She had grown up in Australia and only returned to Germany as an adult. She said that when she saw someone who looks like me, it was strange for her to speak to the person in German.

CHAPTER 5

1. This is true in spite of what Yasemin Sosyal (1994) claims about noncitizen access to social welfare benefits in northern Europe, i.e. that one receives them whether or not one is a formal citizen.

2. As we will see in the next chapter, the arts are not a luxury form of participation, but vital.

3. By pointing to *exclusionary incorporation*, I point to how the states that most forthrightly claim democracy often incorporate noncitizens and radicalized bodies, needing them for their economies and also their arts, while simultaneously systematically forcing then to have limited access to full participation, to face differential forms of regulation and never to fully become citizens, sometimes even to become noncitizens (Partridge 2003).

4. By emphasizing the "actually existing" (see Verdery 1995) nature of democracy in practice as opposed to democracy in theory, I am emphasizing the fact that the actually existing form never meets the ideals people often claim for it. Even in ancient Greek democracy there were slaves. In writing about "actually existing socialism" anthropologist Katherine Verdery distinguishes between socialist ideology and everyday socialism: "[T]he expression 'real' or 'actually existing' socialism came into use, to distinguish its messy reality from its hopes and claims" (4). In her analysis, Verdery cites "Rudolph Bahro's term 'actually existing socialism,' in his *The Alternative in East Europe* (London: Verso, 1978)" (235n4).

5. For more on slow death, see Berlant (2007). My use here is closest to Puar's in *The Right to Maim* (2017).

6. For these insights, I am grateful to the work of Benjamin Rastakoff, particularly a talk he gave on January 30, 2022 on "Du Bois Before Warsaw, Fascism Before Racism" in conversation with Amelia Glaser (see https://www.youtube .com/watch?v = YJ0LkykJMVo, accessed March 17, 2022). See also Du Bois (1952); Rothberg (2001, 2009).

7. Of course, as the qualifications "more," in "more respect" and "more equality" imply, Black equality was not equal, even in Germany. Black military and social occupation, though, played a significant role in the reception of Blackness in post-World War II Germany. The point, then, is not that democracy is adequate as an end for Black liberation. The point is to trace the systematic reproduction of this limit. If we trace *democratization* as a form of incorporation, we can see how this limit is systematically reproduced.

8. An American journalist friend who lives in Berlin often jokes that the freest moment in the United States was the moment of Reconstruction, when the South was being occupied by Union soldiers. If freedom for Black people requires occupation, including their role as occupiers, then what does that say about freedom? Occupation, at least in the military sense, of course, is also a always a form of vio-

lence. Perhaps, in these cases, it is defensive, but it seems to me that liberation would be the moment after the necessity for that violence. On the other hand, if violence is required to achieve liberation, then one, at least those who have committed the acts of violence, will never be free.

9. See, for example, Kluge et al (2010). Fassbinder's contribution to this collective film project is particularly striking.

10. The Bundesministerium für Familie, Senioren, Frauen und Jugend (my translation).

11. "Zentrales Ziel ist es, durch Einbindung aller gesselschaftlichen Kräfte vor Ort gemeinsame Strategien für eine starke Demokratie zu entwickeln.

Jeder Lokale Aktionsplan erhält dazu eine jährliche Förderung von 100.000 €.

Lokale Koordinierungsstllen verwalten diese Fördermittel, Einzelne Projekte können mit bis zu 20.000 € unterstützt werden" (my translation).

12. "Der Kampf gegen Rechtsextremismus, Antisemitismus und Fremdenfeindlichkeit wird damit dort gestärkt, wo er geführt werden muss: in den Kommunen und Landkreisen vor Ort" (my translation).

13. See Stewart (2017).

14. Here, I recognize Rothberg's (2019) point that even those who are not perpetrators might nevertheless be (and often are) implicated in prior atrocity whether or not they participated in the actual events. Living as a non-indigenous person in a settler-colonial state is one example of implication.

15. See also a recent discussion about the Historikerstreit 2.0 in the blog of the *Journal of the History of Ideas* (Catlin 2022a, 2022b).

16. See also Bunzl (2005) and Özyürek (2005).

17. "Auch die erstinstanzliche Jury der senatseigenen Kulturprojekte GmbH wollte von Kritik zunächst nichts wissen. Sie hatte noch im März der 100.000-Euro-Förderung für Refugee Club Impulse RCI zugestimmt. Erst nach der Intervention des American Jewish Committee und ersten Presseberichten zog der letztinstanzliche Beirat die Zustimmung kurzfristig zurück. Jetzt wolle man besser prüfen, welche Arbeit von und mit Flüchtlingen gefördert wird, sagt der stellvertretende Geschäftsführer der Kulturprojekte GmbH Torsten Wöhlert:

"Natürlich haben wir eigene rote Linien. Das betrifft die Frage Antisemitismus, die Haltung zum Staat Israel, den Umgang mit Xenophobie, die Gleichberechtigung der Geschlechter, und das sind kulturelle Konflikte, die auf uns zukommen werden. Das ist für uns als Kulturfonds auch ein Lernprozess. Es ist die erste Runde, die wir mit solchen Projektbewilligungen haben" (my translation).

18. "Hätte also das American Jewish Committee nicht in sprichwörtlich letzter Minute interveniert, wäre dem RCI-Theaterprojekt eine erhebliche Summe zugesprochen worden. Nach dem Eklat hofft Deidre Berger vom Berliner AJC-Büro nun auf mehr Sensibilität beim Berliner Senat" (my translation).

CHAPTER 6

1. Throughout this book, POC stands for People of Color.

2. The artistic director asked those who expressed explicitly racist positions to leave, or he expressly decided not to invite them back.

3. "Beschäftigung schaffende Maßnahmen sind Teil aktiver Arbeitsmarkt-politik. Sie sollen zusätzliche Arbeit zur Verfügung stellen, Teilhabe am Arbeitsleben für besonders benachteiligte Personen ermöglichen, als Brücke in den 'regulären' 'allgemeinen' Arbeitsmarkt fungieren, aber auch wirtschafts- bzw. strukturpolitische Ziele erfüllen. Unter der Vielzahl unterschiedlicher Instrumente, die zu diesen Maßnahmen zu zählen sind, gehören Arbeitsbeschaffungsmaßnahmen (ABM) und Arbeitsgelegenheiten (AGH, Ein-Euro-Jobs) zu den bekanntesten. . . ." ("The Employment Policy Measures are part of an active job market politics. They are designed to create additional job offerings, to create the possibility of participating in the job market for especially disadvantaged persons, to facilitate a bridge to the 'regular' 'common' job market, but also to achieve economic and political goals. Of the many different instruments that these policies include, Employment Creation Measures (ABM) and Casual Labor Work Possibilities (AGH, One Euro Jobs) are the most well known") (my translation). For more on the history of these efforts and how they have changed over time in Germany, see Oschmiansky 2020.

4. I am paraphrasing here.

5. This was true, with the exception of one blond cast member.

6. See, for example, *Der Braune Mob* (2008). As Priscilla Layne and Elizabeth Stewart (2021) note: "Black Germans' increasing engagement with theatre could possibly be linked to the more public presence they achieved in 2011 with the creation of Bündnis Bühnenwatch (Alliance Stage Watch), which was founded to tackle the problem of blackface on German stages. Beginning with a performance of Herb Gardner's *Ich bin nicht Rappaport* (I Am not Rappaport) at the Schlosspark Theatre in Berlin during the 2011/2012 season, a series of incidents involving blackface in German theatres sparked outrage among Black German activists. Bühnenwatch published a statement on their website, declaring '[i]t is our intention, to prevent any future racist depictions of blackface and racist discrimination against actors of Colour'" (54).

7. In *Buddha is Hiding*, Ong writes about the ways in which east versus southeast Asian immigrants get incorporated into American life. She analyzes this in terms of a Black-White continuum. In this sense, Cambodian immigrants get Blackened, while East Asian immigrants find themselves thought of in terms as being more closely aligned with Whiteness. This is not to say that any of these immigrants become White, but to think about how incorporation, in the American context, works.

8. See work on Afrofuturism, for example, Womack 2018, Layne 2018, and Layne and Stewart 2021.

9. In our conversations in the theater, we also spoke about the critiques of the Black Panthers. The actors learned about and spoke critically about the links between male chauvinism and nationalism. But they also insisted on Blackness as a means for political action. The critique did not foreclose the remaining possibility. It suggested an anti-sexist Black Power and took up Angela Davis as one of its leaders.

10. *KulTür Auf* has been an organization within the theater designed to think about how to make interventions in the cultural landscape where youth of color are often excluded, in part because they are not seen as artists or their art is not seen as "high art." The name of the group is a play on *Kultur* (culture) with the word *Tür* embedded, which references opening the cultural door.

11. For more on the notion that "Everyone is an Artist" (*Jeder mensch ist ein Kulstler*), see Krüger 1979, as well as Beuys 1975.

12. "'Soziokultur' belaufen sich auf einen Bruchteil der Ausgaben für 'Hochkulturförderung,' und ermöglichen in den seltensten Fällen eine langfristige Förderung, was gerade im Theater die Möglichkeiten einer künstlerischen Entwicklung stark beschränkt22" (Haakh 2021). ["'Social Culture' only receives a fraction of the funding given to 'High Culture.' It is also only rare cases when 'Social Culture' receives long-term funding. Especially in theater, this strongly reduces the possibilities for an artistic development."]

13. While I quote Althusser here, I also recognize, call attention to, and condemn the killing of his wife, Helene Rytmann-Légotien. I also note that, while I am aware of this specific case of violence, there are many others (also amongst the authors I cite) of which I am not aware. In addition, I recognize my own failings, but nevertheless work to be better everyday and condemn, in general, what bell hooks (2014) has referred to as "imperialist, white supremacist, capitalist, patriarchy" in a conversation with Cornel West. In his article about Althusser killing his wife, I think that William S. Lewis (2019) misses hooks's point.

14. About debility, Jasbir Puar notes: "In *The Right to Maim: Debility, Capacity, Disability*, I think through how and why bodies are perceived as debilitated, capacitated, or often simultaneously both. I mobilize the term 'debility' as a needed disruption (but also expose it as a collaborator) of the category of disability and as a triangulation of the ability/disability binary, noting that while some bodies may not be recognized as or identify as disabled, they may well be debilitated, in part by being foreclosed access to legibility and resources as disabled. Relatedly, some bodies may well be disabled but also capacitated. I want to be clear here: I am not diluting or diffusing the identity rubrics of disability by suggesting all bodies are disabled to some extent or another, or by smoothing disability into a continuum of debility and capacity. Quite the opposite; I am arguing

that the three vectors, capacity, debility, and disability, exist in a mutually rein-forcing constellation, are often overlapping or coexistent, and that debilitation is a necessary component that both exposes and sutures the non-disabled/disabled binary" (2017, xv). I am grateful to Paula Batista for bringing my attention back to this passage in our discussions. It seems significant that this passage appears in the preface of Puar's book under the heading "Hands Up, don't Shoot," an obvious referent to the protest against the debilitation of Black life, but in a book that also ultimately addresses the purposeful maiming (as opposed to immedi-ate killing) of Palestinians.

15. For the original German see Mind the Trap 2014; this is my translation.

CHAPTER 7

1. I do not mean the United Nations' legal definition of the term "refugee." I am referring to the everyday definition, that is, someone seeking refuge.

2. Here, the boy's death is ultimately read retrospectively as a sacrifice, even if initially unintentional. Unlike Agamben's (1998) noncitizen *Homo Sacer,* who can be killed without being sacrificed, the European contribution to the boy's death, which an analyst might otherwise read as the result of a murderous Euro-pean immigration/refugee politics, is redeemed through the shift in Merkel's position. His death is now given new meaning. He was retrospectively killed so that others might come; however, this re-signification does not undo the horror of his loss. It also cannot completely remove the stains of blood from the hands of those who retroactively sacrifice and now pity.

3. For Arendt's comments see Arendt (1958).

4. See, for example, Susan Buck-Morss's (2000) account of Hegel's thinking about the Haitian revolution in relation to his theorization of the master/slave dialectic (also see introduction). For European Enlightenment philosophers including Locke, Hegel, and Rousseau, theorizing the possibilities for freedom was a central concern. According to Buck-Morss: "[By] the eighteenth century, slavery had become the root metaphor of Western political philosophy, connot-ing everything that was evil about power relations. Freedom, its conceptual antithesis, was considered by Enlightenment thinkers as the highest and univer-sal political value" (821).

5. See http://www.filmingfuturecities.org, accessed December 8, 2021. In various polls over the years through which I conducted this research, Germany was ranked as either the best (see Chew 2016) or the most popular country in the world (see BBC 2013). I would argue that the fact that so many refugees came to Germany during the "crisis" suggests that refugees also saw it as one of the most highly desired destinations.

6. I would note here that speaking as if pitied people and citizens are actually equals in the eyes of the economy or the law glosses over the actual power dynamics.

7. The translation in *The New York Times* (Coburn 2015) uses the word "imagine."

8. The translation here is a mixture of the translation from *The New York Times* (Coburn 2015) and my own. I occasionally changed the words when I thought that alternative words were more important. I also added descriptions in parentheses to give a sense of the scene. Finally, as noted in the text, I added the "umms" heard in the original video to convey the awkwardness of the exchange. Merkel is usually regarded as a well-spoken leader, but, in this moment, she struggled to find the right words.

9. In 2017, the rights to residency for Reem Sahwil were extended indefinitely, but the initial temporariness of this extension remains significant, particularly from the perspective of the fourteen-year-old whose future seemed indefinite.

10. See, for example Terkessidis 2016, where a frequent spokesperson against racism works to substantiate a seemingly racist stereotype about North Africans. See also *Focus* (2016).

11. Here I do not mean the border agent as a specific individual who might also struggle through the contradictions of contemporary life, including the symbolic violence represented in his or her position *vis-à-vis* refugees; rather, I refer to the border agent as a legal category/subject position, under Schengen Law and the Dublin Regulation, intended to control the movement of refugees.

12. While supposedly universal, the terminology is problematically gendered.

CONCLUSION

1. For the Initiative of Blacks in Germany see https://isdonline.de.

2. Buck-Morss (2000) points to a moment of potential light in Hegel's thinking, his inspiration for the Master-Slave Dialectic. But she has to do a lot of background work to make this claim. Hegel, himself, doesn't explicitly acknowledge it. From my perspective, then, Hegel's inspiration from the Haitian revolution reads more like plagiarism, stealing from the liberatory claims of Black life, and not directly supporting them in the efforts towards liberation. That is not enough.

3. Foucault emphasizes biopower (1990), governmentality and the triangle between sovereignty, discipline, and governance, with the production of the population as the main goal under what he calls an "art of governance" (1991). I emphasize sovereignty here, because it is the form of power that is most critical in thinking about the articulations and regulations of Blackness. It is also what

Black people are ultimately up against when thinking about social change. Carl Schmitt (2005 [1922]) defines sovereignty in terms of "he who decides on the state of exception." In *The History of Sexuality* Foucault writes about sovereign power being exercised through the threat of death. Biopower, he argues, is focused on the fostering of life. In that same text, Foucault writes about liberation in terms of an emphasis on bodies and pleasures. Elsewhere, he writes about liberation in terms of "not being governed quite so much" (1997, 29).

4. While Mbembe's analysis is helpful, it does not yet offer a politics to counter these forms. On the other hand, a politics offered or imagined by a single individual also would not be adequate.

5. Although the extent to which Blackness is at the center of Puar's analysis is not clear.

6. The student's film, made as part of the series I direct on Filming the Future of Detroit, was about how to make spaces more accessible for those who experience life as "neurologically atypical" (Levy 2021).

Bibliography

Adelson, Leslie A. 2005. *The Turkish Turn in Contemporary German Literature: Towards a New Critical Grammar of Migration*. New York: Palgrave Macmillan.

Agamben, Giorgio. 1998. *Homo Sacer: Sovereign Power and Bare Life*. Stanford, CA: Stanford University Press.

———. 2005. *State of Exception*. Chicago: University of Chicago Press.

Aikins, Joshua Kwesi. 2008. "Die alltägliche Gegenwart der kolonialen Vergangenheit. Entinnerung, Erinnerung und Verantwortung in der Kolonialmetropole Berlin." In *Afrika. Europas verkannter Nachbar, Bd. 2. Ansichten und Einsichten aus Theorie und Praxis*, edited by Herta Däubler-Gmelin, et al., 47–68. Frankfurt: Peter Lang.

Akin, Fatih, dir. 2004. *Kurz und schmerzlos*. Hamburg, Germany: Universal Studios.

Alsubee, Basil. 2001. "Detroit, the Intersection." In Filming the Future of Detroit film series at the University of Michigan in Ann Arbor, MI. Directed and curated by Damani Partridge.

Althusser, Louis. 2006. "Ideology and Ideological State Apparatuses (Notes Towards an Investigation)." *The Anthropology of the State: A Reader* 9, no. 1: 86–98.

Anderson, Benedict R. 1991. *Imagined Communities: Reflections on the Origin and Spread of Nationalism*. Rev. and extended ed. London: Verso.

Arendt, Hannah. 1958. *The Origins of Totalitarianism*. London: Allen & Unwin.

Arndt, S., and Ofuatey-Alazard, N., eds. 2011. *Wie Rassismus aus Wörtern spricht:(K) Erben des Kolonialismus im Wissensarchiv deutsche Sprache: ein kritisches Nachschlagewerk*. Münster: Unrast-Verlag.

Baer, A., and N. Sznaider. 2016. *Memory and Forgetting in the Post-Holocaust Era: The Ethics of Never Again*. London: Routledge.

Balibar, Étienne, and Immanuel Maurice Wallerstein. 1991. *Race, Nation, Class: Ambiguous Identities*. London: Verso.

BBC. 2002. "Sixty Years Since Holocaust Conference." January 20, 2002. http://news.bbc.co.uk/1/hi/world/europe/1771656.stm.

———. 2013. "BBC Poll: Germany Most Popular Country in the World." May 23, 2013. http://www.bbc.com/news/world-europe-22624104. Accessed April 5, 2022.

———. 2018. "Germany and Turkey Mark Solingen Deadly Racist Attack." May 29, 2018. https://www.bbc.com/news/world-europe-44288642. Accessed April 5, 2022.

Bennett, Andy. 1999. "Hip Hop am Main: The Localization of Rap Music and Hip Hop Culture." *Media, Culture & Society* 27: 77–91.

Berdahl, Daphne. 1999. *Where the World Ended: Re-unification and Identity in the German Borderland*. Berkeley: University of California Press.

Berlant, L. 2007. "Slow Death (Sovereignty, Obesity, Lateral Agency)." *Critical inquiry* 33, no. 4: 754–80.

———. 2011. *Cruel Optimism*. Durham, NC: Duke University Press.

Bernstein, Richard. 2003. "A Bold New View of Turkish-German Youth." *The New York Times*, April 12, 2003. https://www.nytimes.com/2003/04/12/world/the-saturday-profile-a-bold-new-view-of-turkish-german-youth.html.

Beuys, Joseph. 1975. *Jeder Mensch ist ein Künstler*. https://www.youtube.com/watch?v=Obw1zUA7BNo. Accessed April 5, 2022.

Blake, W., and H. Bloom. 1982. *The Complete Poetry and Prose of William Blake*. Berkeley: University of California Press.

Boyer, Dominic. 2005. "Welcome to the New Europe." *American Ethnologist* 32, no. 4: 521–23. doi:

Brauerhoch, Annette. 2003. "Foreign Affairs"—"Fräuleins as Agents," Panel VI. Germanness and Gender. http://www.unc.edu/depts/europe/conferences/Germany_celeb9900/abstracts/brauerhoch_ annette.html. Accessed April 4, 2003.

Braun, Stuart. 2020. "Street Name Change Major Step in Struggle to Decolonize Berlin. *DW.com*, August 28. https://www.dw.com/en/street-name-change-major-step-in-struggle-to-decolonize-berlin/a-54712751.

Brooks, Daphne A. 2008. Amy Winehouse and the (Black) Art of Appropriation. *The Nation*, September 29, 2008. Accessed July 24, 2019.

Brown, Jacqueline Nassy. 1998. "Black Liverpool, Black America, and the Gendering of Diasporic Space." *Cultural Anthropology* 13, no. 3: 291–325.

Brown, Timothy S. 2006. "'Keeping it Real' in a Different 'Hood: (African-) Americanization and Hip Hop in Germany." In *The Vinyl Ain't Final: Hip Hop and the Globalization of Black Popular Culture,* edited by Sidney J. Lemelle Dipannita Basu, 137–50. London: Pluto Press.

Brown, Wendy. 2006. *Regulating Aversion: Tolerance in the Age of Identity and Empire.* Princeton, NJ: Princeton University Press.

———. 1995. *States of Injury: Power and Freedom in Late Modernity.* Princeton, NJ: Princeton University Press.

Buck-Morss, Susan. 2000. "Hegel and Haiti." *Critical Inquiry* 26, no. 4: 821–65.

Bunzl, Matti. 2007. *Anti-Semitism and Islamophobia: Hatreds Old and New in Europe.* Chicago: Prickly Paradigm Press.

———. 2005. "Between Anti-Semitism and Islamophobia: Some Thoughts on the New Europe." *American Ethnologist* 32, no. 4: 499–508.

Buschkowsky, H. 2012. *Neukölln ist überall.* Ullstein eBooks.

Butler, Judith. 1993. *Bodies that Matter: On the Discursive Limits of "Sex."* New York: Routledge.

Çalgar, Ayse. 1998. "Popular Culture, Marginality and Institutional Incorporation: German-Turkish Rap and Turkish Pop in Berlin." *Cultural Dynamics* 10, no. 3: 243–61.

Campt, Tina. 2004. Other Germans: Black Germans and the Politics of Race, Gender, and Memory in the Third Reich. Ann Arbor: University of Michigan Press.

Catlin, Jonathon. 2022a. "A New German Historians' Debate? A Conversation with Sultan Doughan, A. Dirk Moses, and Michael Rothberg (Part I)." *Journal of the History of Ideas* blog. February 2, 2022. https://jhiblog.org/2022/02/02 /a-new-german-historians-debate-a-conversation-with-sultan-doughan-a-dirk-moses-and-michael-rothberg-part-i. Accessed March 18, 2022.

———. 2022b. "A New German Historians' Debate? A Conversation with Sultan Doughan, A. Dirk Moses, and Michael Rothberg (Part II)." *Journal of the History of Ideas* blog. February 4, 2022. https://jhiblog.org/2022/02/04 /a-new-german-historians-debate-a-conversation-with-sultan-doughan-a-dirk-moses-and-michael-rothberg-part-ii. Accessed March 18, 2022.

Chew, Jonathan. 2016. "This Country Was Named the Best in the World." *Fortune.com.* https://fortune.com/2016/01/20/germany-best-country-usnews. Accessed May 22, 2022.

Chin, Rita C-K. 2007. *The Guest Worker Question in Postwar Germany.* Cambridge, UK: Cambridge University Press.

Chin, R., Fehrenbach, H., Eley, G., & Grossmann, A. 2010. *After the Nazi Racial State: Difference and Democracy in Germany and Europe.* Ann Arbor: University of Michigan Press.

Coburn, Jesse. 2015. "Tearful Moment with Merkel Turns Migrant Girl Into a Potent Symbol." *New York Times,* July 21, 2015. https://www.nytimes.com

/2015/07/21/world/europe/legislation-gives-hope-to-girl-who-shared-plight-with-merkel.html.

Combahee River Collective. 1986. *The Combahee River Collective Statement: Black Feminist Organizing in the Seventies and Eighties.* Albany, NY: Kitchen Table: Women of Color Press.

Cox, Aimee Meredith. 2015. *Shapeshifters: Black Girls and the Choreography of Citizenship.* Durham, NC: Duke University Press.

Crenshaw, Kimberlé. 1991. "Mapping the Margins: Intersectionality, Identity Politics, and Violence against Women of Color." *Stanford Law Review* 43, no. 6: 1241–99.

———. 1989. Demarginalizing the Intersection of Race and Sex: A Black Feminist Critique of Antidiscrimination Doctrine, Feminist Theory and Antiracist Politics. *The University of Chicago Legal Forum Volume 1989: Feminism in the Law: Theory, Practice and Criticism:* 139–67.

De Genova, Nicholas, and Nathalie Peutz. 2010. *The Deportation Regime: Sovereignty, Space, and the Freedom of Movement.* Durham, NC: Duke University Press.

De León, Jason. 2015. *The Land of Open Graves: Living and Dying on the Migrant Trail.* Oakland, CA: University of California Press.

Dekel, Irit. "Ways of Looking: Observation and Transformation at the Holocaust Memorial, Berlin." *Memory Studies* 2, no. 1: 71–86.

Der Brauner Mob. 2008. "Germany: New Case of Blackface Advertising." https://blog.derbraunemob.info/2008/07/31/germany-new-case-of-blackface-advertising. Accessed August 9, 2019.

Deutsche Welle. 2019. "Director of Jewish Museum Berlin Resigns." https://www.dw.com/en/director-of-jewish-museum-berlin-resigns/a-49214098. Accessed May 22, 2022.

Deutsche Welle and *Qantara.de.* 2008. "Guided Tours for Muslims in Berlin's Jewish Museum: Discovering a Different Belief."http://www.qantara.de/webcom/show_article.php/_c-478/_nr-805/i.html. Accessed July 3, 2009.

Domentat, Tamara. 1998. *Hallo Fräulein: Deutsche Frauen und Amerikanische Soldaten.* Berlin: Aufbau-Verlag.

Du Bois, W. E. B. 1952. "The Negro and the Warsaw Ghetto." *Jewish Life.* https://perspectives.ushmm.org/item/w-e-b-du-bois-the-negro-and-the-warsaw-ghetto. Accessed May 22, 2022.

DW.com. 2021. "NSU: What you need to know about Germany's neo-Nazi terror group." https://www.dw.com/en/nsu-germany/a-39777036. Accessed May 22, 2022.

Edkins, Jenny. 2003. Trauma and the Memory of Politics. Cambridge, UK: Cambridge University Press.

Eddy, Melissa. 2021. "European Court Backs Germany In Case Over 2009 Killing of Afghan Civilians." *New York Times.* February 16, 2021, https://

www.nytimes.com/2021/02/16/world/europe/european-court-germany-afghanistan-bombing.html. Accessed December 7, 2021.

———. 2019a. "Director of Berlin's Jewish Museum Quits After Spat over B.D.S."New York Times. June 14, 2019. https://www.nytimes.com/2019/06/14/world/europe/berlin-jewish-museum-director-quits-bds.html. Accessed December 7, 2021.

———. 2019b. "What and Whom Are Jewish Museums For?" July 9, 2019. https://www.nytimes.com/2019/07/09/arts/design/jewish-museums-germany-berlin-europe.html. Accessed May 20, 2022.

Ege, Moritz. 2007. *Schwarz werden: "Afroamerikanophilie" in den 1960er und 1970er Jahren, Cultural studies.* Bielefeld: Transcript.

Eisenman, Peter. 2005. Speech http://www.holocaust-mahnmal.de/dasdenkmal/geschichte/reden/redeeisenman. Accessed 3 July 2009.

El-Tayeb, Fatima 2019. "Queering De-Colonial Theory from a European of Color Perspective." Keynote address at *Decolonizing European Anthropology?* Leiden.

———. 2011. *European Others: Queering Ethnicity in Postnational Europe.* Minneapolis: University of Minnesota Press.

———. 2001. *Schwarze Deutsche: der Diskurs um "Rasse" und nationale Identität 1890–1933.* Frankfurt/Main: Campus.

von Eschen, Penny. 2004. *Satchmo Blows Up the World: Jazz Ambassadors Play the Cold War.* Cambridge, MA: Harvard University Press.

Evans, Stephan. 2013. "Germany's 'n-word' Race Debate." *BBC News.* March 13, 2013. https://www.bbc.com/news/world-europe-21702989. Accessed May 17, 2021.

Fanon, Frantz. 1968. *Black Skin, White Masks.* London: MacGibbon & Kee.

Fanon, Frantz. 1963. *The Wretched of the Earth.* New York: Grove Press.

Fassbinder, R. W., P. Märtesheimer, P. Frohlich, H. Schygulla, K. Löwitsch, I. Desny, and P. Raben. 1992. *Die Ehe der Maria Braun.* New York, NY: New Yorker Video.

Fassbinder, Rainer Werner, and Joyce Rheuban. 1986. *The Marriage of Maria Braun.* New Brunswick, NJ: Rutgers University Press.

Fassin, Didier. 2012. *Humanitarian Reason: A Moral History of the Present Times.* Berkeley: University of California Press.

Fehrenbach, Heide. 2005. *Race After Hitler: Black Occupation Children in Postwar Germany and America.* Princeton, NJ: Princeton University Press.

———. 2000. "Of German Mothers and "Negermischlingskinder": Race, Sex, and the Postwar Nation." In *The Miracle Years: A Cultural History of West Germany, 1949–1968*, edited by Hanna Schissler, 164–86. Princeton, NJ: Princeton University Press.

———. 1995. *Cinema in Democratizing Germany: Reconstructing National Identity After Hitler.* Chapel Hill: University of North Carolina Press.

Ferguson, J. 1994. *The Anti-Politics Machine: "Development," Depoliticization, and Bureaucratic Power in Lesotho.* Minneapolis: University of Minnesota Press.

Ferguson, Roderick A. 2004. *Aberrations in Black: Toward a Queer of Color Critique.* Minneapolis: University of Minnesota Press.

Florvil, T. N. 2020. Mobilizing Black Germany: Afro-German women and the making of a transnational movement. University of Illinois Press.

Focus. 2019. Deutlicher Anstieg: Fast jeder zweite Arbeitslose hat Migrationshintergrund. Accessed July 25, 2019.

———. 2018. "Neun Migranten und eine Polizistin getötet—die Geschichten der Opfer." July 11. https://www.focus.de/politik/deutschland/drogen-belaestigung-gewalt-sozialarbeiter-klagt-an-was-in-koeln-geschah-passiert-hier-in-berlin-taeglich_id_5229067.html.

———. 2016. "Köln passiert hier täglich." January 31. https://www.focus.de/politik/deutschland/drogen-belaestigung-gewalt-sozialarbeiter-klagt-an-was-in-koeln-geschah-passiert-hier-in-berlin-taeglich_id_5229067.html

———. 2012. Ausländer doppelt so oft arbeitslos wie Deutsche. *Online Focus.* Accessed July 25, 2019.

Foucault, Michel. 1990. *The History of Sexuality.* New York: Vintage Books.

———. 1991. "Governmentality." In *The Foucault Effect,* edited by G. Burchell, C. Gordon, and P. Miller, 87–104. London: Harvester Wheatsheaf.

———. 1997. *The Politics of Truth.* New York: Semiotext(e).

Frankfurter Allgemeine Zeitung. 2001. "Plakat sofort abhängen!" August 6.

———. 2003. "Der Spike Lee von Kreuzberg." September 3. https://fazarchiv.faz.net/faz-portal/document?uid=FAS__SD1200303091787460. Accessed May 22, 2022.

———. 2008a. "Im Gespräch mit Neco Çelik: Ich bin bestimmt nicht deutschenfeindlich." https://www.faz.net/aktuell/feuilleton/debatten/im-gespraech-mit-neco-elik-ich-bin-bestimmt-nicht-deutschenfeindlich-1513097/er-will-jugendliche-1520509.html. Accessed August 29, 2011.

———. 2008b. "Muslime im Jüdischen Museum." July 3, 2008. http://www.faz.net/s/RubCF3AEB154CE64960822FA5429A182360/Doc~ECA738C014E3E4420BC8064B375BACE65~ATpl~Ecommon~Scontent.html. Accessed 3 July 2009.

Freie Universität Berlin. n.d. "Kleine Chronik der Freien Universität Berlin." http://web.fu-berlin.de/chronik/chronik_Home.html. Accessed February 28, 2010.

Fremeaux, Isa and John Jordan. 2018. "The Art of Organising Hope." Presentation on La ZAD. http://theartoforganisinghope.eu. Accessed May 9, 2019.

Fuqua, Antoine, dir. 2002. *Training Day.* Warner Brothers.

Gemünden, Gerd. 1998. *Framed Visions: Popular Culture, Americanization, and the Contemporary German and Austrian Imagination.* Ann Arbor: University of Michigan Press.

Georgi, Viola B. 2003. *Entliehene Erinnerung. Geschichtsbilder junger Migranten in Deutschland*. Hamburg: Hamburger Edition.

Georgi, Viola B., and Rainer Ohlinger. 2009. "Geschichte und Diversität: Crossover statt nationaler Narrative?" In *Crossover Geschichte: Historisches Bewusstsein Jugendlicher in der Einwanderungsgesellschaft*, edited by Viola B. Georgi and Rainer Ohlinger. Hamburg: Edition Körberg-Stiftung.

Gilman, Sander L. 1985. *Difference and Pathology: Stereotypes of Sexuality, Race, and Madness*. Ithaca, NY: Cornell University Press.

Gilmore, Ruth Wilson. 2007. Golden Gulag : Prisons, Surplus, Crisis, and Opposition in Globalizing California. Berkeley: University of California Press.

Göktürk, Deniz. 2003. "Turkish Delight—German Fright: Migrant Identities in Transnational Cinema." In *Mapping the Margins: Identity, Politics, and the Media*, edited by Karen Ross and Deniz Derman, 177–92. Creskill, NJ: Hampton Press.

Gryglewski, Elke. 2009. "Diesseits und jenseits gefühlter Geschichte: Zugänge von Jugendlichen mit Migrationshitergrund zu Schoa und Nahostkonflikt." In *Crossover Geschichte: Historisches Bewusstsein Jugendlicher in der Einwanderungsgesellschaft*, edited by Viola B. Georgi and Rainer Ohlinger. Hamburg: Edition Körberg-Stiftung.

Guerrero, Ed. 1993. *Framing Blackness: The African American Image in Film*. Philadelphia: Temple University Press.

Güvercin, Eren. 2008. From "Educated Kanakster" to Literary Star. Qantara. De, April 12, 2009. https://en.qantara.de/content/portrait-feridun-zaimo-glu-from-educated-kanakster-to-literary-star. Accessed March 2, 2010.

Haakh, N. 2021. *Muslimisierte Körper auf der Bühne: Die Islamdebatte im postmigrantischen Theater*. Transcript Verlag.

Hakami, Muntaser. 2015. *Please Take My Money*. In Filming the Future from Berlin film series at Theater X in Berlin. Directed and curated by Damani Partridge, Ayla Gottschlich, and Ahmed Shah.

Hall, Stuart. 1990. "Cultural Identity and Diaspora." In *Identity: Community, Culture, Difference*, edited by Jonathan Rutherford, 222–37. New York: New York University Press.

Halle, Randall. 2008. *German Film After Germany: Toward a Transnational Aesthetic*. Urbana: University of Illinois Press.

Hammad, Suheir. 2010.*Born Palestinian Born Black*. Brooklyn, NY: UpSet Press.

Hartman, Saidiya. 2020. "Saidiya Hartman on Insurgent Histories and the Abolitionist Imaginary." *Artforum*. https://www.artforum.com/interviews /saidiya-hartman-83579, accessed November 30, 2021.

———. 2019. Wayward Lives, Beautiful Experiments: Intimate Histories of Social Upheaval. New York: W. W. Norton & Company.

———. 2006. *Lose Your Mother : A Journey Along the Atlantic Slave Route*. New York: Farrar, Straus and Giroux.

———. 1997. *Scenes of Subjection: Terror, Slavery, and Self-making in Nineteenth-Century America*. New York: Oxford University Press.

Heine, Matthias. 2016. "Wie 'Kanake' zum rassistischen Hasswort wurde." *Die Welte*. April 18. https://www.welt.de/kultur/article154409100/Wie-Kanake-zum-rassistischen-Hasswort-wurde.html. Accessed December 1, 2021.

Heldmann, Eva. 1999. *Fremd Gehen. Gespräche mit meiner Freundin*. Deutschland.

Herbert, Ulrich. 1990. *A History of Foreign Labor in Germany, 1880–1990: Seasonal Workers, Forced Laborers, Guest Workers*. Ann Arbor: University of Michigan Press.

Höhn, Maria. 2002. *GIs and Fräuleins: The German-American Encounter in 1950s West Germany*. Chapel Hill: University of North Carolina Press.

———. 2008. "'We Will Never Go Back to the Old Way Again': Germany in the African-American Debate on Civil Rights." *Central European History* 41, no. 4: 605–37.

Hull, Akasha Gloria, Patricia Bell-Scott, and Barbara Smith. 1982. *All the Women are White, All the Blacks Are Men, But Some of Us Are Brave: Black Women's Studies*. Old Westbury, NY: Feminist Press.

hooks, bell. 2014. "A Public Dialogue between bell hooks and Cornel West." Eugene Lang College, The New School, New York, NY. October 8, 2014. https://www.youtube.com/watch?v=_LL0k6_pPKw. Accessed April 5, 2022.

James, C. L. R. 1938. The Black Jacobins. Toussaint Louverture and the San Domingo Revolution. London: Secker and Warburg.

Julien, Isaac, dir. *The Darker Side of Black*. New York: Filmmakers Library, 1994.

Kanak Attak. 1998. "About." https://www.kanak-attak.de/ka/about/manif_eng.html. Accessed December 1, 2021.

Kapadia, Asif, dir. 2015. *Amy*. Lionsgate Films.

Kello, Mohammed. 2015. *Pity No More*. In Filming the Future from Berlin film series at Theater X in Berlin. Directed and curated by Damani Partridge, Ayla Gottschlich, and Ahmed Shah.

Klatt, Thomas. 2016. " Wie antisemitisch ist der Refugee Club Impulse?" *Deutschlandfunk Kultur*. May 20, 2016. https://www.deutschlandfunkkultur.de/streit-um-foerdergelder-in-berlin-wie-antisemitisch-ist-der-100.html. Accessed April 4, 2022.

Kluge, Alexander, et al, dirs. 2010. *Deutschland Im Herbst Germany in Autumn*. Chicago: Facets Video.

Koensler, Alexander. "Acts of Solidarity: Crossing and Reiterating Israeli-Palestinian Frontiers." *International Journal of Urban and Regional Research* 40, no. 2: 340–56.

Kopp, Kristin Leigh. 2012. Germany's Wild East : Constructing Poland as Colonial Space. Ann Arbor: University of Michigan Press.

Kosnick, K. 2019. "New Year's Eve, Sexual Violence and Moral Panics." In *Refugees Welcome? Difference and Diversity in a Changing Germany*, edited by Jan-Jonathan Bock and Sharon Macdonald, 171–90. New York: Berghahn.

Krüger, W. 1979. *Joseph Beuys: Jeder Mensch ist ein Künstler*. Arte Media Edmund Schmidt.

Langhoff, S. (2011). Die Herkunft spielt keine Rolle.„Postmigrantisches "Theater im Ballhaus Naunynstraße. *Bundeszentrale für politische Bildung, 10*.

Layne, Priscilla. 2018. "Space Is the Place: Afrofuturism in Olivia Wenzel's *Mais In Deutschland Und Anderen Galaxien* (2015)." *German Life and Letters* 71: 511–28.

Layne, Priscilla, and Elizabeth Stewart. 2021. "Racialisation and Contemporary German Theatre." In *The Palgrave Handbook of Theatre and Race*, edited by Tiziana Morosetti and Osita Okagbue, 39–60. London: Palgrave Macmillan.

Levy, Emily. 2021. *Nothing About Us Without Us*. In Filming the Future of Detroit film series at the University of Michigan in Ann Arbor, MI. Directed and curated by Damani Partridge.

Lewis, William S. 2019. "But didn't he kill his wife?" *Verso Books* blog. May 29. https://www.versobooks.com/blogs/4336-but-didn-t-he-kill-his-wife.

Lorde, Audre. 1992. "Foreword." In *Showing Our Colors: Afro-German Women Speak Out*, edited by May Opitz, Katharina Oguntoye, and Dagmar Schultz. Amherst: University of Massachusetts.

Maase, K. 1992. *BRAVO-Amerika. Erkundungen zur Jugendkultur der Bundesrepublik in den fünziger Jahren* [BRAVO-America: Soundings in the West German Youth Culture of the 1950s]. Hamburg: Junius Verlag.

Macdonald, Sharon. 2009. *Difficult Heritage: Negotiating the Nazi Past in Nuremberg and Beyond*. London: Routledge.

Malik, Sarita. 1996. "Beyond "The Cinema of Duty"? The Pleasures of Hybridity: Black British Films of the 1980s and 1990s." In *Dissolving Views: New Writings on British Cinema*, edited by Andrew Higson, 202–15. London: Cassel.

Mani, B. Venkat. 2007. *Cosmopolitical Claims: Turkish-German Literatures from Nadolny to Pamuk*. Iowa City: University of Iowa Press.

Margalit, Gilad. 2009. "On Being Other in Post-Holocaust Germany—German-Turkish Intellectuals and the German Past." In *Juden und Muslime in Deutschland: Recht, Religion, Identität*, edited by J. Brunner.Göttingen: Wallstein Verlag.

Massaquoi, Hans Jürgen. 1999. *Destined to Witness: Growing Up Black in Nazi Germany*. New York: William Morrow.

Mbembe, A. 2008. "Necropolitics." In *Foucault in an Age of Terror: Essays on Biopolitics and the Defence of Society*, edited by Stephen Morton and Stephen Bygrave, 152–82. London: Palgrave Macmillan.

Mehta, Uday S. 1990. "Liberal Strategies of Exclusion." *Politics and Society* 18 (December): 427–53.

Mennel, Barbara. 2002a. "Local Funding and Global Movement: Minority Women's Filmmaking and the German Film Landscape of the Late 1990s." *Women in German Yearbook* 18: 45–66.

Mennel, Barbara. 2002b. "Bruce Lee in Kreuzberg and Scarface in Altona: Transnational Auteurism and Ghettocentrism in Thomas Arslan's Brothers and Sisters and Fatih Akın's Short Sharp Shock." *New German Critique* What 87.

Mignolo, Walter D. 2007. "DELINKING." *Cultural Studies* 21, no. 2–3: 449–514.

Mind the Trap. 2014. "Intervention im DT." January 9, 2014. https://mindthe-trapberlin.wordpress.com/intervention-im-dt. Accessed April 5, 2022.

Mora-Kapi, Idrissou. 1999. *Falsche Soldaten*. Benin: Hochschule fu r Film und fernsehen "Konrad Wolf."

Müller, Ray, dir. 1995. The Wonderful Horrible Life of Leni Riefenstahl. New York: Kino International Corp.

Naficy, Hamid. 2001. *An Accented Cinema: Exilic and Diasporic Filmmaking*. Princeton, NJ: Princeton University Press.

Olick, Jeffrey, K. 1998. "What Does It Mean to Normalize the Past? Official Memory in German Politics since 1989." *Social Science History* 22, no. 4: 547–71.

Omi, Michael, and Howard Winant. 1994. *Racial Formation in the United States: From the 1960s to the 1990s*. 2nd ed. New York: Routledge.

Ong, Aihwa. 1996. "Cultural Citizenship as Subject-Making: Immigrants Negotiate Racial and Cultural Boundaries in The United States." *Current Anthropology* 7, no. 5: 737–62.

———. 1999. *Flexible Citizenship: The Cultural Logics of Transnationality*. Durham, NC: Duke University Press.

———. 2003. *Buddha is Hiding: Refugees, Citizenship, the New America*. Berkeley: University of California Press.

———. 2006. *Neoliberalism as Exception: Mutations in Citizenship and Covereignty*. Durham, NC: Duke University Press.

Opitz, May, Katharina Oguntoye, and Dagmar Schultz, eds. 1991. *Showing Our Colors: Afro-German Women Speak Out*. Translated by Anne V. Adams. Amherst: University of Massachusetts Press.

Oschmiansky, Frank. 2020. "Beschäftigung schaffende Maßnahmen." *BPB*. September 1, 2020. https://www.bpb.de/themen/arbeit/arbeitsmarktpolitik/317166/beschaeftigung-schaffende-massnahmen. Accessed April 5, 2022.

Özyürek, Esra. 2018. Rethinking Empathy: Emotions Triggered by the Holocaust Among the Muslim-Minority in Germany. *Anthropological Theory* 18, no. 4: 456–77.

———. 2016. "Export-import Theory and the Racialization of Anti-semitism: Turkish-and Arab-only Prevention Programs in Germany." *Comparative Studies in Society and History* 58, no. 1: 40–65.

———. 2009. "Convert Alert: German Muslims and Turkish Christians as Threats to Security in the New Europe." *Comparative Studies in Society and History* 51, no. 1: 91–116.

———. 2005. "The Politics of Cultural Unification, Secularism, and the Place of Islam in the New Europe." *American Ethnologist* 32, no. 4 (November): 509–12.

Parker, B. A. "The Miseducation of Castlemont High." *This American Life*. April 27, 2018. https://www.thisamericanlife.org/644/random-acts-of-history /act-one-11. Accessed February 14, 2022.

Parkinson, J., and D. George-Cosh. 2015. "Image of Drowned Syrian Boy Echoes around World." *The Wall Street Journal*. September 3, 2015. https:// www.wsj.com/articles/image-of-syrian-boy-washed-up-on-beach-hits-hard-1441282847.

Partridge, Damani J. 2013. "Occupying American 'Black' Bodies and Reconfiguring European Spaces—The Possibilities for Noncitizen Articulations in Berlin and Beyond." *Transforming Anthropology* 21, no. 1.

———. 2015. "Monumental Memory, Moral Superiority, and Contemporary Disconnects." In *Spaces of Danger: Culture and Power in the Everyday*, edited by Heather Merrill and Lisa Hoffman, 101–31. Athens: University of Georgia Press.

———. 2012. *Hypersexuality and Headscarves: Race, Sex, and Citizenship in the New Germany*. Bloomington: Indiana University Press.

———. 2008. "We Were Dancing in the Club, Not on the Berlin Wall: Black Bodies, Street Bureaucrats, and Exclusionary Incorporation into the New Europe." *Cultural Anthropology* 23, no. 4: 660–87.

———. 2011. "Exploding Hitler and Americanizing Germany: Occupy- ing 'Black' Bodies and Postwar Desire." In *Germans and African Americans: Two Centuries of Exchange*, edited by Anke Ortlepp and Larry A. Greene, 201–17. Jackson: University of Mississippi Press.

———. 2003. "Becoming Non-citizens: Technologies of Exclusion and Exclusionary Incorporation after the Berlin Wall." PhD diss., University of California, Berkeley.

Partridge, D. J., and M. Chin. 2019. "Interrogating the Histories and Futures of "Diversity": Transnational Perspectives." *PUBLIC CULTURE* 31 (2):197–214. doi: 10.1215/08992363-7286777.

Patterson, Orlando. 1982. *Slavery and Social Death: A Comparative Study*. Cambridge, MA: Harvard University Press.

Peck, Jeffrey. 1994. The 'Ins' and 'Outs' of the New Germany: Jews, Foreigners, Asylum Seekers. In *Reemerging Jewish Culture in Germany*, edited by Sander L. Gilman and Karen Remmler, 130–47. New York: New York University Press.

Poiger, Uta G. 2000. *Jazz, Rock, and Rebels: Cold War Politics and American Culture in a Divided Germany*. Berkeley: University of California Press.

Pred, Allan. 2000. *Even In Sweden: Racisms, Racialized Spaces, and the Popular Geographical Imagination*. Berkeley: University of California Press.

Puar, Jasbir K. 2017. *The Right to Maim: Debility, Capacity, Disability, Anima*. Durham, NC: Duke University Press.

———. 2012. "'I would rather be a cyborg than a goddess': Becoming-Intersectional in Assemblage Theory." *PhiloSOPHIA* 2, no. 1: 49–66.

Rastakoff, Benjamin. 2022. "Du Bois Before Warsaw, Fascism Before Racism." In conversation with Amelia Glaser. https://www.youtube.com/watch?v=YJ0LkykJMVo. Accessed March 17, 2022.

Roediger, David R. 2002 [1991]. The Wages of Whiteness: Race and the Making of the American *Working Class*. London: Verso.

Rogin, Michael Paul. 1996. *Blackface, White Noise: Jewish Immigrants in the Hollywood Melting Pot*. Berkeley: University of California Press.

Rothberg, Michael. 2019. The Implicated Subject : Beyond Victims and Perpetrators. Stanford, CA: Stanford University Press.

———. 2009. *Multidirectional Memory: Remembering the Holocaust in the Age of Decolonization*. Stanford, CA: Stanford University Press.

———. 2001. "W. E. B. DuBois in Warsaw: Holocaust Memory and the Color Line, 1949–1952." *The Yale Journal of Criticism* 14, no. 1 (2001): 169–89.

Ryback, Timothy W. 1993. "Evidence of Evil." The New Yorker, November 15, 68–81.

Sandel, M. J. 2020. The Tyranny of Merit: What's Become of the Common Good? London: Penguin UK.

Sarrazin, Thilo. 2010. *Deutschland schafft sich ab: wie wir unser Land aufs Spiel setzen*. München: Deutsche Verlags-Anstalt.

Schmitt, C. 2005. *Political Theology: Four Chapters on the Concept of Sovereignty*. Chicago: University of Chicago Press.

Schroer, Timothy L. 2007. *Recasting Race After World War II: Germans and African Americans in American-Occupied Germany*. Boulder: University Press of Colorado.

Scorsese, Martin, dir. 1973. *Mean Streets*. Warner Brothers.

Scott, Julius S., and Marcus Rediker, 2018. *The Common Wind : Afro-American Currents in the Age of the Haitian Revolution*. London: Verso Books.

Selasi, Taiye. 2014. TED Talk. https://www.youtube.com/watch?v=LYCKzpXEW6E. Accessed May 22, 2022.

Sexton, J. 2010. "People-of-color-blindness: Notes on the Afterlife of Slavery." *Social Text* 28, no. 2: 31–56.

Silverman, Kaja. 1996. *The Threshold of the Visible World*. New York: Routledge.

Spiegel Online. 2005. "How Long Does One Feel Guilty?" September 5. https://www.spiegel.de/international/spiegel-interview-with-holocaust-monument-architect-peter-eisenman-how-long-does-one-feel-guilty-a-355252.html. Accessed May 22, 2022.

Spiegel, Paul. 2005. Speech. http://www.holocaust-mahnmal.de/dasdenkmal /geschichte/reden/redespiegel/?highlight=paul%20spiegel. Accessed July 3, 2009.

Spolar, Christine. 1994. "The Kids Who Laughed Till It Hurt." *Washington Post*, March 10, C1.

Stewart, L. 2021. "The Cultural Capital of Postmigrants Is Enormous." *Postmigration Studies* 4: 87.

———. 2017. "Postmigrant Theatre: The Ballhaus Naunynstraße Takes on Sexual Nationalism." *Journal of Aesthetics & Culture* 9, no. 2: 56–68.

Stiftung Denkmal für die ermordeten Juden Europas. 2008. http://www .stiftung-denkmal.de/dasdenkmal/geschichte/reden/redeeisenman. Accessed 15 May 2008.

Subramanian, A. 2019. The Caste of Merit: Engineering Education in India. Cambridge, MA: Harvard University Press.

TAZ, Die Tageszeitung. 2008. "Ein Moslem erklärt die Schoah; Ufuk Topkara macht Fürungen im Jüdischen Museum—auf Türkische. Als Ansprechpartner vor allem für muslimische Kreuzberger Schüler versucht er ihre Vorurteile gegen Juden und Israel abzubauen." May 7.

Terkessidis, Mark. 2004. *Die Banalität des Rassismus: Migranten zweiter Generation entwickeln eine neue Perspektive*. Bielefeld: Transcript.

———. 2016. "Atmosphäre in Kreuzberg ist ähnlich wie Silvester in Köln." *Der Taggesspiegel*. https://www.tagesspiegel.de/berlin/kriminalitaet-in-berlin-atmosphaere-in-kreuzberg-ist-aehnlich-wie-silvester-in-koeln/12840514. html. Accessed May 22, 2022.

Ticktin, Miriam Iris. 2011. *Casualties of Care: Immigration and the Politics of Humanitarianism in France*. Berkeley: University of California Press.

———. 2006. "Where Ethics and Politics Meet." *American Ethnologist* 33, no. 1: 33–49.

Till, Karen E. 2005. *The New Berlin: Memory, Politics, Place*. Minneapolis: University of Minnesota Press.

Todorov, Tzvetan. 2001. "The Uses and Abuses of Memory." In *What Happens to History: The Renewal of Ethics in Contemporary Thought*, 11–22. New York: Routledge.

Topkara, Ufuk. 2009. "Interkulturelle Museumsarbeit mit Kindern und Jugendlichen: Erfahrungen aus dem Jüdischen Museum Berlin." In Crossover Geschichte: Historisches Bewusstsein Jugendlicher in der Einwanderungsgesellschaft, edited by Viola B. Georgi and Rainer Ohlinger. Hamburg: Edition Körberg-Stiftung.

TRAP, MIND THE. 2014. Stellungnahme im Rahmen der Intervention im Deutschen Theater am. *MIND THE TRAP*. Accessed May 24, 2019.

Verdery, Katherine. 1996. *What Was Socialism, and What Comes Next?* Princeton, NJ: Princeton University Press.

Weheliye, Alexander G. 2014. *Habeas Viscus: Racializing Assemblages, Biopolitics, and Black Feminist Theories of the Human.* Durham: Duke University Press.

Weinthal, Benjamin. 2016. "Berlin government allegedly supports Hezbollah activists through refugee project." *The Jerusalem Post,* April 20. https://www.jpost.com/international/berlin-government-supports-hezbollah-activists-through-refugee-project-451747, accessed March 19, 2022.

WELT. 2014. 90 Festnahmen bei Protest gegen den „Zwarte Piet". *WELT.* Accessed July 24, 2019.

Werthschulte, Christian. 2017. "'Nach' Köln ist wie 'vor' Köln. Die Silvesternacht und ihre Folgen." *APuZ.* June 1, 2017. https://www.bpb.de/shop/zeitschriften/apuz/239696/nach-koeln-ist-wie-vor-koeln-die-silvester-nacht-und-ihre-folgen. Accessed March 19, 2022.

Wiedmer, Caroline Alice. 1999. *The Claims of Memory: Representations of the Holocaust in Contemporary Germany and France.* Ithaca: Cornell University Press.

Wilderson, Frank B., III. 2020. *Afropessimism.* New York: W. W. Norton.

Williams, Robert Gooding. 1993. "Introduction: On Being Stuck." In *Reading Rodney King/Reading Urban Uprising,* edited by Robert Gooding Williams, 1–12. NewYork: Routledge.

Womack, Ytasha. 2013. *Afrofuturism: The World of Black Sci-fi and Fantasy Culture.* Chicago: Lawrence Hill Books.

Wright, Fiona. 2016. "Palestine, My Love: The Ethico-politics of Love and Mourning in Jewish Israeli Solidarity Activism." *American Ethnologist* 43, no. 1: 130–43.

Yildiz, Yasemin. 2009. "Turkish Girls, Allah's Daughters, and the Contemporary German Subject: Itinerary of a Figure." *German Life and Letters* 62, no. 4: 465–81.

Young, James Edward. 1993. *The Texture of Memory: Holocaust Memorials and Meaning in Europe, Israel, and America.* New Haven, CT: Yale University Press.

Zaimoglu, Feridun. 2000. *Koppstoff: Kanaka Sprak vom Rande der Gesellschaft.* 3. Aufl. ed. Hamburg: Rotbuch.

———. 1995. *Kanak Sprak : 24 Misstöne vom Rande der Gesellschaft.* Hamburg: Rotbuch Verlag.

Zaimoglu, Feridun, and Imran Ayata. 2008. *Literature to go: Feridun Zaimoglu im Gespräch mit Imran Ayata, Maxim Biller, Neco Çelik, Ralf Fücks, Maybrit Illner, Marius Meller, Albert Ostermaier, Peter Siller, Benjamin von Stuckrad-Barre, Moritz von Uslar, Klaus Vater und Volker Weidermann, Edition AL.* Berlin: Edition AL.

Index

Founded in 1893,
UNIVERSITY OF CALIFORNIA PRESS
publishes bold, progressive books and journals
on topics in the arts, humanities, social sciences,
and natural sciences—with a focus on social
justice issues—that inspire thought and action
among readers worldwide.

The UC PRESS FOUNDATION
raises funds to uphold the press's vital role
as an independent, nonprofit publisher, and
receives philanthropic support from a wide
range of individuals and institutions—and from
committed readers like you. To learn more, visit
ucpress.edu/supportus.

CPSIA information can be obtained
at www.ICGtesting.com
Printed in the USA
JSHW021507070223
37419JS00001B/40